WITHDRAWN
HARVARD LIBRARY
WITHDRAWN

Poverty and Power

LATIN AMERICA AFTER 500 YEARS

Edited by George Gelber

Poverty and Power
Latin America after 500 years

Published in Great Britain 1992
by CAFOD
Romero Close
Stockwell Road
London SW9 9TY

Copyright © CAFOD 1992

Cover photos by
Sue Cunningham, Carlos Reyes and Marj Clayton
Photo opposite by Mo Fini/Tumi

Printed in Great Britain by
Billings Book Plan Ltd, Worcester

contents

- **The continuing conquest**   1
  george gelber

- **A short history of Latin America**   7
  jenny pearce

- **Crushing Burden: Latin America's foreign debt**   69
  seamus cleary and george gelber

- **Environmental destruction and popular resistance**   101
  jutta blauert

- **Land rights and land reform**   129
  george gelber

- **Against all odds: Indigenous people and the battle for survival**   147
  george monbiot

- **Through the eyes of artists**   181
  john king

- **The Church in Latin America**   199
  george gelber

- **Appendix 1**   229
  country profiles

- **Appendix 2**   251
  fact files

george gelber
THE CONTINUING CONQUEST

Nineteen ninety-two, the fifth centenary of Columbus's arrival in the Americas, is no more than an anniversary. And it will remain no more than an anniversary, briefly remembered and soon forgotten, if it does not make us look critically at the impact of Europeans on the peoples and continents of the 'New World'. These essays deal with the present and today's legacy of the five hundred years that have passed since Columbus, because for the peoples of Latin America and the Caribbean a better future depends on what they – and the rest of the world – can do in the present.

Nevertheless, there is certainly a battle to reclaim the past. Historians speak of the 'dark' and 'rose-tinted' legends of the Conquest, implying that the truth must lie somewhere between the two. Attempts to smooth away the cruel, rough edges of the past can be found everywhere: the official Spanish campaign of commemoration of the fifth centenary is titled 'Meeting between Two Worlds', suggesting that the Conquest was an encounter of equals. A mural in Madrid's Barajas airport celebrates the event with the declaration that, 'the discovery of America gave humanity a new company of men, a mixture of Iberian and Indian, son of the Sun, and a new culture – which today is bringing forth a new approach to life.' Most countries in Spanish-speaking Latin America still celebrate 12 October – Columbus Day in the United States – as the Day of the Race (*Día de la Raza*), commemorating the 'enrichment' of native American blood with that of the conquerors. Unfortunately, this mingling of genes was all too often the product of rape.

José Carlos Mariátegui, a Peruvian writing in the 1930s, called upon his compatriots not to dwell on the past:

'... the Conquest, bad as it was, is a historical fact. The Republic [of Peru], as it is today, is another historical fact. Abstract speculations of the intellect and pure concepts of the spirit can do little or nothing against historical facts. The history of Peru is no more

Growing up in Columbus's shadow. This statue, commemorating the arrival of Christopher Columbus, stands in the centre of Santo Domingo in the Dominican Republic. Photo by Jenny Matthews.

introduction

than a scrap of human history. In four centuries a new reality has been formed. The avalanches of the West created it. It is a weak reality, but it is, nevertheless, a reality. To decide to ignore it would be an act of excessive romanticism.'[1]

The past, however, *is* important, because a common understanding of the past is the first step towards changing the present. The battles of the historians are not entirely irrelevant to the present. For this reason native American groups are organising throughout the Americas to remind the descendants of the settlers of the harm they and their forebears have done, and are still doing; to rediscover their own culture; and to recover the lands they see as rightfully theirs. They view the fifth centenary as a commemoration of five hundred years of resistance and have called their campaign the 'Campaign of Self-Discovery', reminding their own peoples of their roots in the lands that have become Latin America and the pride they can take in their culture and heritage.

Columbus, a Genoese seafarer in the service of the Spanish Crown, is a Latin figure. The British never established more than footholds on the mainland of Latin America (in Belize and Guyana) and see Latin America, with its history of destruction, plunder and exploitation, as the exclusive creation of Spain and Portugal. On the one hand, this attitude ignores the enormous benefits that Britain derived from the Conquest, the substantial British influence in Latin America in the nineteenth century and contemporary patterns of trade and finance which give the countries of the industrialised world a decisive advantage over the poor countries of the southern hemisphere. On the other hand, one can find in this attitude a sort of anti-Spanish and anti-Portuguese racism, attributing to their *conquistadores* and *bandeirantes* unique characteristics of cruelty, greed and ruthlessness. But one has only to look at the British control of the slave trade in the Caribbean and North America, and the treatment meted out by them to native Americans of the United States and Canada, to find similar shameful episodes. Throughout the eighteenth century the slave code of Virginia read,

'Whereas many times slaves run away and lie hid and lurking in swamps, woods and other obscure places, killing hogs, and committing other injuries to the inhabitants ... if the slave does not immediately return, anyone whatsoever may kill or destroy such slaves by such ways and means as he ... shall think fit ... If the slave is apprehended ... it shall ... be lawful for the county court to order such punishment for the said slave, either by dismembering, or in any other way ... as they in their discretion shall think fit, for the reclaiming any such incorrigible slave, and terrifying others from the like practices ...'[2]

continuing conquest

In Dutch-ruled New York, Governor Kieft sent his troops against a Hackensack village to punish Indians for taking peaches from a farmer's orchard. Eighty sleeping Indians were killed and infants were torn from their mothers' breasts, then hacked to pieces in the presence of their parents and the pieces thrown on the fire.[3]

Similar excesses are perpetrated today against the surviving indigenous peoples of the Amazon basin. Systematic torture, arbitrary execution and disappearances were a feature of the military régimes of Latin America during the 1970s and 1980s, and today political violence still disfigures too many countries.

Such extreme cruelty may cause people in richer and more peaceful countries to turn away from this unwelcome reality as something alien and different, defying comprehension. But they are part of economic and social processes taking place in Latin America and the Caribbean today in which we all participate through the workings of world trade and international financial markets.

These processes are the modern continuation of the Conquest, which was organised to funnel profits and wealth to interests outside Latin America and the Caribbean. The beneficiaries again are largely outside interests: international companies, banks (which hold the bulk of the region's debt) and the citizens of industrialised countries who gain access to cheap commodities that are now seen as an essential element of their high standard of living. The most marked consequences for Latin America and the Caribbean are poverty, inequality and environmental destruction.

Throughout these five hundred years of Latin American and Caribbean history there have been rebellions of native Americans, slaves and the poor, whose labour was – and is – essential to the production of the commodities consumed by the industrialised countries. Modern guerrilla conflicts have not always been uprisings of the poor as such, but have often been undertaken by middle-class people on behalf of the poor. Many of these ventures were misconceived, inflicting untold suffering not only on those directly involved but also on others who, while sharing their desire for change, did not support their methods. These conflicts are nevertheless symptoms of the injustices built into Latin American and Caribbean societies and the frustration at the seeming inability of even 'democratic' institutions to bring about fundamental changes. The role of the Latin American military has too often been to shore up the status quo, favouring the rich, and to remove governments which were seen as responsive to the needs of the poor.

3

introduction

The issues which brought about such extreme social conflict have not been resolved. Distribution of wealth and income remains disastrously skewed in favour of the rich. The poor have little access to education, health and social welfare. There is, however, some awareness on the part of political and business leaders that countries with uneducated, unhealthy and exploited workforces will not experience economic growth on the same scale as those which invest more in their human resources. This awareness has yet to be translated into effective programmes that signify a redistribution of income.

In terms of absolute poverty, Latin America and the Caribbean cannot compete with Africa and Asia. Yet the region is remarkable for the enormous gap between the rich and the poor, and the tensions which this provokes in all areas of life. In the poorer countries of the region, those who would regard themselves as 'poor' amount to half the population or more. The exclusion of the poor from economic participation has driven settlers and gold-prospectors to the most remote corners of Brazil; is forcing people from the *altiplano* (the high Andean plateau) of Bolivia to become slash-and-burn farmers in the lowland rainforest; and has made millions of Mexicans and Central Americans into illegal immigrants in the United States. Latin American countries will not be able to deal squarely with the problems of pollution and environmental destruction until they give real priority to tackling poverty.

Even supposing that the foremost priority of governments were the fight against poverty (which it is not) the region's foreign debt would be an overwhelming constraint. The pressures created by the debt burden are pushing Latin America towards a more thorough exploitation of its natural and, indeed, human resources. 'More thorough' does not necessarily mean more destructive of the environment, but clearly the desperate quest for exports and foreign exchange is a constant incentive to cut corners and to disregard environmental safeguards and the interests of the poor. And, increasingly, it appears that there is no intermediate solution to the exploitation of Latin America's remaining rainforests: either they are left alone as a treasure-house of biological diversity, a legacy for future generations, or they are destroyed.

Religion and culture in Latin America are deeply conditioned by the Conquest and its aftermath. After all, Christianity did arrive in the New World with the *conquistadores*. In recent times, however, the poverty of Latin America and the exclusion of the poor from the mainstream of society have been the context for the emergence of new movements within the Catholic and Protestant Churches and have brought about the innovations known as Christian base communities and liberation theology. These have attracted the attention of church-people – and others – throughout the world and have made liberation theology itself something of an export success for Latin America. But in the fields of religion and culture, as in economics, there are imports to weigh against exports: a tide of US consumer values and habits, transmitted through television, and fundamentalist Christian beliefs and practices, spread by groups connected with the United States. So, even though it may be more difficult to calculate the balance of payments, here too we see the continuing 'conquest' of Latin America and the Caribbean.

George Gelber has wide experience of development issues in Latin America and the Caribbean, especially in Chile and Central America. His published work includes a study of human rights in Nicaragua under the Sandinistas, Right to Survive (CIIR, 1987), and a co-edited collection of essays on El Salvador, A Decade of War (CIIR/Monthly Review Press, 1991). Currently George Gelber is Latin America Consultant to CAFOD for its 'Land, Hope and Glory' education campaign.

References

1. Mariátegui, J.C., *Peruanicemos al Peru*, quoted in Gustavo Gutiérrez, *Dios o el oro en las Indias*, CEP, Lima, 1989.

2. Quoted in Howard Zinn, *A People's History of the United States*, Longman, New York, 1980, p35.

3. Dial, Adolph L., 'A Look at the Past – a Lesson for the Future', in *IDOC Internazionale*, February 1989.

chapter one

jenny pearce
A SHORT HISTORY OF LATIN AMERICA

In the space of half a century, a few thousand men from the Iberian peninsula conquered an area perhaps forty times the size of their homeland, and came to dominate a population of many millions – about 21 million in the case of Mexico and 11 million in the case of Peru, the two most densely populated regions at the time of the Conquest. Hernán Cortés conquered the Aztec empire in three years with a mere 508 soldiers and 110 sailors.

The Spaniards refer to 1492 as the year they 'discovered' the New World. But for the indigenous population, the word 'destruction' better describes the character of Spain's expansion. The scars are still apparent five hundred years later. The motivations of the Spaniards and the way the Conquest was organised can help us to understand the nature of these persistent scars.

The Crown, the Church and the armed entrepreneur

Columbus's first voyage to the West Indies in 1492 coincided with the fall of Granada, the last Moorish stronghold on the Iberian peninsula. Many historians have seen continuity between the *Reconquista*, the 'Reconquest' of the peninsula from the Moors which began in the eleventh century, and the Conquest of the New World in the early sixteenth century.

The Conquest was carried out using practices similar to those evolved over centuries of trying to expel the Moors. The Reconquest was largely undertaken by small, autonomous military forces officially sanctioned by the Church and the peninsula's Christian kingdoms, notably Castile-Leon, Aragon and Portugal. The kings promised lands and privileges to the victors. The pursuit of wealth and adventure in the name of a Holy War was thus the basis of the Reconquest and all subsequent military expeditions overseas.

By the end of the thirteenth century all but Granada had been won for Spain and the expansion overseas began, starting with the Canary Islands and North Africa. Once again, these expeditions

Value human life! Slogans on the placards at a march by street children in Brazil repeat a cry which has echoed through Latin America for the past five centuries. Photo by Maria Luiza Carvalho.

were undertaken by bands of warrior-adventurers – usually a military leader and his *campaña*, or followers – under rules that granted feudal rights over the lands to be seized and laid down the basis for the distribution of booty, including the *Quinto Real*, or Royal Fifth, which the Crown took.

Loans to finance these enterprises were secured from commercial companies. The leaders of the expeditions then formed their own trading companies. The privileges granted to the adventurers who joined the expeditions were enshrined in legal instruments called *capitulaciones*. The idea of a Holy War against Islam was extended to include the peoples of Africa and the offshore islands. The same procedures were followed in the expeditions to the Indies, which began with Columbus's voyage of 1492.

The Spanish expansion overseas was thus the latest manifestation of an historic collaboration between Crown, Church and the armed entrepreneur, as Bernal Díaz described it in his account of the Conquest of Latin America: 'To serve God and his Majesty, to give light to those in darkness and also to get rich.'

The search for gold

The Spanish Conquest of the New World differed in very important ways from the processes of European conquest and settlement in Africa and Asia in the nineteenth century. Europe in the fifteenth and sixteenth century was just beginning the prolonged process of transition from feudal to industrialised, capitalist society which was to take at least four hundred years. Mercantilism – the search for wealth through trade rather than manufacturing – dominated Europe at the time of the Spanish Conquest. Demand was high for the exotic luxuries and foodstuffs of the East and, in particular, for the gold needed to pay for them. The search for gold was the principal human motivation of the Conquest, and this fact alone was to have important implications for the future development of Latin America.

While the advance of the Ottoman empire threatened Europe's eastern flank, the Iberian peninsula was well situated geographically to lead the process of westward expansion. It was close to Africa and had a long Atlantic coast and a strong maritime tradition. New navigational techniques (the magnetic compass, improved map-making skills, and so on) and advances in shipbuilding enabled seafarers to venture over unknown waters.

By the middle of the fifteenth century the Portuguese had reached 1,500 miles down the West African coast and had pushed into the Atlantic as far as the Cape Verde islands. On the African coast they established *feitorias* (fortified trading posts) and avoided costly journeys into the interior. Meanwhile, Seville in southern

Spain had become a maritime and trading centre, attracting a growing number of settlers from within and beyond the peninsula. The Genoese merchants who had settled there were to play an important role in financing Spanish overseas expansion, in the hope of finding alternative supplies of the valuable commodities of the East.

It was from Seville that Columbus set out in 1492. The first phase of the Conquest centred on the Caribbean and lasted until 1519, when Cortés organised his expedition to Mexico. Initially, the Crown's objective was to set up trading posts for the trade in gold, rather like the Portuguese *feitorias*, with only a small garrison. The term 'conquest' was actually used initially in its strict etymological sense as the 'search' for something worth acquiring. For the Spanish adventurers this was primarily treasure, although arable lands and the labour to work them subsequently became important as conquest gave way to settlement.

The tragedy of Hispaniola

Columbus's first major landfall was in Hispaniola, the largest Caribbean island, now divided between Haiti and the Dominican Republic. Hispaniola was the nucleus of Spanish settlement, and it was here that between 1493 and 1505 the idea of a permanently populated colony, where the Spanish settlers would be serviced by Indian labour, began to emerge. It was to have disastrous consequences for the indigenous population.

If the Spaniards were to be persuaded to settle, they had to be given a stake in the human and natural resources of the area. This was especially true for those adventurers who arrived in the New World with aspirations to noble status. Among the nobility, manual labour was deeply disdained so, with this in mind, the Crown agreed to distribute the 'Indians' to the settlers in return for certain obligations – namely that the Indians should be instructed in the Catholic faith. The Indians were thus 'entrusted' to the settlers under a system known as *encomienda,* which was based on the practice of assigning Moorish villages to members of military orders in medieval Spain.

A Castilian model of settlement soon began to establish itself: landowning Spanish settlers, with their right to compulsory Indian labour, paid the Crown its one-fifth share of precious metals, customs duties and tithes for the maintenance of the Church. Santo Domingo (now the capital of the Dominican Republic) became the first true city of the Spanish overseas empire, and efforts were made to encourage cattle-raising and sugar production to free new settlements from over-dependence on the rather elusive pursuit of gold.

chapter one

Hispaniola also provided the first example of the destructive impact of Spanish policies. Less than twenty years after Columbus's arrival the indigenous population had been virtually wiped out by disease, ill-treatment and the shock of the complete disruption of time-honoured lifestyles. The population of the island is estimated to have been between 200,000 and 300,000 in 1493; by 1548 there were only about 500 indigenous people left. The Spaniards raided neighbouring islands to replenish their labour supply, but the indigenous population continued to decline, while yet more adventurers from the mainland arrived to settle the island and claim their share of Indian labour.

The fate of the Indians, however, shocked many. Two churchmen in particular denounced what was happening: in 1511 Antonio de Montesinos refused communion to the *encomenderos* most responsible for ill-treating the Indians, and in 1514 Bartolomé de las Casas gave up his *encomienda* on the island, and devoted the next half-century to the defence of the Indians.

But while there were moves to defend the Indians, such as the Law of Burgos in 1512, the implementation of these measures was very limited, with no local authority prepared to enforce them in the face of local demands for forced labour. In fact, recognising this dependence on forced labour, the Crown sent a commission from Spain to govern Hispaniola and stop abuses against the Indians. The commission recommended that negro slaves be brought to the island to replace the Indians. Bartolomé de las Casas supported this recommendation in the belief that negroes were more suited to work in the tropical climate. In his old age, las Casas admitted how wrong he had been and regretted his advocacy of introducing slavery to Hispaniola.

The Portuguese had been importing black slaves from the Barbary coast of Africa since the mid-thirteenth century. Negro slaves seemed a 'natural' solution to the labour problems of the New World; and so began the systematic exploitation of black labour which became one of the characteristics of European expansion into these regions.

Conquering the mainland

The search for treasure was the dominant motivation for a great number of the Spaniards who sailed to Hispaniola. Many also found that access to *encomiendas* was limited by the decline in the Indian population and the reduced labour force. This fuelled the wave of expeditions aimed at conquering new territories and finding new sources of treasure. It was from Hispaniola that bands of *conquistadores*, the armed entrepreneurs of the Spanish Conquest, first set out to conquer the rest of the Caribbean and

Central and South America, beginning with Puerto Rico in 1508. The expeditions were costly affairs, so the conquerors often struck up partnerships with investors. This meant that it was ultimately the great banking houses of Genoa and Augsburg which provided the financial backing for the Conquest.

After Cuba was taken in 1511, Havana replaced Santo Domingo as the starting point for expeditions. It was from here that Cortés set out for Mexico, destroying the Aztec confederation between 1519 and 1522. The Conquest then moved south, with expeditions through present-day Guatemala and El Salvador.

Another wave of expeditions set out from Panama, taking Nicaragua in 1523-24 and going further south to Peru to conquer the Inca empire in 1531-33. From Peru, the conquerors went north, founding Quito in 1534 and Bogotá in 1536. Francisco Pizarro set out from Quito in 1541 to explore the Amazon basin, while Pedro de Valdivia went south to Chile, founding Santiago in 1542. An expedition left Europe in 1535 to take the River Plate region, but only succeeded in establishing an outpost in Paraguay. It was from Asunción in Paraguay that an expedition finally set out for the River Plate, founding Buenos Aires in 1580.

The Conquest was a brutal affair. Most of the adventurers that led the expeditions were interested only in booty, and slaughtered many Indians in their search. This was not merely the casual brutality of desperate men. Their leaders deliberately massacred communities in order to terrorise entire peoples into submission. Those Indians who were not killed usually died of disease or trauma. This, in turn, led the invaders to carry out slave-raiding expeditions to replenish the labour needed to grow their crops, carry their loads and pan for gold.

There was a great diversity of Indian cultures at the time of the Conquest. This variety made the act of conquest easier for the Spaniards despite the numerical superiority of the indigenous population. There were the densely populated centres of Meso-America (Mexico and present-day Central America) and the Andes; semi-nomadic peoples on the periphery of these regions; and hunters and gatherers, such as those in Uruguay and Argentina and in the lowland regions of the Amazon basin.

The Aztec and Inca empires were quite sophisticated surplus-producing societies, but the surplus was mostly used in tribute for consumption by a caste of nobles rather than in enhancing productivity. The empires were fairly loose confederations of conquered tribes. Deep resentments against their overlords allowed the Spanish invaders to play off the tribes against each other. By the time of the Spanish Conquest, there was evidence

chapter one

that both empires had overreached themselves and decline was underway. These facts and the technological superiority of Spanish weaponry, in particular the use of gunpowder, help to explain the comparative ease of Conquest. The Spaniards had weapons of steel; the Indians had weapons of stone and wood. The Spaniards also had ships, with which they could bring reinforcements, and horses – animals that the indigenous population had never seen before.

Nevertheless, the Spaniards did encounter resistance. In some places, such as Chile where they clashed with the Araucanian Indians, they experienced crushing defeats. The Araucanians managed to adapt their fighting techniques to those of the Spaniards, and they continued to resist them into the seventeenth century. The Chichimeca Indians, meanwhile, successfully held up the northward advance of the Spaniards from central Mexico.

Spiritual conquest

The Church was to play a central role in the Spanish Conquest of the New World. The Conquest was spiritual as well as military, in the tradition of the *Reconquista*. Spanish America was to be integrated into the European cosmos in accordance with the notion of Christendom, which unified the spiritual and the temporal. Mass conversion of the indigenous population of Central America by the Spaniards was, in any case, as much a political as a spiritual necessity. The acceptance by the vanquished of the beliefs and values of the conquerors enormously facilitated control of their territories.

The Spanish Crown sought legitimacy for the Conquest from the Pope, who was more than willing to sanction the military campaign as an essential prerequisite for the winning of new souls for the faith. After 1517, the rise of Protestantism gave a new urgency to the opening up of fresh territories to Spanish rule and to the spread and consolidation of the Catholic faith. To achieve this, the Pope was willing to give to the state unprecedented powers of patronage and control over the Church in the Americas.

The initial process of evangelisation was carried out by members of regular religious orders. The first missionaries to reach Mexico were Franciscans; they were followed by the Augustinians and Dominicans. These orders were motivated by considerable idealism and humanism, seeing their mission as one of divine importance. They began the process of conversion with great enthusiasm, baptising thousands of Indians at a time. The Indians' receptivity to Christianity, however, was not as straightforward as it first appeared. Many found in Christianity certain similarities to their own beliefs: some Christian saints, for instance, bore resemblance to Indian gods. In addition, among the subjugated peoples the act of conquest had created a spiritual and ceremonial vacuum which Christianity was able to fill. The Indians took what they needed or wanted from Christianity and adapted it to their own religious beliefs, creating a syncretic faith. The religious orders began to realise what was happening. Some missionaries began to study the Indian customs and belief systems. But this attitude was to shift when the secular or diocesan clergy arrived.

The first missionaries tried to protect the Indians. Las Casas waged his battle to defend the Indians. He denied the theory of the military 'mission', seeing the Crown as having a tutelary trust over Christian Indian kingdoms. But by the middle of the sixteenth century, the religious orders were challenged by the arrival of the secular or diocesan clergy, who were based in towns and subject to the control of the now well-established institutional Church. Other religious orders were allowed to establish themselves in the region in the latter part of the sixteenth century, including the Jesuits, who were to play an especially important role in missionary work in the more remote frontier areas. By 1574, however, when the Crown established limits to the work of the secular clergy and brought them under episcopal control, the missionary phase of the Conquest was virtually over.

Land and labour in the conquered territories

In the course of the sixteenth century, there were major social, demographic, economic and political changes in the newly conquered territories as they became settled colonies. The legacy of this period was to be long-lasting in Latin America.

Occasionally, during the early years of the Conquest, a *conquistador* emerged with a wider vision. One such was Hernán Cortés, who saw the need to settle, establish cities and set up central authorities. Francisco Pizarro was another, though he had great difficulty controlling the other *conquistadores*. As a system of settlement slowly began to emerge, Cortés's vision was to play an important role in its development.

Cortés foresaw a society in which the Crown, the conquerer and the Indian each had obligations and duties to the other. Cities would be defended by the *encomenderos* who lived in them and controlled the *cabildos* (city-councils) which administered them. The Indians would be protected and their workloads regulated to avoid the disaster of Hispaniola. They would remain under the authority of their *caciques*, or chiefs, and would give their labour to the new lords of the land.

chapter one

Cortés had wanted the *encomienda* to be hereditary, hoping that this would give the *encomendero* a longer term view of the value of their Indian labour. But the Crown never accepted this idea, fearing that it would give rise to an overly powerful colonial aristocracy. Nor did the Crown accept the idea that the Indians should be obliged to give personal service to the *encomendero*, as this resulted in terrible abuses against the Indian population. In 1549 the Crown issued a decree in an effort to change the system to one based on tribute rather than labour. These were years of some tension between settlers and the Crown, as the Crown began to assert and institutionalise its authority over the colonies, and offer some defence for the indigenous peoples.

The *encomiendas*, which were given out to the conquerors as a prize of conquest, provided the framework for the emerging colonial society and created the ruling élites of the New World. An *encomienda* did not itself involve a grant of land (the Crown independently made grants of land to the conquerors). Rather, the *encomienda* was the right to forced Indian labour, enabling the *encomendero* to make a profit from the land. If this land was not the subject of a separate grant it remained in the hands of the Indian communities or the Crown.

The conqueror's main interest was the search for precious metals. Gold and silver opened the door to riches, luxury and ennoblement. The Indian labour entrusted to him was the means by which he could discover, mine and transport these precious metals. Initially, the Indians were sent on expeditions to rivers and streams to track down the alluvial gold deposits, which were the source of many Indian gold artefacts.

The Portuguese, by way of contrast, found no precious metals in Brazil (gold was discovered there only at the beginning of the eighteenth century), which was first visited in 1500 by Pedro Alvares Cabral but not seriously colonised until 1531. They therefore began commercial production of a tropical crop, sugar, using experience they had gained in the Atlantic islands and importing African slave-labour. This produced a very different pattern of settlement which required considerable investment from the colonisers.

In Spanish America the discovery of rich silver deposits in Mexico and Peru in the 1540s added a major new dimension to the colonial economy. With the introduction of the amalgamation process (using mercury) the settlers were able to mine poorer-quality ores and still obtain very high levels of production. The discovery of a local supply of mercury in Huancavelica, Peru, meant that the local silver mines could be supplied as well as those of Mexico.

The struggle over the shrinking supply of Indian labour now intensified. By 1568 the indigenous population of Mexico had fallen to 2.65 million from an estimated 21 million at the time of the Conquest, and that of Peru to 1.3 million from more than 11 million.

The abolition of personal service obligations in the *encomienda* – though not the obligation to provide tribute in kind or cash – meant that Indian labour had now to be mobilised through the Crown. Individual colonists had to apply to the Crown for labour, and the Crown supplied it through levies on Indian villages (a system known as *mita* in Peru and *repartimiento* in Mexico). In the silver mines of Potosí, this involved an annual forced migration to work for a very low fixed wage. The result was that Indian communities had to provide the basic subsistence for their members taking part in the *mitas*. The conditions in the mines were so bad that thousands died carrying out their duties.

The growth of the silver mines affected the organisation of land. As more settlers arrived, demand grew for land and increased food production. Two sorts of territory emerged, linked by regulations laid down by the Crown. The first was indigenous territory, namely the communal Indian villages, which no longer produced the surplus that had been important in the initial phase of the Conquest. It was now an area of subsistence peasant agriculture. Often these villages were relocated and the best land given to the Spaniards. Here the Indians produced new generations of labourers for the mines, agricultural enterprises and towns.

The second was Spanish territory, in which food production for the settlers and the production of surplus for the purposes of trade was concentrated. The Spaniards mostly lived in the new cities, but their control of the large agricultural estates, or *latifundios,* was to set a lasting pattern for rural Latin America. The Spanish Crown controlled the movement of indigenous labour between the two territories.

Special grants of land were made to settlers, and they were encouraged to grow new crops. The settlers, for example, preferred wheat bread to the indigenous maize, although wheat was more costly to produce and needed a larger acreage. They wanted meat, so European livestock was introduced. In some areas, crops were eventually found that could establish a market in Europe, such as indigo in El Salvador and cocoa in Venezuela.

As the era of the *conquistador* ended and a colonial economy emerged, so the Spanish Crown imposed its administrative structure. The Viceroy was the head of the administration, appointed for three to five years and directly responsible to the monarch. Below him was the vice-regal court or *audiencia*, with broad judicial and administrative powers. At the base of the hierarchy was the *corregidor de indios* or *alcalde mayor*, who controlled the indigenous populations usually through the Indian chiefs, or *caciques*.

Over the years, the Church served the Crown so closely that it almost fossilised as an institution. A key event in this process was the expulsion of the Jesuits from Brazil in 1759 and eight years later from other parts of Latin America. By that time the Jesuits alone claimed independence from the Crown, acknowledging allegiance only to their General in Rome. The expulsion of more than two thousand Jesuits devastated the centres of learning in the Americas. Henceforth, the Church in Latin America was uniformly subservient to the state, from which it received protection and many material privileges.

The colonial legacy

The fundamental features of present-day Latin America were established in the sixteenth century. The ethnic composition is one such feature and, in particular, the relationship between ethnic origins and social status. The foundations of a firmly hierarchical social pyramid based on race had been laid down.

The white settlers, the so-called *criollo* (creole) élite, were at the apex of this pyramid. As there were few women in the initial phase of the Conquest (although by the 1560s, 28 per cent of emigrants from Spain were women) there were many mixed marriages, as well as rape and concubinage. As a result, a substantial *mestizo* or *ladino* (mixed race) population began to emerge, some of whom managed to scale the social pyramid, at least to become small traders and artisans. The arrival of African slaves also affected the ethnic composition of society. They in turn had offspring with whites and Indians, producing *mulattos* and *zambos*, both remaining very low in the social hierarchy.

The extent of racial mixing varied throughout Latin America, with geography playing a significant part. El Salvador's relatively gentle terrain produced a predominantly *mestizo* society, while neighbouring, mountainous Guatemala retained a large population of pure Indian blood.

There were also a variety of mechanisms by which Indian communities managed to preserve their identity. Some historians speak of virtually 'closed corporate communities', which have continued to exist in parts of highland Central America and the Andes. Although these were never completely closed to outside forces, some peasant communities managed to develop a complex set of institutions and customs that helped to preserve both their own identity and a measure of autonomy in their dealings with the outside world.

Within these communities, the male heads of households participated in an elaborate system of civil and religious offices – the *cargo* system – by which membership of the community was earned. Prestige in the community was derived from the number of *cargos* performed. Often these offices involved time-honoured religious practices that had their origins in pre-Christian rites. They enabled the indigenous population to hang on to an identity which linked them with their pre-Columbian past, despite the efforts of the Catholic Church to stamp out such links.

Communities were able often to resist the control of the Church, which in any case did not have enough priests to serve the thinly spread population of vast rural areas. Such customs could not, however, prevent the widespread disruption to their way of life caused by the demands of the colonial economy for land and labour.

Other aspects of the colonial legacy help us to understand the shape of Latin America's society and economy today. The region was brought into the international economy of the time to serve the interests of Spain and Portugal. Neither Spain nor Portugal were accumulating wealth to invest in their own productive potential. On the contrary, the Spanish and Portuguese nobility saw the wealth of the New World primarily as a means to purchase luxury goods produced elsewhere. The result was a growing tension within the colonial system: the *criollo* élite often saw trading opportunities thwarted by the efforts of the Crown to maintain a strict monopoly of trade with the colonies.

Independence and its limits

The emergence of independence movements in the colonies was part of a complex historical process that was gathering momentum throughout Europe during the eighteenth century. The response of the Spanish Crown was to seek to preserve the old order at whatever cost. But its empire in the New World had been organised around the exploitation of precious metals.

The world was changing rapidly in the eighteenth century, as first agricultural and later industrial revolution gathered pace in Britain. By the end of the century Britain was the focus of an irresistible process of economic and social change, stemming from its increasing technological superiority and manufacturing capacity, which was to reach its peak during the nineteenth century.

Britain already had won virtual control of world shipping. It was thus inevitable that the South American ports would eventually be opened up to international trade.

This is the context in which independence was won from Spain and Portugal. Britain was emerging as a dominant world power, with no desire to exert direct control over the newly independent republics, for it had already won most of the local élites over to the philosophy of free trade which secured their markets for its manufactured goods.

Independence is won

During the eighteenth century, Spain and Portugal fell ever further behind as other European nations, notably Britain, developed the manufacturing base of their economies. In response to the decline of mining as the major economic activity and the rise of British commercial interests, Spain attempted to diversify the economies of its colonies. Spain, however, was unable to supply the needs of the colonies for manufactured goods.

The colonies, meanwhile, found their own ways of circumventing colonial restrictions by finding direct markets elsewhere in Europe through contraband or by producing their own goods. Mounting frustrations among the local élites found expression in the liberal ideas emanating from Britain and France: the emphasis on rationality contrasted starkly with the intolerant rigidities of the Spanish Crown, providing the ideas around which to mobilise rebellion.

In the case of Portugal, there had been early recognition of the rising commercial power of Britain. In 1703 the Portuguese signed the Methuen treaty, which opened up the Portuguese market and that of her colonies to British manufactures in return for advantages for Portuguese wine on the British market. Nearly all Brazil's gold ended up in Britain. Portugal became an increasingly irrelevant intermediary between Brazil and Britain.

Demonstrations against Spanish rule began to spread rapidly after 1810, as war in Europe isolated Spain from her colonies. The independence movement was focused in three places: Caracas, Buenos Aires and Mexico. Caracas and Buenos Aires were the most prosperous parts of the empire, the former with a thriving export economy and the latter a flourishing trading centre.

Mexico was still a centre for silver mining. The Indian population there was beginning to resist the power of the large landowners. As a result, Mexico was virtually the only country where the struggle for independence contained an element of social rebellion. This element was to erupt one hundred years later in the Mexican revolution. Mexico is also notable for the number of priests who joined the independence struggle. About a hundred priests headed battalions, with some, such as Miguel Hidalgo, specifically championing the Indian cause. Elsewhere the Church tended, always with exceptions, to ally itself with the Crown rather than with movements that openly espoused eighteenth-century European rationalism. The books of the French revolutionary writer Jean Jacques Rousseau had been proscribed by the Inquisition, but were smuggled into South America by young *criollo* students when they returned from Europe.

The struggle for independence culminated in the Battle of Ayacucho in 1824, which virtually ended Spanish power in the New World. It was, despite the liberal and liberating ideals of many prominent in the independence movement, essentially a struggle of the local élite for freedom to create and control their own wealth.

A new age was dawning with the rise of capitalism in Europe. The local élites wished to share in the fruits this new age would generate, integrating their economies into the expanding flow of international trade. In the most developed colonial regions, there was already a rich merchant class which champ- ioned free trade and was anxious to wipe out the colonial past. But there was almost no political vision of how best to organise the newly independent republics. It took half a century (and more in some cases) of intense struggles for these republics to begin the construction of what could be called nation states.

Latin America fragments

One of the first issues of the newly independent colonies was the size and composition of each unit. Simón Bolívar, one of the major leaders of the struggle for South American independence, had a vision of the political future of the region as a federation of Spanish-speaking South America. His bitter fight against local and regional interests ended in defeat, and he died in isolation and poverty, a visionary whose ideas had not matched the times. Even *Gran Colombia* – a federation of what are now Venezuela, Ecuador, Colombia and, for a time, Panama – lasted only from 1819 to 1830, and never extended to Peru and Bolivia, as was originally intended. South America eventually broke up into the countries we know today.

Central America briefly became part of Mexico from 1822 to 1823, before it too opted for a federation, which lasted from 1823 to 1839-40. The federation was riven by conflict between rival political forces over the extent of federal and local powers. These groups increasingly identified themselves as either Liberals or Conservatives. In the 1840s the defeat of the last president of the

chapter one

federation, the Honduran-born Liberal Francisco Morazán, marked the collapse of the federation. By this time Morazán, in some respects the Central American equivalent of Bolívar, had the backing only of El Salvador.

Once Latin America had been defined as a region of independent political units, with only Brazil managing to emerge intact from its colonial past, the next challenge was the creation of viable political authorities. This proved exceptionally difficult. The nation states of Latin America were, in general, constructed only after their economies had been built around one or two key exports, with political power being held by the particular regional group which controlled the export sector concerned. This was a long, drawn-out and bitterly contested process. Immediately after independence Latin America sank into regional and local conflicts which were often resolved only on the battlefield.

The economics of political stability

The context in which nations were formed in Latin America was very different from the European experience. Latin America first had to contend with its colonial legacy. It then faced independence at a time when Britain was emerging from a truly dramatic process of economic transformation with such confidence that it could open up its economy (and encourage or force the rest of the world to follow suit) to a world unable to compete with its technological prowess.

The earlier transition from feudalism to capitalism in England[1] had greatly benefited from the precious metals extracted from the Spanish and Portuguese empires, as well as from the capital accumulated through the use of slave labour to produce first sugar and then cotton. This wealth found its way to England in the form of plunder, contraband or more legitimate commerce and financial transactions. The rising class of English independent merchants and later manufacturers put it to productive use. The Spaniards and the Portuguese used it for consumption and to preserve the old order.

The availability of indigenous or imported black labour and of large expanses of land to reward settlers played a major role in the way the Spaniards and Portuguese exploited their colonies. The plentiful supply of forced labour enabled huge profits to be made in the mining of precious metals. The combination of forced labour with the ready availability of land created an élite of wealthy landowners, in contrast to the peasant smallholders who settled the eastern coast of the United States. The concentration of wealth in the hands of a tiny minority, while the mass of the people lived a life of bare subsistence, discouraged the emergence of an effective domestic market for industrial products and made exports a more attractive way of generating wealth.

With little capital – and in the wake of the destruction of the independence wars – the local élites in the nineteenth century turned to exports as a way of generating wealth. There were comparatively few advantages to be had from developing local manufactures, given that cheaper, mass-produced goods were now available from Britain (as long as the foreign exchange could be found to buy them). The status attached to European products as well as European culture by Latin American élites fuelled the demand for foreign rather than locally produced goods. The city-based traders of Latin America were, naturally, the first to see the potential; many had been long-associated with the British through contraband. Gradually they won over a sector of the landowning class, while other landowners remained wedded to traditional and mostly subsistence production. The rise to political dominance of the 'progressive' and 'liberal' class was a protracted, uneven and often bloody affair.

But one country, Paraguay, did embark on a process of development based on local manufacturing and a strong, authoritarian government. Under Dr José Gaspar Rodríguez de Francia (1814-40), all foreigners were banned from Paraguay. While Europeans were pouring into other countries in search of economic gain, Rodríguez's policy of isolation led the Paraguayans to develop and diversify their internal economy. He was succeeded by Carlos Antonio López, who allowed in foreigners but very much on his own terms. Roads were built, along with one of the first railways in South America. Primary education was expanded and foreign surgeons, engineers and mechanics were invited to settle in Paraguay and pass on their skills.

Francisco Solano López succeeded his father in 1862, by which time Paraguay was one of the most stable and developed countries in South America. Its continued independence, however, roused the suspicions and hostility of its neighbours as well as Britain, which played a major role in building an anti-Paraguayan alliance of Brazil, Uruguay and Argentina. The War of the Triple Alliance (1865-70) decimated Paraguay's male population, and ensured that the Paraguayan market was once more open to British manufactured goods. Its independent path of development was no longer a model that other nations might emulate. Indeed, Paraguay subsequently became a byword for backwardness.

In the first half of the nineteenth century, most Latin American countries had great difficulty in finding profitable exports. The British had concentrated at first on organising the import trade

chapter one

and setting up import houses to distribute British-manufactured goods. This had a very adverse effect on such handicraft-type 'industries' as did exist in the region and weakened the arguments of those who continued to support the need to develop a local manufacturing base. Many countries were forced to devalue their currencies and to apply for foreign loans in order to pay for imported goods. British banking houses again stepped in to offer their assistance. The situation encouraged an export drive, but Britain had its own colonies to supply tropical products, while cotton, which along with wool was the basis of the textile industry that led the industrial revolution, was produced by slave labour in the United States.

The Brazilian economist Celso Furtado, in his economic history of Latin America, argues that it was the difficulty of finding markets for exports that left the urban groups who had led the fight for independence unable to organise a stable political order.[2] This is the exact opposite of the view, often expounded, that persistent instability was the cause of the failure of post-independence Latin America to expand its exports. Colombia, for instance, failed to find a suitable export crop for the international market until the early twentieth century. The country was chronically unstable and backward in the nineteenth century, because of the inability of any one part of the élite to exert its dominance over others. Relations within the élite were characterised alternately by bloody warfare and compromise, and by party politics and civil war, in which the forces of tradition were never really defeated. The nineteenth century holds many clues to the nature of the Colombian political order today, with its formal adherence to constitutions and electoral politics and use of violence to resolve political differences.

Chile, on the other hand, is an exceptional case. It had not been a producer of precious metals in colonial times but an agricultural and cattle-raising region supplying the needs of the silver mines of Peru. Local Chilean interests had therefore arisen within the legal framework imposed by Spain, rather than through smuggling and under strong British influence. The conflicts which bitterly divided élites in other countries did not emerge in Chile and a relatively stable system of political power was constructed soon after independence. Even today, Chile prides itself on having the longest tradition of 'democracy' in Latin America.

Export-led growth

During the nineteenth century two factors emerged that can help us understand contemporary Latin America. The first is the role of élites – that is, ruling groups who look outside their own countries for the means to generate wealth, rather than building up local productive forces. These groups were quick to adopt the British ideas of free trade. The second factor is the formation over the years of an international economy based on a division of economic tasks. Britain, and later those nations hot on its heels in the process of industrialisation, dominated this international economy, while Latin America was led by its élites into a subordinate role of exporter of raw materials.

An international economy could not properly emerge until there was a world market. For this, a revolution in transport was necessary. The mechanisation of shipping, with the development of the steamship and the invention of the propeller in 1840, brought major changes in international trade. As well as increasing the volume and speed of shipping, it drastically cut freight charges. The yearly value of world trade rose from $1.5 billion in the 1820s to $3.5 billion in the 1840s, and to $40 billion just before the outbreak of the First World War.

There was a strong incentive to specialise within this system of world trade. The technological supremacy of the industrialised or industrialising nations was very great. Meanwhile, markets for raw materials expanded rapidly from the mid-nineteenth century onwards. Populations were growing and other nations began to challenge Britain in the industrialisation process.

Each Latin American country sought an export crop with which to respond to the new demand, sometimes with much experimentation and with the help of government incentives. In El Salvador the government gave preferential treatment to producers of cocoa, balsam, rubber, coffee, wheat, tobacco, vanilla and agave. These were referred to as *frutas de más esperanza* (fruits of most hope), that is, crops thought to have export potential. Coffee later proved itself to be the 'golden bean' that linked the nation to the international economy.

The goods which each Latin American country produced affected its pattern of development. Argentina and Uruguay, for instance, produced wool, beef and wheat, all of which were in high demand to feed as well as clothe the rapidly growing urban populations of the industrialising nations. Extensive use of good agricultural land resulted in high productivity. This was increased further by technological changes (developed mainly in the United States) in the farming, storage and shipping of cereals. Uruguay and Argentina enjoyed high growth-rates as their exports expanded.

Ecuador, Central America, some parts of Mexico and Venezuela, Brazil and Colombia became exporters of tropical produce. Coffee and cocoa were particularly significant commodities for these countries, with demand coming mostly from the United States and the newly industrialised nations of Europe. Only in certain situations did tropical commodities stimulate development, however, because they did not require an advanced infrastructure or technology. Indeed, banana production in Central America remained a foreign-controlled enclave, with very little impact on the local economy. In the case of the coffee regions of São Paulo in Brazil and Antioquia in Colombia, where the crop was largely in the hands of local producers, coffee did play a significant role in promoting infrastructural development and the expansion of a domestic market.

Mexico, Chile, Peru and Bolivia (and Venezuela when it became an oil exporter in the 1920s) all became exporters of mineral products. Demand for industrial metals was growing rapidly, but the scale of the capital investment and technology required meant that, in most cases, these exports were mined by foreign companies in a virtually closed economic system.

Liberals vs Conservatives: the separation of Church and state

The divisions within the Latin American élites following independence settled into a consistent pattern of opposition and conflict between Liberals and Conservatives. Historians differ over the precise meaning of each term. Liberals, however, are normally identified with the rising class associated with new export crops, and Conservatives with the forces of tradition, particularly the less commercially-minded landowners. Such divisions are often not as clear-cut in practice. But the one defining feature between the two which all can agree on is their attitude towards the Catholic Church. The Liberals wanted a modern and secular state, which meant stripping the Church of its often vast temporal powers.

The Latin American Church recovered only slowly from the trauma of the independence struggles, which had greatly weakened its structures. Separation from Spain, for example, stopped the flow of clergy from the Iberian peninsula. Rome was unwilling to grant the post-independence governments the same rights of patronage enjoyed by the Spanish Crown, leaving some countries without bishops for years.

The Church had hitherto relied on its close association with colonial government to protect its interests. Having lost this means of support, it turned to the most conservative forces in society for protection from the rise of liberalism.

Those wishing to bring Latin America into the modern age felt that the Church was a bastion of tradition, privilege and conservatism.

The Liberals were not opposed to all religion but they were against the Church influencing the institutions of the state. Education in particular, it was felt, had to be freed from church control. The confiscation of church property, often including large tracts of fertile land, was another major cause of conflict between Conservatives and Liberals.

In general, the Liberals emerged victorious from these nineteenth-century political struggles. And their victories did indeed seem to coincide with the consolidation of the export economy, the creation of modern state institutions, the building of basic infrastructure and the dismantling of the Church's secular power. Gradually the Church was forced to come to terms with its reduced role, often renegotiating with the state until a *modus vivendi* was found. Religion was still important to the state as a transmitter of values supportive of authority. However, the Church was soon facing new challenges posed by alternative religious influences and secular political ideologies.

It is interesting to look again at an exception to this history: the case of Colombia. Here the battles between Conservatives and Liberals were never resolved as finally as in other countries. The 1886 Constitution was promulgated in a spirit of compromise between the competing forces. A Concordat the following year reversed previous anti-clerical measures which had provoked many bloody battles between the parties. Church privileges were restored and the Catholic Church was recognised as an essential element of social order and given control of education and most civil ceremonies. The consequence of this protected role within the state was a lack of interest on the part of the Church in internal renewal, either social or religious. Even today, the Colombian Church remains one of the most conservative and traditional in Latin America.

Into the twentieth century

The fifty years of export-led expansion between 1880 and 1930 provoked social upheavals of all kinds as mining companies, plantation owners and the first industrial enterprises of Latin America sought to mould the labour force to new economic requirements. They often met resistance from dispossessed peasants drawn into wage and non-wage labour for the first time. The transition from pre-capitalist to capitalist forms of agriculture was uneven. One consequence was large-scale migrations to urban areas beginning Latin America's transformation to the highly urbanised region it is today. In Latin America, unlike Europe, export-led agriculture rather than a sustained industrial growth, acted as the motor for these changes. The migration of

chapter one

unskilled labour to the cities was not matched by a corresponding growth of manufacturing jobs. The consequence was the creation of a heterogeneous urban population of skilled and semi-skilled workers and a mass of underemployed and unemployed.

The creation of a workforce. The consequences of the social changes described above varied greatly from country to country. They differed according to the predominant economic activities – plantation agriculture, extensive ranching or mining enclaves – and upon incipient industrialisation where labour, capital and market conditions were appropriate. They were also influenced by the degree to which the workforce resisted its adaptation to new processes of production, which were designed to extract the largest possible profit for the smallest possible cost.

In the towns, small craft workshops and print shops were established to serve the rapidly growing and increasingly literate middle class. Their workers, together with workers in the railways and ports built to serve the export economies, formed the region's first labour unions. In countries with mining enclaves there was a much larger labour force that often formed the basis for the region's strongest labour organisations.

Argentina and Uruguay (and to a somewhat lesser extent Brazil, Chile and other countries) were affected by the considerable immigration of Europeans. A study by Paul A. Ladame in 1958 estimated that between 1865 and 1914 around 20 million people emigrated to Latin America from Europe. Although some migrants returned home, the majority stayed, making a lasting impact on their new countries. Argentina and Uruguay, for instance, received hundreds of thousands of Italian and Spanish immigrants. Most ended up in the cities of Buenos Aires and Montevideo, as there was limited access to jobs or land in rural areas given over to cattle-raising, sheep-rearing and cereal production. Many provided the skills and some capital for the early processes of industrialisation, particularly in Argentina with its large population and domestic market. They also brought with them the European ideas of anarchism and syndicalism, around which the first unions were created.

In Brazil, immigrant labour subsidised by the state provided the solution to the labour needs of the São Paulo coffee estates after the abolition of slavery in 1888. The coffee planters, who now represented the most powerful group of landowners in Brazil, saw economic advantages in a labour force of free workers who had to provide their own food and often their agricultural tools as well. But the conditions for the workers were very harsh and, as soon as they were able, many moved to new jobs in the city. The abolition of slavery brought significant growth in the internal market and a sudden spurt of industrialisation. New jobs were created in the textile and food factories and in the railways and ports. Here European immigrants again brought anarcho-syndicalist ideas that influenced the formation of early unions.

The new organisations of the workers in Brazil and Argentina met with harsh repression. During the 1930s and 1940s their unions were brought under state control. In Uruguay they were seduced by the creation of an advanced system of state welfare provision in the second decade of the twentieth century.

The Chilean experience was different because the dependence of the state on revenues from nitrate exports gave the workers in this sector particular power. As the state was not considered to have the right to intervene in the economy, including labour relations, labour and capital fought out their battles virtually without government regulation. Both sides took tough positions: militant strikes by workers, and blacklists and sackings by bosses. Anarcho-syndicalists gained control of most labour unions in Santiago and Valparaíso, while in the 1920s the Communists won control in the nitrate and coal mining areas. But the tradition of independent labour organisation was maintained, and the anarcho-syndicalist tradition was strong enough to prevent absorption by the Communist Party and contributed to the formation of Latin America's only significant socialist party in 1933.

These examples are from the southern part of Latin America, which industrialised and urbanised earlier than other regions. The Central American experience was quite different. Export economies based on tropical produce, notably coffee and bananas, remained very backward in comparison. Most backward of all was Honduras, where a US company, United Fruit, controlled virtually its only export crop, bananas, with few benefits for the rest of the economy.

Elsewhere in the region, where a local élite or oligarchy controlled at least a part of the export sector, the problem of creating a suitable labour force and labour market was a major factor in the social transformations of the late nineteenth and early twentieth centuries. The need for labour, which was mostly seasonal, was a major issue for plantation owners. In the 1870s indigenous communities were dispossessed of their lands to make way for coffee plantations, creating a new source of labour: many Indians became workers on the plantations in exchange for a plot of land and sometimes a very small wage. Vagrancy laws were introduced in Guatemala (where they were not abolished until 1944), El Salvador and Nicaragua, to force people back into work when they drifted away from their villages.

chapter one

Throughout Central America, the commercial estates made use of various pre-capitalist forms of labour relations as well as free-wage labour. Subsistence farming by peasants continued on land unsuitable for export crops. In a number of other regions of Latin America, such as the Andean highlands and parts of Brazil and Chile, small peasant farmers continued to eke out a living on tiny plots, or provided labour for traditional estates through debt-bondage or sharecropping, forms of labour relations which originated in colonial times. Debt-bondage (by which labourers were tied to estates through debts incurred to landowners) and sharecropping arrangements (by which peasants gave landowners a share of their crop in return for land) persisted into the twentieth century alongside rapidly evolving commercial agriculture.

Some of the most backward and impoverished conditions for peasants and rural workers were in Mexico. In 1910, 96.6 per cent of rural families were landless and many worked for landowners in conditions of semi-slavery. Historians still fight over how to interpret the Mexican revolution which broke out that year, but at one level it was clearly a massive uprising of peasants – a quintessential peasant revolution. Looked at from the perspective of history, however, the revolution actually paved the way for the development of capitalism in Mexico. Peasants were no longer tied unproductively to the old *hacienda,* or estate, and could move to the urban areas. Land reform was not fully implemented until the 1930s, and even then it was unable to halt the advance of the new entrepreneurial landowners. It did, however, largely destroy the old, traditional landowners. The state took on the task of modernisation, but the legacy of the revolution was such that it had constantly to refer to the 'masses', in order to institutionalise the moment when they burst into history so that it would no longer be an active threat but a passive memory.

The creation of a labour force in Latin America therefore took place against a background of uneven development and capitalist growth. Social transformations, though usually partial, were mostly deeply disruptive. The emerging labour movements conducted their struggles against this background, and it often influenced their outcome. In Colombia, for instance, the 1920s are known as the 'Heroic Years' for the labour movement. But the power of labour was limited by the fact that the most strategic area of the economy, the coffee sector, was in the hands of relatively prosperous peasants – with their small and medium-sized farms – rather than large-plantation owners. At the same time, the labour movement was unable to link up with the many other sectors of the peasantry who were disaffected and impoverished by the process of economic change.

Along the Magdalena River, oil, rail and river-port workers organised in independent unions that looked increasingly to the Revolutionary Socialist Party (PSR) for leadership. The famous orators of the party, such as María Cano, toured the river winning supporters in the bordering towns and villages. A revolutionary culture emerged in which people baptised their children in the 'holy name of oppressed humanity'. Militancy reached its high point in the strike of the banana plantation workers in 1928, which resulted in a massacre of some 1,000 workers and the loss of the insurrectionary momentum the party believed was building up. The workers' movement then fell under the influence of first the Liberal Party and later the Conservative Party. The rebuilding of an independent union movement had to await the 1980s.

By the end of the 1920s, it was clear that 'the people' were taking an active role in the shaping of Latin American history as never before. They were protagonists, and there was a ferment of ideas around which they could mobilise and which gave them a sense of confidence and power: from Marxism, through various forms of socialism, to anarchism, syndicalism and indigenous forms of Marxism, such as that of José Carlos Mariátegui in Peru.

For traditional institutions, such as the Church, these ideas were a major challenge to its unquestioned authority in the realm of beliefs and ideas. If Catholicism was to retain the allegiance of the rising urbanised (and increasingly secularised) populations it had to come to terms with the changing nature of the world.

Élite politics and the challenge of the middle classes. The élites of Latin America had no sooner organised their economies around one or two exports and consolidated political domination than they were faced with the emergence of the new social forces described above. There was no long, drawn-out process of erecting a liberal, competitive political system for the propertied classes (as in England) so that democratic aspirations from below could eventually be incorporated without threat. Mechanisms to resolve peacefully the many conflicts among the ruling groups, such as well-organised political parties, free elections, established rules of the political game and an independent judiciary, had little chance to develop.

Each Latin American country boasted progressive constitutions and had electoral systems and political parties whose very names were taken from European political parties, all mostly within the context of strongly presidential forms of government. But the reality was, with only a few notable exceptions, a parody of the liberal-democratic model they aspired to replicate. Politics was almost entirely an affair of the élite. The mass of the people, still mostly rural, represented votes to be bought in various ways.

chapter one

Local leaders, or *caudillos,* would organise the vote using powers of patronage or intimidation to ensure compliance. Such practices continue to operate in many backward rural areas of Latin America, while many of them were adapted in the course of the decades to the needs of the rapidly growing urban populations.

One institution did emerge with the coherence and strength to decide conflicts within the élite: the armed forces. By the early twentieth century, most Latin American countries already had – or were in the process of forming – professional military institutions. They received training and arms from foreign (mostly European) armies and navies. In the weakly formed political institutions of early twentieth-century Latin America, the armed forces' internal discipline and unquestioning loyalties to leaders made them a powerful force.

Civilian politicians in many countries turned to the army for support at crucial moments. Military coups would organise transfers of power when the results of the ballot failed to please. Central America provides the crudest examples of military intervention and dictatorship, reflecting the chronic failure of the élite to build itself a stable political order. A similar pattern was evident in all the Andean republics, with the exception of Colombia. Here two strong political parties survived into the twentieth century, maintaining loyalties sealed in blood during many conflicts fought out on the battlefield during the nineteenth century and dominating even the armed forces.

Elsewhere in Latin America, particularly in the Southern Cone (a term that includes Argentina, Chile, Uruguay and sometimes Paraguay) and some Andean countries, the social changes of the first decades of the twentieth century had created a middle class as well as an industrial labour force. Civil servants, professionals and the owners of small businesses and landholdings, all aspired to participate in the political system. Élites were sometimes forced to grant them this right.

In Argentina, it was partly the conspiracies of the Radical Party (founded at the turn of the century) with the military which forced the dominant class to grant universal suffrage in 1912 and allow the election of the party leader, Hipólito Yrigoyen, to the presidency in 1916.

In Uruguay the middle classes gained control of the state early in the twentieth century. This small and prosperous country could afford to use the surplus from its thriving export sector to finance a powerful state, giving jobs and pensions to the rising middle classes, labour legislation and welfare benefits to the workers, and 'class harmony' to the landed élite which financed it.

In Peru a middle-class movement against the rule of the traditional élite began with student demonstrations for university reform in the early 1920s. One of the leaders of this movement was Victor Raúl Haya de la Torre, who went on to found the American Popular Revolutionary Alliance (APRA) – a movement of considerable importance to twentieth-century Peruvian politics. APRA expressed the rise of the new social classes of early twentieth-century Latin America and their frustrations at the exclusivity of the oligarchic political order.

APRA was led by the middle classes but attempted to draw the working class into an alliance against the traditional élite and foreign interests. It was particularly successful amongst the sugar workers in the north of the country. Its nationalist and populist character led it to look to the Mexican revolution as a model rather than the Russian revolution. The Marxist, José Carlos Mariátegui, on the other hand, founded the Socialist Party around his vision of a revolutionary socialism led by the workers but also acknowledging the importance of Peru's large Quechua-speaking indigenous population.

The debate inherent in these two parties recurred time and time again over the ensuing decades in Latin America. Should workers be forging their own revolutionary path? Or should they be making alliances with the middle classes and 'progressive' industrialists against traditional oligarchs and the influence of external interests, with a view to building a modern form of national capitalism?

Populism, nationalism and the state

Between the Great Depression (1929-32) and the immediate aftermath of the Second World War, Latin America experienced two more decades of rapid change. The period began with a severe economic crisis, but it is notable for the pursuit, at first through force of circumstance and later more systematically, of a national path to development, based on a locally owned industrial sector producing for the domestic market. This strategy usually demanded a certain kind of class alliance to support it, which ultimately proved elusive. Industrialists were too weak and fearful of the 'masses' to consider alliances with them, and the still powerful agro-exporting interests were totally hostile to them. When 'populist' leaders were in power, efforts to build such an alliance were often undertaken by the state. These leaders used their charismatic appeal to mobilise the masses. Cárdenas of Mexico (1934-40), Perón of Argentina (1946-52 and 1952-55) and Getulio Vargas of Brazil (1930-45 and 1950-54) are particularly associated with this strategy.

chapter one

The chronology is by no means exact, and the political expression of the idea of national industrialisation and development varied greatly between countries. Both Peru's military government of 1968 and the socialist Allende in Chile (1970-73) attempted such a strategy; the Central American republics, apart from a brief experiment in Guatemala in the 1940s, ignored the idea; and in Colombia it was extinguished when its leader, Jorge Eliecer Gaitán, was assassinated in Bogotá in 1948. In Colombia, where oligarchic power was deeply entrenched, state-led populism would have meant revolution.

The Great Depression

The Great Depression was the result of the stock market crash in 1929 which led to recession in the industrialised countries. It also had disastrous effects on poor countries which were dependent on the industrialised world for markets for their raw material exports and for imports of manufactured goods. It was the most serious crisis the world capitalist system had hitherto experienced.

In most of Latin America the uncertainties of the export-led growth model were already apparent, and vulnerability to fluctuating world prices for their exports had caused considerable insecurity in the 1920s. The Depression was not, therefore, a sudden cataclysmic event for otherwise buoyant economies. But its unprecedented severity and impact on the volume and value of international trade heralded a number of political upheavals in Latin America. Its effects were felt throughout the continent, both in the most impoverished countries, such as El Salvador, and the wealthiest, such as Argentina.

As the price of coffee tumbled in the world market, the meagre wages of the coffee-plantation workers of El Salvador were cut. Farabundo Martí, the founder of the Salvadorean Communist Party, had begun organising among coffee workers and by 1932 had laid the ground for an uprising. But the leaders were arrested before it started and the uprising itself – the occupation by starving peasants and coffee-pickers of several towns in the west of the country – was suppressed with the savagery for which the Salvadorean rulers and their military protectors have become notorious. It is estimated that between 20,000 and 30,000 peasants were killed in cold-blooded reprisals.

In Argentina, the crash occurred just one year after the re-election of Yrigoyen. Low international prices for beef and grain threatened the economic dominance of the cattle ranchers, who had never lost economic power during the rule of the Radical Party. The military coup of 1930 allowed them to recapture some of their political leverage. But the old order had been changing since the

First World War, with a declining Britain being supplanted as the dominant world power by the United States. In Argentina the old order was the close alliance between the cattle ranchers – especially those who fattened cattle for sale to the slaughter houses rather than the cattle breeders – and British political and commercial interests.

The Depression revealed the extent to which the economic foundations of this alliance had been eroded: Argentina, still excluded from access to US markets, was forced in mid-depression to negotiate humiliating treaties with Britain to maintain its access to the British market. Unable to earn sufficient foreign exchange to import the manufactured goods from the industrialised world, cattle ranchers were forced to accept an accelerated process of national industrialisation led by an increasingly interventionist state.

Industrialisation

Argentina, Brazil, Chile, Mexico and even Cuba had all achieved some level of basic industrial development – particularly in textiles, clothing, footwear and some metal tools – by the beginning of the First World War. The issue for these countries was how to expand from the production of non-durable consumer goods into higher levels of industrialisation which would have greater power to generate sustained growth. The larger economies (Argentina, Brazil, Mexico and Chile) began to make rapid strides in the local manufacture of previously imported goods during the 1930s and 1940s. This has been called import-substitution industrialisation.

TABLE 1: Industrial output as % of Gross Domestic Product

	Argentina	Mexico	Brazil	Chile
1929	22.8	14.2	11.7	7.9
1937	25.6	16.2	13.1	11.7
1947	31.1	19.8	17.3	17.3
1957	32.4	21.7	23.1	19.7

(Source: Celso Furtado, *Economic Development of Latin America*, Cambridge University Press, 1970, p86.)

Other countries were much further behind, but driven by the effects of the crisis of the 1930s and two world wars, industrialisation gathered pace in Colombia, Peru, Uruguay, Costa Rica and

Bolivia. After the Second World War, industrialisation began in even the poorest countries of Latin America. The process of industrialisation often started out of necessity because international trade had been disrupted by war and recession. It was not until the late 1940s that import-substitution industrialisation began to be advocated as a coherent strategy for development.

Its main proponent was Raúl Prebisch, who headed the United Nations Economic Commission for Latin America (ECLA) set up in Santiago, Chile, in 1949. Prebisch drew attention to the structural obstacles to development in Latin America, including the adverse terms of trade for primary commodity exports in relation to manufactured goods. He advocated a state-led strategy of national industrialisation, protected by tariff barriers to shield local industry from cheap manufactured imports from the industrialised countries. He also supported agrarian and other reforms needed to create a market for industrial goods.

Variants on this strategy began to be implemented in most Latin American countries in the late 1940s. The common element in these industrialisation processes was the role of the state. But whom did the state represent in each country? Behind the economic process of industrialisation lay complex webs of social relations and political struggles. The interests which profited from the export of agricultural exports were sometimes incorporated into industrial strategies; sometimes they held them back. Countries with small markets had to expand them by seeking access to neighbouring countries or through income redistribution and agrarian reform. The structural and political tensions inherent in this type of industrialisation manifested themselves most clearly in the larger, more advanced economies during the 1930s and 1940s.

The politics of industrialisation. The building of an industrial base requires considerable mobilisation of human and material resources. In countries dependent largely on income earned by exports, the accumulation of a surplus to invest in industry is hugely problematic. Those who control the export sector retain considerable economic and political power, while those in the manufacturing sector cannot obtain the resources needed to take industrialisation forward to higher levels. In these circumstances, the state often plays a crucial role in transferring resources to industry and empowering the industrial classes by winning the support of the mass of the people for industrialisation which, in political terms, means jobs, higher incomes and social security.

In the most advanced Latin American countries, notably Mexico, Argentina and Brazil, the state was a powerful force during the 1930s and 1940s as these countries sought to build on the gains of their early industrialisation. Many associate these years with the rise of 'populism', the mobilisation through the state of an unwieldy alliance of industrialists, the urban middle class, urban workers and recent migrants from the countryside to the city in an assault on old agrarian oligarchies.

As with all attempts at tidy definitions of socio-political processes, there are many problems with the term 'populist' to describe the governments of Cárdenas, Perón and Vargas, each of which had its own unique features and reflected the distinct realities of each country. But the term does emphasise the common element in their attempts to build appropriate alliances between classes in order to develop import-substitution industrialisation.

Vargas in Brazil, for instance, was a distinctly demobilising, authoritarian figure during his first period of government (1930-45). In Brazil, unlike Argentina, the 1930 revolution ousted the powerful coffee oligarchy but did not restore explicitly conservative interests. There was no Radical Party of urban middle class interests with experience of government in Brazil, so the forces which then rose to prominence in Brazil, including the growing middle classes, did so within an authoritarian framework in which their leader, Vargas, openly adopted much of Mussolini's fascist thinking in his construction of what he called the 'New State'. Labour legislation, for instance, was built around corporatist conceptions of controlled worker-participation and rules tying labour unions to the state.

In Argentina and Mexico, on the other hand, the independently organised unions initially gave their support to Perón and Cárdenas respectively. But as these leaders began consciously to court organised labour in order to establish state control over it, the unions lost their autonomy, creating a lasting association of labour with Perónism in Argentina and with the state under the Institutionalised Revolutionary Party (PRI) in Mexico.

In all three countries populist appeals to the masses came to play an important role in mobilising support for state-led industrialisation. In Brazil, this sort of populism was a feature of the entire period from 1945 to 1964, the year of the military coup, including Vargas's second presidency (1950-54).

In Argentina, Colonel Juan Domingo Perón, helped by the consistently high prices for Argentina's main exports caused by the Second World War and the Korean War, used his post as Minister of Labour (1943-46) in the military government to develop social security programmes very favourable to the labour force. By satisfying many of the demands which organised labour had made unsuccessfully in the 1930s, he built up a solid base of support amongst the workers. In 1946, he won the presidency in free elections against the opposition of the large conservative landowners. Perón's goal as president was an Argentina based on national economic development and social justice, with a strong industrial sector. The contradictions in the Perónist strategy, which eventually brought about its collapse, were inherent in all the Latin American efforts at import-substitution industrialisation and national economic development. High export prices, from which the state benefited through export taxes, had brought in resources which the state channelled to industry with little harm to the traditional export sector. But when the period of high demand for Argentina's exports came to a close at the end of the Korean War, further development of industry could no longer rely on this extraordinary surplus as a way of bringing in the raw materials, fuel, machinery and technology required. And industry could no longer afford to pay the high real wages Perón had hitherto guaranteed the labour force.

Perón's second presidency (1951-55) was marked by a move to the right. Rather than using his base of support among organised labour to challenge the power of the agro-export sector, Perón abandoned his emphasis on national economic development and social justice. Instead, he sought capital from abroad and squeezed the living standards of the workers. He also began to strengthen centralised political control, increasing repression and censorship. By the time Perón was ousted by the military coup of 1955, he had alienated most sectors of society, notably the Catholic Church (whose privileges he had attacked), the landowners, the national industrialists and the army. Only the workers still tried to defend him, but to no avail.

Elsewhere in Latin America, import-substitution industrialisation led by the state ran into similar difficulties. The 'easy' phase of substitution – the domestic manufacture of basic consumer goods – was soon exhausted. Further industrialisation required the production of capital goods. This stage was difficult, as it depended on the ability to import more machines and technology.

The difficulties were as follows: first, the creation of a manufacturing base, capable of producing capital goods such as steel-making plant and machine tools, is a long-term undertaking, requiring consistent investment over a number of years in different sectors of the economy, including electricity generation and transport infrastructure. Second, overall income and demand for industrial products were rising faster than the growth of manufacturing capacity, provoking the high inflation which accompanied the industrialisation processes of Latin America. In addition, local industry, shielded from competition by protective tariff barriers, often proved inefficient and unable to supply sufficient goods of quality to meet the growing demand. Third, most (if not all) of the machines and industrial goods needed for this process had to be imported, so the export sector and its capacity to earn hard currency were as crucial as ever.

At the same time, agriculture in most countries was largely given over to one or two export crops, and was unable to respond to the growing demand for food from rising urban populations. Not only was distribution highly unequal, but resources had also not been invested in the agricultural technologies needed to increase productivity for the domestic market. Over-emphasis on industrial investment thus tightened the bottleneck in the structure of production. Shortages of agricultural products led to price rises, which mostly benefited the large landowners who were better able to respond to market forces than peasant producers. In some cases (Argentina was one of them), home markets for agricultural produce came to compete with export markets, aggravating the general problem of the country's capacity to earn hard currency from exports.

These and many other factors overshadowed Latin America's efforts at state-led national industrialisation. There were inflationary pressures and persistent balance of payments problems. One solution, in theory, would have been to transform the structure of landownership through agrarian reform. But rather than confront the vested interests of the large landowners, governments (particularly in the larger economies) turned towards foreign capital. In the post-war period this was mostly available from increasingly powerful US-based transnational corporations. The search for a national process of industrial development continued into the 1970s, often with the state espousing radical social policies. The 1973 coup against Salvador Allende in Chile virtually marked the end of this quest.

Latin America's 'glorious thirty years'

The economist Albert O. Hirschman described the period 1950-81 as the 'glorious years' of Latin American history. This coincided with the post-war growth of Europe and Japan (1950-73). Latin American countries used foreign borrowing to maintain growth even after the oil shocks of 1973 had halted growth elsewhere. Growth ended in 1981. Mexico announced in 1982 that it could no longer maintain interest payments on its foreign debt, and the debt crisis was at last formally acknowledged in Latin America.

Between 1950 and 1981, gross domestic product (GDP) in the region increased fivefold, while the population rose from 155 million to nearly 400 million. Latin America enjoyed faster and

chapter one

more stable growth than the more advanced countries of the Organisation for Economic Co-operation and Development (OECD).[3] Between 1938 and 1980, Brazil, Colombia and Mexico did not experience a single year in which GDP declined.

In the space of a few decades, nearly every Latin American country shifted from a predominantly rural to a largely urban society. The share of industry in GDP increased from 17 per cent to 24 per cent between 1950 and 1980.

Agriculture also changed, with the introduction of modern, capital-intensive techniques of production and advances in the organisation and marketing of products. Many countries diversified their export sectors with new crops, while agro-industrial development grew apace.

On average, agriculture accounted for almost half of employment in 1950, ranging from 60 per cent in Brazil and Mexico to about 25 per cent in Argentina and Uruguay. But by 1981, only a quarter of the economically active population worked in agriculture. Service sector employment rose from less than one-third to more than half of the total.

There is, however, another side to the 'glorious years' of growth and development in Latin America. The growth failed to bring any real change in Latin America's highly unequal distribution of income. The wealthiest 5 per cent of the population maintained their share of income and there was a notable increase in the urban middle class, who enjoyed a higher standard of living and benefited from greater access to education and, in most countries, participation in political life. (Central America is the exception: until the 1980s middle-class democrats in the region faced assassination squads just as much as working-class revolutionaries.) But at the same time, the numbers of people in urban areas living in extreme poverty also grew. In absolute terms, around 40 per cent of the population of Latin America was estimated to be living in critical poverty by the early 1970s, with little improvement over the subsequent years. And for this population, education was still rudimentary, particularly in rural areas. A full period of elementary education is still not guaranteed to all Latin Americans of school age.

Income disparity does not become apparent in per capita GDP figures, but these comparisons show that Latin America's economic performance was much less impressive than is indicated by the figures for overall GDP growth. Overall figures do not take into account population growth, which is twice as fast as in OECD countries. Birth rates slowed in the 1970s and 1980s, but the population of Latin America has still trebled between 1938 and

1985. No OECD country has ever experienced comparable population growth, with the consequent pressures on housing, education and urban and rural services.

In the rural areas, capitalist agricultural transformation took place alongside the persistence of traditional, peasant subsistence-farming. In many cases the growth of the one seriously disrupted the other: large-scale entrepreneurial farmers growing new export crops took over agricultural frontiers, dispossessing peasant smallholders and forcing them into wage labour at least for part of the year.

Changes in the structure of employment did not match the demand for work from Latin America's growing labour force. Despite the emphasis on industrialisation in these years, the average percentage of employment in this sector rose only from 23 per cent in 1950 to 25 per cent in 1981. Service sector employment in reality covers a host of informal sector activities, from street selling and prostitution to work in small sweatshops – activities which are all unregulated by the state. Measurement of this sector is notoriously unreliable. The Regional Employment Programme for Latin America and the Caribbean (PREALC) estimated in the 1980s that the equivalent of 19.4 per cent of the labour force was underemployed.

Nor did economic growth result in greater autonomy for Latin America or greater bargaining power in its external economic relations. A high percentage of Latin American exports remained primary products. And the region continued to import both products incorporating advanced technology and the technology itself, which was required for further economic development.

The most dynamic sectors of industry had also come under the control of transnational corporations, notably the chemical, basic metals, engineering and car industries. They expanded their operations in Latin America during the 1960s, particularly in the larger countries where there were domestic markets to which their operations were primarily directed.

Latin America is criticised today for its failure to adopt during these years the strategy of export-led manufacturing which was so successful in the East Asian economies. The strategy of maintaining the trade barriers and exchange rate policies designed for an 'anachronistic' policy of inward-oriented growth is seen as a source of many of the region's contemporary problems, although it did result in high growth-rates for a number of years.

But by the mid-1960s it was apparent that the region was missing opportunities for trade. Between 1950 and 1973 exports from OECD countries grew in volume by an average of 9.4 per cent a year, while Latin American exports grew by only 3.2 per cent. During the 1970s military régimes in a number of Latin American countries began to shift towards more open economies, aided by the transformation in external financing which occurred in the 1970s. Private banks began to channel large amounts of funds to the region, and external loans became much more important than the direct foreign investment that had dominated the 1950s and 1960s. Transnational banks became deeply involved in the Latin American economies in the 1970s, with disastrous results only apparent in the ensuing decade.

Thus, while the 'glorious years' brought major transformations and growth, they simultaneously brought disruption and misery to the lives of millions. A technologically advanced sector emerged in most Latin American economies alongside a backward, traditional sector. A formal, measured economy could genuinely convey signs of growth and development, while most men and women lived and worked in the unregulated, informal sector. Latin America did not achieve either technological or productive self-reliance. Financial and commercial relations continued to favour overwhelmingly the industrialised nations.

This extraordinary unevenness of growth and economic development provided the context for the rise of challenging political and social movements and new ideas. The Cuban and the Nicaraguan revolutions belong to this period, as do a variety of theories and experiences of armed struggle. In addition, radical economists developed the theories of economic 'dependency'; the Chileans elected a Marxist government; peasant and worker movements flourished; and base Christian communities and liberation theology emerged to challenge traditional practices and thinking in the Catholic Church.

Ranged against them were heavily entrenched vested interests. The agro-exporting élites, progressive in their heyday, were now the standard bearers of the old order: with their control of key export sectors they remained very powerful, while manufacturing classes (not always as distinct as theory would dictate) remained relatively weak. The Latin American ruling class proved itself capable of extreme brutality, often relying, at least initially, on the ambivalence of the middle classes, who were fearful of the radicalism below which might threaten their own more limited access to the fruits of growth. Torture, 'disappearances', mass arrests and murder were all used to ward off the (real or imagined) threat of revolution.

This period coincided with the Cold War. The efforts of the United States, particularly after the Cuban revolution in 1959, to preserve its Latin America neighbours from any social unrest which might lead to revolution is a constant theme in the political ferment of these years. Successive governments in the United States used the armed forces of Latin America to guarantee stability, building them up to defend the status quo.

The Cold War. The post-war dominance of the United States affected Latin America in many ways. Always considered part of the US 'sphere of influence', Latin America now became a region to be assiduously defended from encroachments by the rival super-power, the Soviet Union. It was also a region ripe for investment by large and powerful companies anxious to expand overseas.

Latin America, in common with many areas of the Third World, became the terrain in which East-West rivalry was frequently fought out. Conflicts which, taken by themselves, would be seen as the result of legitimate grievances of oppressed and marginalised peoples, were viewed only in the light of the Cold War. Even efforts at moderate reform ran aground, particularly in the Central American countries where entrenched, US-supported oligarchies and dictators had not yet faced the challenge of social change on the scale of most other Latin American countries. Here proponents of a modernised economic and political order were seen as a major threat to the agro-exporting élites.

US organisation of the overthrow of the Arbenz government in Guatemala in 1954 was an early example of the effect of the Cold War on Central America. Jacobo Arbenz attempted to modernise his country, which was deeply polarised by class and ethnic divisions. Part of his programme was a limited agrarian reform, which would have expropriated idle lands owned by the United Fruit Company. This was interpreted as a 'communist-inspired' attack on US interests.

The Cuban revolution. It was the Cuban revolution, however, that unleashed the full force of Cold War politics on Latin America. Fidel Castro's revolution of 1959 was not at first seen as a major threat. The dictator, Fulgencio Batista, had become extremely unpopular and even large sectors of his army were disaffected. Cuba was known as the 'whorehouse of the Caribbean', a centre for corruption and a playground for American racketeers of all kinds. 'Our revolution is neither capitalist nor communist,' Castro declared in May 1959.

But tensions between the United States and Cuba began to mount as Castro introduced measures affecting US companies. Cuba, dependent for 80 per cent of its foreign exchange earnings on sugar exports, two-thirds of which went to the US market, was seeking massive aid to finance a programme of reform and modernisation. The United States would only give aid with stringent political conditions. Castro did not back down; rather, he went on the offensive with a more radical programme of nationalisation. By early 1960, President Eisenhower had accepted a CIA recommendation to train and arm Cuban exiles for an invasion, similar to that launched against Arbenz in Guatemala in 1954.

Castro was now turning increasingly to the Soviet Union, which agreed to supply the country with oil in return for sugar. The US government retaliated by imposing a trade embargo on Cuba. The Bay of Pigs invasion followed, a fiasco in which 1,400 Batista supporters and mercenaries launched an abortive assault on the island. Then, in 1962, the missile crisis forced a pledge from the United States not to invade Cuba in return for a Soviet undertaking not to place missiles on the island.

The United States now had to adjust to living with a communist state in the Caribbean basin, a region which it looked upon as its own 'backyard'. It never really made that adjustment, and throughout the 1960s organised numerous attempts to assassinate Castro and subvert the revolution.

The impact of the Cuban revolution on the rest of Latin America was profound. The idealism of the early revolutionary years and the dramatic advances in health, education and social welfare, achieved with the help of generous Soviet aid, made many Latin Americans overlook the political control that permeated Cuban society (justified constantly as a necessary defence against US aggression) and the vengeful treatment of early political opponents which lasted years after they had ceased to be any sort of threat to the régime. Even though a mythology developed around the revolution, which over-emphasised the role of the small group of revolutionaries around Castro in bringing down a pro-US dictatorship, Cuba did represent an alternative model of society for the disillusioned and frustrated peoples of Latin America. It made the 1960s a decade of radical, anti-capitalist movements in Latin America, of struggle between competing classes and opposing ideologies.

Revolution in theory. In the realm of ideas, the growing radicalism found expression in a school of thought which went way beyond the ECLA formulation of national reformism. The 'dependency' theorists were mostly Latin Americans, although André Gunder Frank, one of the best known exponents, was European. They argued that development along the lines advocated by ECLA thinking was not possible, as Latin America's relationship with the developed world was the source of its state of underdevelopment. Development could only take place after a radical restructuring of internal class relations, as well as relations with the international economy. Dependency on the industrialised world, it was argued, conditioned all the options open to Latin America, and only a radical rupture could make real development possible.

Within the 'dependency' school of thought, there were many divergent views: the more sophisticated, such as Fernando Henrique Cardoso, a Brazilian, and Enzo Faletto, a Chilean, saw the possibility of some form of development for Latin America, although it would remain dependent; they invented the term 'associated dependent development'. Cardoso and Faletto also gave more emphasis to class and class struggle within countries, while others stressed relations between nations.

Despite the diversity of opinion within the school, a basic body of ideas began to spread among Latin American intellectuals and radical political activists. They supported the idea of revolutionary political change, both anti-imperialist and anti-capitalist. They challenged the traditional Communist parties of Latin America, for whom the immediate task was to build up modernised capitalism in the region through alliances between the workers and the so-called 'national bourgeoisie', a class of nationalist industrial entrepreneurs. The national bourgeoisie was a theoretical construct modelled on the bourgeoisie that displaced the feudal land-owning classes of Europe. The revolutionary left disputed its existence, claiming that capitalism already existed in Latin America and the next stage of struggle was directly to socialism.

Revolution in practice. The Cuban revolution was the inspiration for the revolutionaries of the 1960s. Che Guevara and the French intellectual Régis Debray declared that the duty of the revolutionary is to create the revolution. It was a call to action which contrasted sharply with the cautious pragmatism of the Communists, who urged patience until conditions were appropriate for revolutionary change.

Armed struggle to bring about revolution was taken up in a number of countries of Latin America. The *foco* theory of guerrilla warfare, developed largely by Debray and based on the events of the Cuban revolution, advocated setting up in rural areas small nuclei (*focos*) of guerrilla-held territory which the surrounding peasants would soon welcome and join.

These efforts ended in unmitigated disaster. Coming largely from urban, middle-class backgrounds, the early guerrillas combined radical theory with a lack of knowledge of the realities of peasant life. They failed to find any support amongst peasant populations, while US-inspired counter-insurgency tactics adapted sophisticated and brutal techniques of repression from Vietnam to the

Latin American countryside. Large tracts of land in Guatemala were napalmed in an effort to eliminate small groups of guerrillas. The end of this period of rural guerrilla warfare came with the death of Che Guevara in Bolivia in 1967. Guevara's Bolivian adventure was an ill-advised attempt to generate revolution in one of the most inappropriate areas of that country. Though grindingly poor, the peasants had already received some land during the 1952 Bolivian revolution.

Guerrilla warfare, however, was not abandoned; it just shifted location. Urban guerrilla war made its appearance in the cities of the highly urbanised countries of the Southern Cone. The Tupamaros in Uruguay and the Montoneros and Revolutionary Peoples' Army (ERP) in Argentina brought a sense of heightened struggle and chaos to societies which were deeply riven by economic crisis. But in the end, they were not capable of building political movements to match their daring and effectiveness as urban guerrillas. Their isolation from the poor whom they aspired to lead made them vulnerable to the ruthless counter-insurgency techniques of security forces trained and armed by the United States. In both Uruguay and Argentina detention without trial, torture, disappearance and murder were systematically used to wipe out the guerrillas and their suspected sympathisers.

Stemming the tide of revolt by reform. The United States soon acknowledged that attempts to repeat the Cuban revolution had to be pre-empted by some measures of reform. The Alliance for Progress signed in August 1961 was a US-sponsored effort to promote reform 'from above' in order to prevent 'revolution from below'. It was a recognition that, in John Kennedy's own words, 'those who make peaceful reform impossible will make violent revolution inevitable'. The Alliance therefore proposed land and tax reforms – considered a small price to pay in order to prevent more radical change.

But the reformers behind the Alliance had not reckoned with the intransigence of the ruling classes of Latin America. They blocked the land reform measures. Rather than abandon the Alliance, the US and Latin American governments shifted the focus away from limited wealth and land redistribution to modernisation – in other words, to increase the productivity of land. Landowners were encouraged through credit and the introduction of new technology to diversify as well as improve their existing cash-crop production. Colonisation schemes, awarding tracts of uncleared forest to landless families, were devised to deal with the pressure for land from dispossessed peasants.

The Catholic Church, as well as the United States, was fearful of the political ferment around it. Since the 1890s the Church had been formulating a social doctrine to enable it to respond to the demands of the modern age. In his encyclical *Rerum Novarum*, published in 1891, Pope Leo XIII had criticised the abuses of liberal capitalism while simultaneously condemning socialism. Denying the existence of class conflict, he sought to reconcile the different social interests in society. Later Popes, in continuing attempts to find Christian solutions to social problems, defended the rights of workers, including the right to organise. In the 1940s the Church began to lend support to Catholic labour organisations in Latin America.

In the post-war years, newly formed Christian Democrat parties in Europe offered a firmly anti-communist and pro-capitalist alternative to the social democratic movements emerging at the same time. In the 1950s and 1960s Christian Democrat parties also emerged in Latin America, often linked financially and ideologically to their European counterparts. They claimed to offer a 'third way' between the extremes of socially irresponsible capitalism and totalitarian communism.

But the Church was just as divided between advocates of reform and radical change as the society around it. The Second Vatican Council in the early 1960s and second conference of Latin American Bishops held in Medellín, Colombia, in 1968 were milestones in the process of rethinking the Church's social role. At Medellín the Latin American Church acknowledged the need for radical transformation of society in order to meet the needs of the poor. Christian Democracy, representing the moderate wing of Christian thinking on social issues, had its high point in Latin America in the 1960s and early 1970s with the election of President Eduardo Frei in Chile (1964-70) and later Dr Rafael Caldera in Venezuela (1969-74). José Napoleon Duarte was deprived of his electoral victory in El Salvador in 1972 by blatant fraud.

The Frei government in Chile was the most coherent attempt to implement an 'Alliance for Progress'-style of political and economic change. It introduced a limited agrarian reform and made efforts to modernise Chile's capitalist economy. But the programme foundered on the inherent difficulties of the 'third way', with the reforms failing to satisfy the demands of the poor and at the same time alienating the wealthy. Society began to polarise further, a process expressed in the Christian Democrat Party itself, which by the end of Frei's presidency had split into left and conservative wings. A generalised disillusion with the capitalist model of development was apparent amongst the poor and marginalised sectors of society as well as amongst the radical intellectuals who led the Chilean left. These groups joined Popular Unity (UP), a coalition of socialist forces that managed to win the 1970 elections under the leadership of Salvador Allende.

chapter one

Socialism through the ballot box

The Chilean election of 1970 reflected the country's deep divisions. Salvador Allende won by a tiny margin: 36.3 per cent of the vote compared to the 34.9 per cent of his nearest rival, the conservative Jorge Alessandri. The Christian Democrat, Radomiro Tomic, took third place with 27.8 per cent. The final decision had to be taken by Congress, where the Christian Democrats controlled the decisive vote.

In return for their favourable vote, the Christian Democrats forced Allende to agree to a range of constitutional guarantees and restrictions. But at the same time right-wing extremist groups and US businessmen and diplomats were plotting to prevent Allende from taking power. International Telephone and Telegraph (ITT), one of the largest US multinationals in Chile, approached the CIA with a plan to destabilise the Chilean economy through international economic pressure and sowing the seeds of panic within the business community. Congressional hearings later revealed the active role in the destabilisation played by President Nixon and Henry Kissinger, who shrugged off the issue of Chilean sovereignty by describing the Chileans as 'irresponsible' for electing a Marxist government.

Allende's government, regarded as a test for the viability of elected Marxist governments, was beset by problems from the start: the UP coalition was far from united and did not have a majority in Congress; Allende also faced a hostile US government.

His programme was certainly a challenge to the old order, though it was more an attempt to modernise it than destroy it. The UP had no armed wing with which to attack opponents or defend itself, but forces within the government and the MIR (Movement of the Revolutionary Left – an armed group) pressed vociferously but unsuccessfully for the radicalisation of the government's programme and the arming of the people.

The government hoped to combine income redistribution, increased demand and reduced unemployment to stimulate the economy. But Chilean industry could not respond to the increased demand and the government, using socialist rhetoric to mobilise its own supporters, never won the confidence of the small shopkeepers and businessmen whom it sought to incorporate in an alliance against big, monopolistic producers. The Allende years were characterised by shortages, rising prices and black markets. Externally and internally generated destabilisation added to the atmosphere of chaos which grew during the three years of the government. Opposition groups began to unite, bringing together middle-class professionals, small-business owners and shopkeepers. A strike was organised in mid-1972, winning the support of ex-President Frei and the Christian Democrat Party. The 40,000 independent lorry-owners, a key group of people in the distribution of goods in Chile, joined the strike in protest against government plans to create a state-owned trucking enterprise.

Meanwhile, factory workers organised in Santiago's industrial belts, the *cordones industriales*, and threatened to form popular militias in a challenge to the moderate course favoured by Allende and the Communist Party leadership. Congressional elections in March 1973 failed to give the right an electoral means of re-establishing their control, and the coalition they had built actually lost seats to the UP coalition, which increased its vote over 1970. March to September 1973 brought rampant inflation and a series of political and economic crises, including an abortive coup attempt in June 1973. Allende himself continued to trust his armed forces. On 11 September 1973, General Pinochet, supported by the Christian Democrats and the conservative National Party, and with heavy involvement from the CIA, led the military coup which overthrew the Allende government.

Military solutions

Military coups have been a commonplace feature of Latin American political life – except in Chile and Uruguay, which both prided themselves on their civilian democratic traditions and had been known respectively as the England and Switzerland of Latin America. They both, however, fell under military rule in 1973.

Although the military intervened frequently in Latin America, the types of intervention and the contexts in which they occurred varied considerably. But the military coup in Brazil in 1964, and those in Uruguay, Chile and Argentina in 1976, shared certain similarities.

The Brazilian military established the pattern. The 1964 coup initiated twenty-one years of uninterrupted military rule. It was the first time that the military had taken over with a view to remaining in power in Brazil. The idea that they should rule rather than hand over to civilians after a certain period was new in South America, as was the emergence of an institutional ideology of the armed forces.

The ideology of the Brazilian military was derived from what was known as the 'doctrine of national security', a set of ideas which can be traced back primarily to the thinking of the Pentagon. A US mission helped to reorganise the Superior War College (*Escola Superior da Guerra*) in 1949. But the doctrine was subsequently

chapter one

developed by Brazilian military theorists and came to influence most of the armed forces of South America. In essence, the doctrine represented the world as divided irreconcilably between Western Christendom and communism. The military were given the status of defenders of the former and interpreters of 'permanent national objectives'. Since the world was divided ideologically, as well as geographically, there were 'internal frontiers' which had to be defended against the enemy within.

Combined with the Pentagon's offensive of the 1960s, when officers from all over Latin America were trained in counter-insurgency and the military were provided with weapons, the doctrine was a powerful motivating force for security forces throughout Latin America. It justified their intervention in political life when the objectives they defined for the nation appeared threatened. It placed the ideas of security and development in an international rather than national context, making foreign capital an ally rather than a threat.

The military coup of 1964, therefore, also represented an option in terms of economic development. Opinion on Brazil's economic direction had been polarising throughout the 1950s. The country had already begun to open its economy to foreign investment as the old model of inward-oriented growth became exhausted. Imports continued to rise, while the export sector failed to develop sufficiently to finance them; the rate of inflation was accelerating and lack of business confidence was reflected in the low rates of investment. Under these conditions, the idea of independent national development through locally owned industrialisation gradually ceased to be the aspiration of ruling élites. 'Nationalism' was replaced by 'Developmentalism', and agreements were made with foreign capital to develop a car industry, chemical plants, heavy and light engineering and other sectors.

The call for independent national development was now taken up more by the radicalised middle classes. There was growing political ferment in early 1960s. Radical politicians such as Leonel Brizola in the south and Miguel Arraes in the north-east were attempting to mould the government programme into an assault on traditional bastions of power in Brazil. The military, backed by multinational companies and the country's most powerful economic groups, intervened as agitation intensified. The nationalists within the military had already been defeated by those who favoured the 'developmentalist' path.

In contrast, the Peruvian coup of 1968 was led by nationalists, who were influenced in part by historical anti-US sentiment and radical teachers in the Peruvian war college (the Centre for Advanced Military Studies). But the Peruvian military experiment lasted only a little longer than any other Latin American attempt at independent national development. The radical phase of the Peruvian military government ended with the death of General Velasco, its leading protagonist, in 1975. By this time it was already beset by difficulties and had unleashed a deep conservative antagonism towards itself. It had also attempted to control the level of mobilisation of the people, so as not to destabilise the capitalist order in Peru. It was thus a 'top-down' approach to development, which ended up alienating nearly all sectors of society as well as international capital.

The Brazilian military government pursued a more coherent plan: it was not hostile to foreign capital and sought to demobilise opposition. Their plan involved the production of consumer durables, notably cars, for a market of middle-class consumers in the more prosperous south of Brazil. Volkswagen, Fiat, General Motors and Ford all set up factories. For them the low wages offered to the workforce, whose unions were essentially controlled by the state, were a major attraction. This was the basis of the Brazilian 'economic miracle'. The country did establish a broad industrial base but failed to improve the lives of the majority of the people. Agrarian structures were left intact, laying the basis for intense and violent land struggles in the decade to come.

But the Brazilian military were trying also to achieve a better balance between production for the domestic market and for export. The state assumed the task of providing resources to stimulate this change and the economy in general, rather than wait for the domestic private sector to gain sufficient confidence to invest. In 1965 alone, government investment rose by 7.9 per cent and that of state enterprises by 70.5 per cent.

Human rights

One feature of the 'new' military régimes of the 1970s in Latin America was the harshness of the measures taken against the population in the interests of programmes of economic restructuring. In Brazil resistance to the military dictatorship was viciously repressed, particularly in the years 1968-73. The Uruguayan and Chilean military dictatorships of 1973 and the Argentine dictatorship of 1976 surpassed even the Brazilians in the intensity of their repression. Their harshness was in part a response to the much higher political participation in those countries before military intervention, and the existence in all three countries of armed opposition groups of varying degrees of effectiveness.

Systematic torture, death squads, long-term imprisonment and murder were all part of the armoury of these military régimes. In Argentina at least 9,000 people 'disappeared', while in Uruguay some 70,000 people were at one time or another arrested – and usually tortured – for political offences. In Chile a presidential commission published details in 1991 of 2,279 known murders and 'disappearances' under the dictatorship between September 1973 and 1988. Given the standard of proof required by the commission, this figure is inevitably an underestimate.

Repression of one form or another touched thousands of people with little or no involvement in any socialist or radical alternative. The voice of civil society as a whole was silenced in all these countries through intimidation, the suppression of political parties, censorship of the press, the banning of trade unions and the right of association in general.

The scars of this period are still evident in all four countries of the Southern Cone. When the military governments were replaced by civilian ones in the 1980s, mass graves were found where victims had been buried; torture chambers were discovered; the children of victims were found living with their parents' murderers; and relatives of the 'disappeared' still awaited confirmation that their loved ones were indeed dead so that they could grieve and mourn.

The military in Chile, Argentina and Uruguay sought to push through radical economic changes to counteract the trend of long-term economic decline. They were heavily influenced by the ideas of the free-market Chicago school of economics associated with Milton Friedman. It is doubtful whether any democratically elected government could have survived the cuts in living standards which they inflicted on wage-earners to achieve these changes. As protective tariffs were removed, vested economic interests (hitherto protected by the state) were forced to become efficient or die. The economies were made more open and non-traditional exports encouraged.

The results were uneven, and though the policies pursued followed a similar pattern, they were implemented with pure ideological rigour only in Chile. Inflation proved more difficult to combat than economists had first thought: after nearly five years, inflation in Chile was still running at a yearly rate of 40 per cent, and in Argentina it was still 150 per cent after four years. High inflation also coexisted with recession; per capita income fell in Argentina and Chile in real terms; unemployment rose sharply, particularly in Chile, where it exceeded 20 per cent of the labour force. Wages fell 20-40 per cent in all the countries, while income distribution was skewed sharply towards the rich. At the end of the 1980s – the end of the period of military rule – only Chile had a relatively successful economic restructuring to show for the huge social cost inflicted on its people.

Armed struggle: the second generation

In the late 1970s guerrilla war flared up in Central America and the Andean countries. These new conflicts were accompanied by new ideas about political mobilisation and guerrilla warfare. Some long-established guerrilla movements which had been militarily weakened during the 1960s and early 1970s, such as the National Army of Liberation (ELN) of Colombia, were also invigorated by this new thinking. In Colombia the M-19 Movement (commemorating 19 April 1970 when the Popular National Alliance Party – ANAPO – was allegedly deprived of an electoral victory through fraud) and the Sandinista National Liberation Front (FSLN) in Nicaragua, tried to make a broad appeal to nationalist and democratic forces and were prepared to build wide, multi-class coalitions.

Conditions in the two countries varied greatly. The Colombian economy is much larger and more highly developed. But political power was highly exclusive in both countries. In Nicaragua power rested in the hands of the family dictatorship of the Somozas. In the 1970s the greed, brutality and corruption of the Somozas alienated business leaders and the traditional opposition, making possible the construction of a broard anti-dictatorial alliance.

When the Sandinistas won power in 1979, therefore, they did so in uniquely favourable conditions. They had won the support of broad sectors of the population and, by the time of their final offensive in June 1979, it was clear that the United States would not intervene on the side of the dictatorship. While President Jimmy Carter's human rights policy prevented him from supporting Somoza, he could not bring himself to apply the effective sanctions that would force the dictator from power.

The situation in Colombia was much more complex: a formal democratic order rested on the domination of two traditional political parties, the Liberals and the Conservatives. Both were archaic institutions that were holding on to power by means of a political pact which excluded other parties from access to government and relied upon political patronage and favours to manipulate the ever-decreasing sector of the population which bothered to vote. But the political order was stable enough to allow the economic élites to get on with running the country to serve their own interests. The Colombian economy was able to function without the swings in policy typical of other countries of Latin America.

The M-19 Movement was led by Jaime Bateman (a flamboyant figure from the Caribbean coast) until his death in a plane-crash in

chapter one

1983. The M-19 Movement won a following in the sprawling urban shanty towns of some cities, such as Cali in the south, but was unable to build a sufficiently broad-based political movement which would threaten seriously the ruling order. The powerful army, meanwhile, launched a ruthless counter-insurgency war, using torture, disappearance and mass arrests to eliminate the guerrilla movement and its suspected sympathisers.

Other Colombian guerrilla movements grew in the late 1970s, but were mostly unable to break out of their entrenched rural strongholds into the more politically-strategic urban centres. The armed movements had largely preceded the emergence of popular organisations and had little experience of working politically with the people. For instance, Manuel Marulanda (known as *Tirofijo*, or 'Dead Shot') who led the Revolutionary Armed Forces of Colombia (FARC) had been 'in the mountains' since 1949.

Popular organisations of peasants, workers and town dwellers frustrated by the gross neglect of urban services also grew in the 1970s so rapidly that they outstripped the capacity of the armed movements to work with them politically or militarily. By the early 1980s (fearful of the emergence of movements no longer controlled by the traditional political parties) businessmen, landowners, political bosses and army officers allied themselves with powerful new drug barons to eliminate the organisations' leaders and activists.

The Popular Forces of Liberation (FPL) in El Salvador, another 'second generation' guerrilla movement, grew out of disaffection with the politics of the local Communist Party. It was founded in 1971 by a former baker and General Secretary of the Communist Party, Salvador Cayetano Carpio. The FPL attempted to combine political organisation and military actions in a conscious rejection of the élitism and militarism of the old *foquista* school. As a result of this emphasis on political organisation, El Salvador during the 1970s generated one of the most combative and best organised popular movements in the history of Latin America. Two other guerrilla organisations, the National Resistance (RN) and the Popular Revolutionary Army (ERP), competed with the FPL for the support of this popular movement.

Though neither the FPL nor the other movements with which it formed the Farabundo Martí National Liberation Front (FMLN) in 1980 had a very powerful or well-armed guerrilla force, the victory of the FSLN in Nicaragua created strong currents of optimism throughout Central America. The FMLN launched what it claimed was a final offensive in January 1981, to coincide with the presidential inauguration of Ronald Reagan in the United States. Although the offensive failed and was subsequently renamed a 'general' offensive, it still represents a high point of the many struggles that characterised the thirty 'glorious' years of Latin America, struggles which mobilised tens of thousands of Latin Americans who were excluded and marginalised from growth and change. Some took up arms in complete frustration at the intransigence of the élites; some took up arms to fight for a new socialist order; and some took up arms to force the élites to democratise and allow the participation of all social classes in the political system. Others simply took to the streets, went on strike, took over land and reclaimed their civic rights in all sorts of different ways. And everywhere the response of élites, supported by the United States, was rejection and intransigence. The struggle from 'below' and the ferocity of the response of the Latin American right are both hallmarks of this 'glorious' period.

Debt and counter-revolution

The 'glorious' thirty years gave way to Latin America's 'lost decade' – the 1980s. For most of Latin America, they were ten years of economic stagnation. Per capita GDP fell at the rate of 1 per cent per year from 1980 to 1990. Investment fell 5 per cent a year over the same period. In all but five of the Latin American countries per capita incomes in 1987 were lower in real terms than those of 1980, and in six they were lower than in 1970. Latin America's share of world trade also declined, falling from 5.5 per cent of world exports in 1970 to 3.9 per cent in 1987.

The debt crisis was the single most important cause of this deterioration. It laid bare the structural problems of Latin American development that had been camouflaged by easy access to external borrowing in the 1970s. Although it was clear in the 1970s that the world economy was entering a period of instability and change, access to credit allowed Latin American governments to postpone the major structural changes needed to enable their economies to compete in the world economy. By the end of the 1980s, efforts to bring renewed growth to Latin America were hamstrung by the yearly transfer of $25-30 billion in interest payments to the commercial banks of the industrialised countries.

Struggles which had begun in the years of growth were now being waged amidst crisis and economic recession. The decade 1980-90 was one of growing poverty. In 1991 the United Nations Economic Commission of Latin America (ECLA) concluded in its 'Preliminary Balance of the Economy in Latin America and the Caribbean for 1990', that one in three people in the region lived in conditions of absolute poverty and that the number of poor had actually risen to 270 million, 62 per cent more than five years previously.

Some cases were particularly shocking. In Guatemala, for instance, according to a study by Inforpress (31 January 1991), the number of people living in poverty rose from 63 per cent of the population at the beginning of 1986 to 85 per cent in 1989, and those living in extreme poverty rose from 32 per cent to 72 per cent over the same period.

Economic survival became the priority for the poor. Cocaine was one route to that survival. Although the coca leaf has a long history in Andean Latin America, during the 1980s its production expanded hugely to meet a growing demand, particularly from the United States. It is estimated that some 35 tonnes of cocaine were consumed worldwide in 1982, rising to 70 tonnes in 1985 and to 270 tonnes in 1988.

Bolivia illustrates dramatically how vulnerable a country is if it depends on one commodity, in this case tin, and how coca production provided an alternative for the victims of the collapse of the world tin market in the mid-1980s. Income per head in Bolivia fell to $840 in 1985 when the tin crash devastated the economy, $150 lower than it had been in 1970. It was estimated that about a quarter of Bolivia's 20,000 tin miners subsequently headed for the Chapare coca-growing region to make a living as *pisadores*, treading the leaf to release the narcotic alkaloid.

The political economy of cocaine

The crisis in Latin America's formal, measured economy resulted in a mushrooming of its informal, unregulated economy. People dismissed from 'proper' jobs as miners or factory workers sought a living as street sellers, odd-job men and domestic employees. Illegal activities also grew enormously and crime and violence rose as living standards fell.

The rise of the cocaine economy in the Andes is linked to this generalised crisis. Over four-fifths of South America's coca originates in Peru and Bolivia. Peru is the world's largest producer: the US State Department estimates that 100,000 hectares of land are devoted to coca in Peru, of which 85,000 are located in the Upper Huallaga valley.

During the 1980s, this valley fell under the virtual control of the *Sendero Luminoso* ('Shining Path'), a messianic revolutionary movement inspired by the Long March of Mao Tse Tung in China. *Sendero Luminoso* took advantage of the frustrations of Peru's Quechua-speaking highland peasants, long neglected by the Lima-based central government and living in conditions of primitive misery. *Sendero Luminoso*'s influence grew through the crisis-ridden 1980s.

In Bolivia 70-80 per cent of the country's coca production comes from the Chapare. Like the Upper Huallaga valley, Chapare is an isolated area where peasants receive little support from the government. Bolivia's Gross National Product declined by 2.3 per cent a year from 1980 to 1986, while coca production rose by about 35 per cent in each of those years. Official unemployment tripled over the same period, from 5.7 per cent to 20 per cent.

Coca production produces far higher returns than any other crop; it is a hardy and reliable crop which peasants grow for rational reasons. But the rewards to the peasants who grow, mash and soak the leaves to release the narcotic alkaloid are as nothing compared to the profits of those who control the rest of the processing and the distribution of the drug. These are largely in the hands of the Colombian drug traffickers.

The 1980s saw the emergence in Colombia of an extraordinarily wealthy and powerful élite of cocaine entrepreneurs. The leading drug barons, such as former gravestone- and car-thief, Pablo Escobar, are amongst the richest men in the world. They have used their wealth to build up vast criminal empires. The political implications of this power and wealth for Colombia have been more significant than the economic consequences. Only a very small part of their drug earnings find their way back into Colombia, and much of this has gone into real estate, consumption of luxury items and land deals. The cocaine dollars help to finance Colombia's trade deficit but are not a decisive factor in the national economy.

The political impact of cocaine, however, has been very great. The corruption and violence associated with the increasing power of the drug mafias have destabilised an already weak and vulnerable political order. The drug mafias have penetrated the Colombian political establishment, forging alliances with right-wing figures against movements of the left. Cocaine-funded death squads killed over 8,000 people between 1986 and 1990. They have also assassinated leading members of the political establishment when threatened with criminal proceedings or extradition to the United States. Judges, policemen and community leaders are routine victims of their death squads. But they have also killed a Minister of Justice; the editor of *El Espectador*, a major daily newspaper; an Attorney-General; and, in August 1989, Luis Carlos Galán, the man most likely to have won the 1990 presidential election for the Liberal Party.

The assassination of Galán triggered a sustained offensive by the political establishment against the drug barons. This killing convinced the government and the business community that the cocaine barons had become a virtual state-within-a-state. The

United States urged the government on; the war on drugs was becoming increasingly important for US political leaders as the Cold War thawed.

Colombia entered a period of terrible violence. The Medellín cartel, most associated with drug-mafia brutality, was weakened by the onslaught. A number of its members accepted government deals, by which they could avoid extradition to the United States if they gave themselves up. Others, such as those associated with the town of Cali, continued to operate, but in a more sophisticated fashion so that they were rarely targeted either by the Colombian government or the United States. Their operations have penetrated Colombian political and economic life more deeply, with less publicity and less bloodshed. Cocaine is likely, therefore, to continue to have a major impact on the country, while capturing fewer headlines. There will be suppliers of cocaine as long as demand continues. For many Latin Americans the coca leaf and cocaine are a means of survival, while for a few, they are the high road to enormous wealth.

Revolution and counter-revolution in Central America

The failure of the offensive in El Salvador by the FMLN (Farabundo Martí National Liberation Front) in January 1981 initiated a decade of civil war. It took ten years of fighting to convince the rulers of El Salvador that the political forces represented by the guerrillas could not be crushed by military means. In 1981 the French and Mexican governments had recognised the FMLN and their political allies, the Revolutionary Democratic Front (FDR), as a 'representative political force' in order to encourage a negotiated settlement. But, as the likelihood of such an outcome faded, international opinion backed away from the guerrilla movement. The Reagan administration, meanwhile, declared that El Salvador would be the test-case of its commitment to hold back the tide of 'communism'.

The Salvadorean guerrillas subsequently became a very effective military force, capable of inflicting high casualties on the army. To bolster the military, the United States began pouring aid into the country. Some $3.5 billion in military and economic assistance was granted between 1981 and 1988. Military repression against the civilian population knew no limits. Some 30,000 people were killed between 1980 and 1983, the year that Vice-President Bush finally visited El Salvador to demand publicly that the Salvadorean army behave with more respect for human rights.

The achievements of the FMLN over the decade were significant. They instituted their own civilian administration in guerrilla-controlled territory, despite aerial bombardment by the

Salvadorean air force. Although death squads were used to kill and silence human rights activists, trade unionists and critics of the government, the civilian population continued throughout the decade to demand its civil rights. In the mid-1980s the popular movement (the non-military civilian opposition) in San Salvador began to reorganise. By the end of the decade, internal and exiled refugees were returning to their land and rebuilding their bombed and war-damaged towns.

But the international and regional context was hostile. Whatever the military strength of the FMLN, it was clear that the US government would never permit them to seize power. Moreover the exigencies of war, with its demands for clear structures of authority, command and obedience, had also undermined the guerrilla movements' initial revolutionary ideals which stressed the importance of participation, criticism and awareness. And, operating as a clandestine military force, the guerrillas lacked the means to rebuild the political movement on the scale it had reached in the late 1970s.

The collapse of communism in Eastern Europe and the Soviet Union, together with the end of Ronald Reagan's presidency in the United States at the beginning of 1989, drastically changed the international situation. The US government moved rapidly from seeking military victory over the FMLN to looking for a way out of a conflict now regarded as unwinnable. The FMLN, militarily as effective as ever, could no longer be portrayed as the instrument of Soviet expansionism in the Americas. At the same time, the FMLN themselves had adapted to the tide of democracy and market economics sweeping Latin America: they became pragmatic political moderates, not unlike the social democratic parties of Europe, acknowledging that the people of El Salvador were tired of war and realising that they would become isolated if they were not seen to be making strenuous efforts to end the fighting. The stage was set for the twenty months of negotiations which ended with the peace agreement signed in January 1992. This promises an effective civilian government, with full authority over the armed forces, and social, economic and political reforms within the framework of a competitive electoral system and a free-market economy.

Central America remained a deeply divided region, with the active encouragement of the United States. Honduras became a base for US military operations and Costa Rica a platform from which to launch various US political initiatives aimed at isolating the Sandinista government in Nicaragua. In Guatemala, the military government's counter-insurgency campaign of 1982, which targeted Mayan Indian villages for virtual extermination, all but crushed support for the guerrillas amongst the largely indigenous peasant population. The security forces killed thousands of civilians in the early 1980s and subsequently sought to control the Indian population by herding them into 'model villages', based on the strategic hamlets of Vietnam. They also set up local 'civil patrols', forcing Indians to report on guerrilla movements and sometimes to fight them and even execute prisoners.

US hostility towards the revolutionary government in Nicaragua was particularly relentless. After the 1979 insurrection the Sandinistas faced huge problems in trying to reconstruct the economy to meet the needs of the people. They aimed to create an alliance between the state and the private sector through which they could generate economic reconstruction and growth. Initially they took over only the business interests and the land which had belonged to Somoza and his closest associates. This left a substantial portion of the economy in private hands, including key areas of export agriculture. The private sector accounted for 37 per cent of export agriculture under the Sandinista government and 64 per cent of production from medium-sized and large farms.

Priority was given to maintaining the export sector, the earnings of which were essential for all the government's development plans. To avoid alienating private owners, the Sandinistas actively reined in popular demands for radical reform, especially for a more sweeping land reform. To avoid fuelling inflation, peasants and workers were to benefit by improvements in health and education rather than direct increases in purchasing power. The mistakes of the Allende government in Chile were still a fresh memory. Some peasants were organised into co-operatives and others became workers on state farms, but there were still many individual peasant farmers who disliked these options.

Many peasants who had hoped that the revolution would give them their own plot of land were disappointed. At the same time peasant farmers suffered from heavy-handed state control over the distribution and pricing of their produce. They felt that urban supporters of the Sandinistas gained from the availability of cheap food to the disadvantage of the producers.

The United States was able to take advantage of discontent brewing among the peasants, especially among the conservative cattle farmers of central Nicaragua, to fund and build a counter-revolutionary army. The *contras,* as they were called, never succeeded in gaining sufficient support to establish a strong base within the country and seriously challenge the government. But they attracted enough support from the disaffected peasantry to undermine the government's plans and force changes in policy. The land reform measures of 1985, which for the first time granted individual farmers title to their land, were a response to the erosion of support for the Sandinistas among the peasants. At the same time, however, the United States was undermining the economy. Nicaragua, in common with other Latin American countries, saw its export earnings from coffee, cotton and beef decline during the 1980s. But Nicaragua also had to face the refusal of the International Monetary Fund (IMF), under pressure from the United States, to make funds available despite regular payment of its debt. US bilateral finance ended in 1981, that of the World Bank in 1982 and that of the Inter-American Development Bank in 1983. The US trade embargo was imposed in 1984. Foreign aid fell from $772 million in 1984 to $384 million in 1987. Meanwhile the escalation of *contra* activities led to a rise in defence expenditure from 6 per cent of GDP in 1980 to 21 per cent in 1987 – over half the budget of the central government.

The Sandinistas continued to court the private sector and moved to open up the political system rather than become more authoritarian. Elections were held in 1984, offering the conservative opposition an opportunity for political representation if not political power. But the majority of large agricultural and business interests refused to collaborate, knowing that the United States was prepared to fund an army to overthrow the Sandinistas in order to give them total political mastery in Nicaragua.

Economic crisis and war forced the Sandinistas to abandon many of their social objectives. There were major changes in economic policy in the late 1980s to liberalise the economy. One Sandinista likened the policy to the application of an IMF structural adjustment programme without the benefit of an IMF loan.

Various regional initiatives, such as the Contadora peace initiative and the Arias plan, seemed for some time to offer hope for a negotiated Central American solution to the regional conflicts. The Sandinistas were able to take advantage of the various peace plans to negotiate with the *contras*, eventually offering them an amnesty and an opportunity for reintegration into political life. The United States meanwhile, continued to finance the war.

The elections of 1990 took place against the background of severe economic decline. The great majority of the population were worse off than they had been under Somoza. People realised that, given US hostility, while the Sandinistas were in government war and deprivation would continue. Military conscription, which sent children off to an uncertain fate in the *contra* war, was vastly unpopular. The Sandinista vision no longer had the same mobilising force. Their initial idealism had been eroded by the practicalities of government and power itself. Nevertheless, the electoral defeat of the FSLN in April 1990 was a blow to those

chapter one

who hoped that Nicaragua might provide a model for a new social order in Latin America. At the end of the 1980s, Central America was in a sorry state. One of the poorest regions in Latin America, with a population of 30 million, it had a regional income in 1990 of $23 billion – smaller than that of Wales. The incomes of all countries (except that of Costa Rica, which grew by just 1.8 per cent during the whole decade) were lower in 1990 than they had been in 1980. In Nicaragua GDP per head in 1990 was less than half of what it had been in 1976, while unemployment was reckoned to be more than 50 per cent. In El Salvador GDP per head in 1990 was about 25 per cent less than in 1978 and corresponded to the level reached in 1970. In a country of 5.2 million people, around 900,000 had left the country and 1 million were internally displaced. Approximately 60 per cent of city dwellers and 70 per cent of the rural population were unemployed or underemployed. In Guatemala unemployment is running at about 40 per cent.

Political violence and civil war have left El Salvador, Guatemala and Nicaragua with scars that will take many years to heal. In El Salvador more than 75,000 people, most of them civilians, died in eleven years of civil war; Nicaragua suffered between 60,000 and 70,000 casualties, including 30,000 deaths, during the *contra* war; in Guatemala it is estimated that over 100,000 people, mainly among the indigenous Maya population, have been killed so far during thirty years of civil conflict.

Democracy and the market: the new rules of the game

The revolutionary aspirations and conflicts of the 1960s and 1970s gave way during the 1980s to the struggle for democracy. This change was in part a response to the reality of dictatorship in so many Latin American countries and, in part, a reassessment of the values of democracy. International events also played a part in this process. The 1980s appear, with hindsight, to have been a decade of fundamental political and economic transition.

The dictatorships disrupted the established political organisations of the régimes which they overthrew, especially political parties and trade unions. In the course of time, however, ordinary people began to organise at the grassroots, often displaying extraordinary courage in confronting their military rulers. The practical experience of democratic politics in very adverse circumstances is a valuable legacy which has survived the period of dictatorship.

Peasants organised to reclaim their land in north-eastern Brazil; refugees returned to their abandoned villages in El Salvador after years in Honduran camps; Christian base communities reclaimed the meaning of the Bible for the poor all over Latin America;

women organised to demand that the authorities account for their disappeared relatives in Argentina; and indigenous communities set up virtually autonomous communities in southern Colombia. Everywhere in Latin America, organisations and social movements seemed to have created a fragile but none the less real space for themselves.

At the same time, the traditional political organisations of the left, which had tried to win support for radical social change, were drastically weakened. Events in Eastern Europe and the Soviet Union fundamentally challenged the thinking of the left in Latin America, which had always looked to the countries of the Socialist Bloc as a beacon of progress, even when they were critical of their own pro-Moscow Communist parties. Their own bitter experience of US actions and policies in Latin America made them overlook the faults of its sworn enemies on the world stage.

In the late 1980s guerrilla movements, with the exception of *Sendero Luminoso* in Peru, began exploring the possibilities of re-entering the political arena. The M-19 Movement in Colombia led the way: it negotiated its way back into politics in 1990 and enjoyed some early electoral success with its kindred political movement, the Democratic Alliance-M-19 (AD-M-19).

Throughout Latin American society, realignments were reshaping the political scene. As the traditional parties of the left underwent crisis or adapted themselves to new realities, they were joined by new political movements emerging more directly from the experience of dictatorship. The Brazilian Workers Party (PT), for instance, grew out of the struggle in the late 1970s to build a union movement independent of the state. By the late 1980s, under the leadership of the metalworkers' leader, 'Lula' (Luis Inacio da Silva), the PT had built an organisation strong enough to mount a serious challenge for the presidency.

Changes were also taking place on the right: there were signs that the 'modernisers' amongst the ruling groups in countries where right-wing violence was still very common, such as El Salvador and Colombia, were gaining greater influence. These were more rational leaders for whom it was not taboo to negotiate with the left to bring guerrilla violence to an end. Some notable outsiders, such as Fernando Collor in Brazil in 1989 and Alberto Fujimori in Peru in 1990, won presidential elections against more traditional politicians of the right.

But the depth and significance of the changes were much debated. The military had withdrawn from government almost everywhere by the end of the 1980s, but remained a powerful force. Traditional political bosses, manipulating local peasants or shanty-town dwellers to ensure their election, continued to dominate backward rural areas as well as cities in some countries, raising questions about the quality of the democratic processes taking place. Human rights violations continued at very high levels, especially in Central America and Colombia where a number of former M-19 guerrillas were gunned down and even their presidential candidate in the 1990 elections, Carlos Pizarro, was assassinated.

In other countries, too, political systems were showing signs of opening up to wider participation. In El Salvador, for instance, the Democratic Convergence, an organisation led by Rubén Zamora, who had previously been a leading force in the FDR (Democratic Revolutionary Front), the political wing of the FMLN, was able to participate in elections. In the 1991 legislative elections, in spite of fraud by right-wing parties, Democratic Convergence won eight seats.

Events in Argentina, Brazil, Chile and Uruguay, however, were the most decisive in terms of the re-emergence of competitive party politics. The way the transition took place varied from country to country and affected the nature of the subsequent governments. In Brazil, the transition was the result of a pact with the military, while in Argentina it came about through the collapse of the military following their defeat in the Malvinas-Falkands war. In Uruguay there was also a pact, but the military had almost no basis of support in the country – in the plebiscite of 1980 the people rejected the proposed Constitution, which would have given the military a permanent supervisory role in political life. And in Chile in 1982, the year of the collapse of Chile's first 'economic miracle', widespread demonstrations and middle-class disenchantment began to undermine General Pinochet's efforts to create a base of political support. With the exception of Chile, the military in the late 1980s were discredited everywhere for their mishandling of their nations' economies.

In all four countries the people played a role in the struggle for democracy. In Brazil a sector of the labour movement had begun to challenge the government-appointed leaders and had set up independent unions. In Argentina it was the mothers and grandmothers of the 'disappeared' who, even before the Malvinas-Falklands War, had overcome their fear and started to protest against human rights violations in the Plaza de Mayo, the main square of Buenos Aires.

In Chile and Brazil the Catholic Church, and some Protestant Churches, played a very important role in the struggle for democracy. The Catholic Church was one of the few institutions which stood up to the dictatorships. In Argentina, on the other hand, the institutional Church offered little support to the victims of human rights violations and even senior bishops applauded the military for their crusade against 'communism'.

This mosaic of experiences should be sufficient to inspire caution when drawing conclusions about the return to democracy. While the experience of the transition to democracy differs in each country, there is considerable uniformity in the economic changes which are taking place in Latin America. The return to market economics, the reduction of the role of the state in the economy and the opening of domestic markets to international capital are happening throughout Latin America, except in Cuba. These structural changes were forced on governments by the debt crisis and their impact on the poor was, and continues to be, disastrous even in the more successful Latin American economies. And, even in Cuba, the withdrawal of Russian support, announced in September 1991, must herald far-reaching changes, even though Fidel Castro, whose personal preferences still determine major political choices, appears to have set his face against significant liberalisation of the economy or the political system.

The changes have also hastened the process of social and economic polarisation, that is, the rich getting richer and the poor poorer. In the great cities of Latin America today the richest live in fortified enclaves while huge working-class areas and shanty towns are no-go areas. In parts of São Paulo, car drivers are reluctant to stop at red lights at night for fear of assault. ECLA forecasts that by the year 2000 the poor in Latin America will make up 62 per cent of the population.

The mere fact that the new governments of the 1990s are civilian and not military constitutes an enormous political advantage. It is not clear, however, how much longer the civilian politicians will be able to benefit from this factor. At the same time, the left has largely accepted the new realities of market economics and offers no ideological challenge to the centre and right-wing politicians who now govern in Latin America.

The transition to democracy

By the late 1980s even sectors of the ruling groups who had initially supported the military governments had come to resent the arbitrary use of power by the military. In Brazil, Argentina and Uruguay they were disillusioned by the failure of the military to bring them out of economic crisis. They also came to recognise that effective government had to have some degree of popular legitimacy. Moreover, the intense conflicts and social upheaval which had provoked military intervention in the first place had passed after years of repression.

chapter one

A sigh of relief went up from the people of the Southern Cone countries when the military withdrew. Years of terror and enforced political silence, exile or imprisonment, had left people yearning for the end of dictatorial rule. The precise political composition of the new civilian governments mattered less than the mere fact that people no longer lived in fear. But the issue of justice illustrates the limits of civilian power. Many wanted, and still want, those responsible for human rights crimes to be punished. The military made clear, however, that they would not tolerate a serious investigation into their record in this respect, although in all countries efforts were made to acknowledge publicly some of the worst excesses of the military régimes. Nowhere, however, was the full truth revealed or were more than a handful of those responsible forced to stand trial for their crimes.

The democracies which emerged in the Southern Cone were circumscribed, therefore, by the continued shadow of the armed forces. These countries also bore the collective memory of years of terror, from which trade unions, social organisations and political parties have still not recovered. In Chile, the caution of the transitional government elected in 1989 under the Christian Democrat, Patricio Aylwin, was endorsed by an alliance of left parties which gave priority to the consolidation of civilian democracy rather than the struggle for social justice. Chile was also the economic success story of Latin America. The economy had been remodelled to make best use of its competitive advantages in the international economy and was exporting an array of 'non-traditional' exports – such as grapes, apples, kiwi fruit and timber products – well as its traditional copper. Wages remained very low, the trade union movement weak, and the poor and marginal populations as excluded as ever.

The meaning of democracy in Latin America had undergone considerable change by the end of the 1980s. It no longer contained aspirations of equality and opportunity for all. It meant a competitive party system within a society in which social divisons were more sharply drawn than they had been two decades earlier, and in which the task of representative government was to articulate the interests of different sectors. The degree to which such a system could function smoothly varied considerably according to the different history and traditions of the individual countries. The premise of this new consensus, encouraged by the United States, was that the free operation of the market required the free operation of the political system. The social protest which might threaten such a combination had to be channelled through the political system. If it were not, the institutions of repression and coercion remained intact and available to enforce conformity whenever necessary.

'Free governments and free markets'

In June 1990, President Bush announced his 'Enterprise for the Americas' initiative. He made a political plea for 'free governments and free markets'. The initiative proposed a hemisphere-wide free-trade zone, a new flow of investment capital and a new approach to the debt burden. But its underlying assumption was that Latin America's declining share of world trade was more the product of its restrictive trade barriers than the crippling debt burden and its impact on the region's level of production and ability to import.

A new global capitalist order is being fashioned that will have many implications for Latin America. The industrialised countries themselves are undergoing major shifts, with old manufacturing industries giving way to high technology, flexible production processes and burgeoning knowledge-based service sectors. Regional blocs are replacing the old bi-polar world of the superpowers. The European Community completes its single market in 1993, giving it huge power and influence in the global economy. Japan already dominates much of Asia. The United States, much weakened economically and politically, will be forced to look to its own continent. Already it has completed a free-trade agreement with Canada which Mexico is soon to join. It is anxious to keep the economies of Latin America open and receptive to US capital and influence.

Latin America will have little choice in the 1990s but to accept the foreign capital on offer. The debt crisis has severely weakened its manufacturing base; lack of investment over the years in plant, technology and human capital have seriously affected its economic potential. The region is now once again embarking on systematic policies of export-led growth, with particular emphasis on the export of manufactured goods. Latin America's industries no longer have the protection they once enjoyed and are being forced to become more efficient. The role of the domestic market in this strategy is not yet clear, but it is unlikely to take on the kind of significance which would require a major redistribution of income.

Policies designed to open up markets to competition and reduce the role of the state are preparing the economies of the region for their new role in the international market-place, introducing the 'adjustments' which will enable them to compete. To qualify for debt relief and aid under the 'Enterprise for the Americas' initiative, Latin American countries must already have introduced a programme of structural adjustment, an open-investment reform programme, and an agreement with commercial banks for debt rescheduling.

chapter one

Nevertheless, the burden of debt is still a major obstacle to renewed growth in Latin America. Structural adjustment policies began to be seriously implemented throughout the region in the mid-1980s but, according to 1990 figures compiled by ECLA, the record has not been encouraging. Inflation has continued to grow, fiscal deficits have been reduced in only eleven of the twenty-five countries and have increased in ten. Trade balances have been positive but below what was reached in 1985. Growth in GDP has declined from 3.5 per cent in 1985 to -0.5 per cent in 1990, and per capita GDP growth has continued to fall.

Despite this, the longer-term development options for the larger, semi-industrialised Latin American nations are much greater than for the smaller nations, which have little to offer the world economy, except perhaps the cheapness and flexibility of their labour force. The non-traditional exports encouraged in Central America, such as luxury fruit and vegetables, are unlikely to generate sustained growth and development over a long period. Few countries have the natural resources and climatic advantages of Chile upon which to base a strategy of export-led growth.

As the role of the state diminishes in Latin America, the private sector becomes more dominant and the laws of the market are able to operate unhindered. No-one denies that capitalism of this sort can promote growth. It is unlikely, however, to promote ecologically sustainable or equitable growth. Rather, it allows some to survive, a few to live very well, and condemns the majority to abject poverty.

There has been no challenge to this new consensus from the political left, the Church or anywhere else. The resignation and apathy engendered among the poor by the military régimes live on under democracy. The most active continue to struggle through their organisations and movements, but often without a sense of direction. The challenge for the future is therefore to generate alternatives. Latin America's rich history and constantly renewed enthusiasm for radical and innovative social change give cause for hope that such alternatives will emerge. But there will have to be real recognition of the demands of the new social movements for genuine participation and equal rights and opportunities, particularly on the part of women and ethnic groups. Latin America's political culture is still rife with the old, corrupt, manipulative politics of the past. Those who wish to challenge the new status quo will have to show their clear rejection of practices which manipulate people. They must also build new movements that fulfil aspirations for genuine democracy and social justice.

Jenny Pearce *is a well-known academic and writer on Latin America. She has written books on Uruguay, Central America,*

El Salvador and Colombia. She is now a lecturer in the politics of development in the Department of Peace Studies at the University of Bradford.

References

1. England, as opposed to Britain, is used when referring to events before the 1605 Act of Union. For events after that date, Britain is used throughout – even though, strictly speaking, it was England rather than Scotland that benefited most from trade with Spain, Portugal and the New World.

2. Furtado, Celso, *Economic History of Latin America*, Cambridge University Press, 1970.

3. The OECD member nations are: Australia, Austria, Belgium, Canada, Denmark, Finland, France, Germany, Greece, Iceland, Ireland, Italy, Japan, Luxembourg, Netherlands, New Zealand, Norway, Portugal, Spain, Sweden, Switzerland, Turkey, United Kingdom and United States.

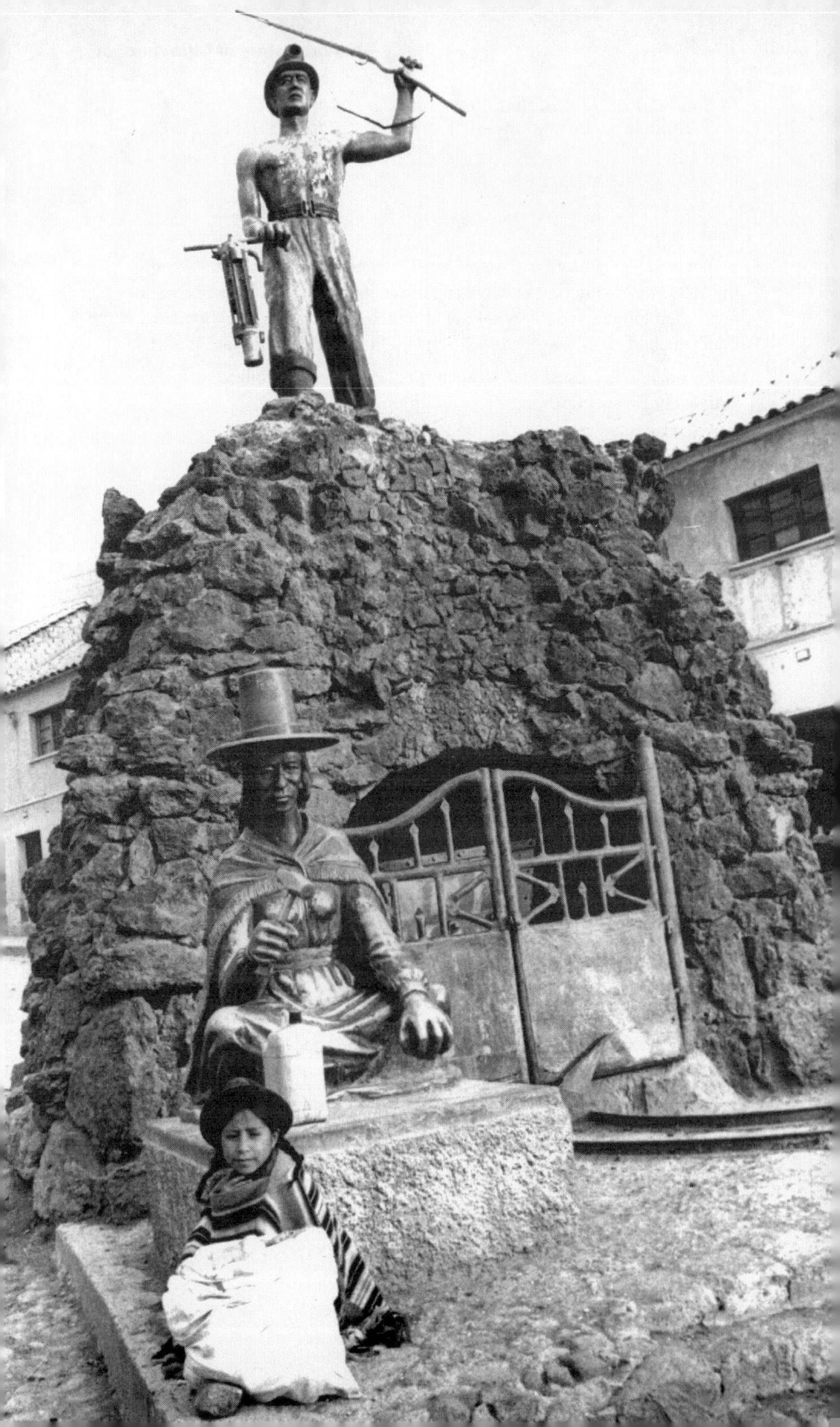

chapter two

seamus cleary and george gelber
CRUSHING BURDEN: LATIN AMERICA'S FOREIGN DEBT

Latin America today is being shaped by the debts which each country owes to the banks and financial institutions of the developed world. Debt determines the economic policies of governments, the wages and benefits of workers, and the exploitation of land and natural resources. Every option is assessed by its contribution to the balance of payments: whether it promotes cheap, competitive exports or reduces imports. The first priority for each country is to pay the interest on its debt. The best land, therefore, is devoted to growing crops for export rather than for consumption at home. Wages are kept down to enable industry to compete not only against the advanced technology of the industrialised countries, but also against other third world countries bidding desperately for export markets.

This does not mean that Latin America's problems would automatically be solved if a magic wand could be waved to cancel the debt, though undoubtedly the poor would benefit. Most Latin American and Caribbean economies are seriously biased towards the rich and the problem of this bias will remain regardless of measures taken to resolve the debt crisis. Significant debt relief, however, would make it easier for countries to address the deep-seated problems of inequality and poverty. As things stand, governments have little choice: right-wing or left, democratic or dictatorial, they are all forced to adopt similar policies.

At the beginning of the 1980s, as the debt crisis was gathering momentum, Nicaragua was in the first flush of the Sandinista revolution after an enormously destructive insurrection. Eleven Latin American governments, including Argentina, Brazil and Chile, were military dictatorships pursuing sharply divisive social and economic policies. The seven civilian governments, with the exception of Costa Rica, were little better. These were the governments under which the greater part of their countries' debts had been contracted. The benefits of the debt in the open-handed 1970s had been unequally divided, with the lion's share going to

---

Testimony to decades of struggle for better working conditions against the logic of international economic markets. A monument to the miners of Bolivia. Photo Jenny Matthews.

the rich. In the 1980s the burden of adjustment was borne mainly by the poor. It is not surprising that throughout Latin America ordinary people are now arguing for the repudiation of these debts on the grounds that they were contracted under unrepresentative governments, that much of the borrowed money was wasted and that the original loans have now been repaid many times over.

In 1990 total Latin American and Caribbean debt owed to private banks and international financial institutions was $428,636 million. At the beginning of the 1980s, as the debt crisis was gathering momentum, the region's debt was $242 billion.[1] What does this increasing burden mean for Latin America? Are the last rites about to be administered to the debt crisis? And if so, who will be celebrating them – the banks, the governments, the rich or the poor?

Most countries, like people and companies, borrow to pay for goods or investments that they do not have the money to pay for immediately. Latin American countries borrowed to fund development long before the crisis of the 1980s. Indeed, throughout the 1960s Latin America was borrowing to pay off existing loans. So what brought the system into crisis? It should be no surprise that a crisis of this magnitude has multiple causes: the selfish and short-sighted economic policies of the rich countries, especially the United States; the development of the Eurodollar and the uncontrolled international market in Eurodollar loans; floating interest rates; and the consequences of the oil price rises of 1973 and 1979.

Import substitution: towards industrialisation

Many Latin American countries experienced their most intense period of industrial development during the Second World War. The countries of the developed world were too involved in their war efforts to export anything to Latin America. In the absence of international competition, Latin American industry, though often producing inferior goods at higher cost, grew rapidly. This industrial expansion in turn generated economic growth and employment. In fact, the move towards industrialisation had received its first impetus in the Great Depression of 1929-32, when the prices of Latin America's traditional exports to North America and Europe plummeted and the continent could no longer afford to buy the manufactured goods traditionally imported from the United States and Europe. This policy, known as import substitution, was intended to save foreign exchange by producing at home goods which had previously been imported. It was, moreover, the strategy adopted by most developed countries, including the United States, Germany and Japan, on their way to becoming industrial powers.

The new Latin American industries were protected by high tariff barriers, which put imported goods out of reach of all but the very rich. It was thought that these industries would, in time, become more efficient, bringing down prices and enabling governments to reduce the tariff barriers. Most of the basic plant and machinery for the new industries, however, was imported. Frequently, too, component parts were imported and the final products merely assembled in Latin America. The cost in foreign exchange of the imported machinery and parts rose inexorably. Latin America began to borrow the necessary foreign currency without any corresponding increase in exports.

The import-substitution strategy was devised before the advent of transnational corporations (TNCs). In practice, the new 'national' industries were often merely subsidiaries of TNCs or their partnerships with local companies. The generally profitable investments by TNCs in Latin America generated a steady outflow of funds as they repatriated profits and interest to their parent companies. Between 1972 and 1974, for example, interest payments on existing public debt in Latin America were between $1 billion and $2 billion per annum; during the same period, according to the Inter-American Development Bank (IADB), yearly remittances by transnationals totalled $4 billion.[2]

Dollars and Eurodollars

At the end of the Second World War, Western political leaders, agreeing that it was vital to expand world trade, decided to value their currencies in terms of the dollar which, in turn, was valued at one thirty-fifth of an ounce of gold. In 1971, however, President Nixon, yielding to inflationary pressures caused by the cost of the Vietnam War, announced that the dollar could no longer be converted into gold and that in future its value would be determined by the market. The dollar fell by over 20 per cent in the next two years, as did the real value of the dollar reserves of Latin American countries. But worse was to follow. The industrialised countries quickly readjusted the prices of their products to compensate for the falling real value of the dollar. Latin America, however, was overwhelmingly dependent on the export of raw materials and agricultural products and could not do likewise. All attempts to set up effective producer organisations, along the lines of the Organisation of Petroleum Exporting Countries (OPEC), for coffee or bananas, for example, ended in failure.

The rise of the Eurodollar. Eurodollars are not a special currency but are simply dollars which are not subject to domestic US banking rules. They do not even have to be held physically outside the United States. The worldwide market in Eurodollars

chapter two

had its beginnings in the foreign reactions to the weakness of the dollar and attempts by US corporations to avoid currency controls. At the end of the 1960s European central banks realised that they would never be able to exchange all their dollars for gold, so they began to convert them into other hard currencies such as Japanese yen, Swiss francs and German marks, thus releasing hundreds of millions of US dollars into commercial banks. At the same time, US multinational corporations managed to side-step restrictions on the amount of capital US citizens could transfer overseas and decided simply to keep their money abroad.

The 1973-74 oil crisis provided the decisive boost for the already burgeoning Eurodollar market. In the space of one year from October 1973 the price of oil almost quadrupled from $2.80 to over $10 a barrel. The surplus of the oil-exporting countries rose from $7 billion in 1973 to $68 billion the following year.[3] The oil producers chose to invest this money in the Eurodollar market.

The banks that received these deposits needed to lend out the money in order to pay interest to their depositors. To safeguard themselves against losses caused by changes in interest rates, they instituted a 'floating' interest rate which they adjusted at six-monthly intervals. This was, of course, enormously advantageous to the banks because it transferred all the risk to the client. As long as the client was not insolvent, the banks were guaranteed a return on their money. And since much of the lending was, directly or indirectly, to sovereign states, such a possibility seemed very remote. Walter Winston, then chairman of Citibank, commented: 'Countries don't go bust.'

The sharp rise in the price of oil was an immediate problem for Latin America. In 1974 only four Latin American countries (Bolivia, Ecuador, Venezuela and Trinidad) were net oil-exporters. In the wake of the oil crisis only Venezuela and Trinidad were able to generate current-account surpluses on their international trade. Other Latin American countries had little choice but to borrow to maintain oil imports. Their economies would have ground to a halt had they tried to restrict oil imports in line with their ability to pay. With the exception of Venezuela and Trinidad, Latin America saw its trade deficit grow from $300 million to $7.9 billion between 1973 and 1974. The cost of Brazilian oil imports doubled in one year.[4] To make matters worse, the oil price rise provoked a recession in the industrialised countries which, in turn, reduced commodity prices (except that of oil) by 19 per cent. While Latin American countries were having to borrow to maintain oil and other imports, their ability to earn foreign currency through exports was simultaneously being sapped by the fall in commodity prices.

Crushing burden: Latin America's foreign debt

The growing participation of private banks in lending to Latin America was made possible by the mushrooming Eurodollar market, fuelled by the dollar surpluses of the oil-producing countries.

Indeed, the banks were so desperate to lend that for foreign borrowers they relaxed many of the rules which they maintained as standard banking practice in assessing domestic loans. One of the innovations of this period was the syndicated loan, a device which enabled banks to club together to spread any risk and to make loans much larger than they would dare to make as sole lenders.

TABLE 1: Total outstanding and disbursed Latin American debt

Year	Total Debt ($ billion)	Official	Private
1970	23	36	64
1971	26	36	64
1972	30	34	66
1973	40	28	72
1974	56	25	75
1975	75	22	78
1976	98	18	82
1977	116	18	82
1978	151	16	84
1979	182	15	85

Source as % of total debt at year end

(Source: UN Economic Commission for Latin America, in Jacobo Schatan: *World Debt: Who is to pay?*, Zed, London, 1987.)

The table shows:

i. The substantial increase in foreign borrowing during the 1970s, almost an eightfold increase.

ii. The declining importance of 'public authorities' as a source for such borrowing.

iii. The overwhelming importance of private sector finance by the end of the decade.

chapter two

Wasted money?

What happened to all these loans? If the money was wasted, who was responsible? Was it governments and state bureaucracies, depicted as villains by monetarists, or the irresponsible rich? Or was the money spent largely on arms by the military dictatorships holding power in thirteen Latin American countries during the 1970s?

There is no clear answer. Investment in the region continued to grow as a percentage of gross domestic product (GDP) during the 1970s, just as it had done in the course of the 1960s, peaking in 1981 at nearly 25 per cent of GDP. But in the 1970s foreign loans replaced local capital rather than supplemented it. Appropriately enough, some of the credits were used by governments or state corporations to tackle the energy crisis. Several of Brazil's major hydroelectric projects date from the 1970s, including Itaipu, the biggest dam in the world. Brazil also started to invest heavily in its programme to use alcohol distilled from sugar-cane as an alternative to petrol. And Mexico used loans to develop its own oil industry. This does not mean, however, that such projects were not wasteful. Budgets spiralled out of control; the completed projects often failed to perform as planned; and many were environmentally and socially disastrous.

At the same time there was substantial capital flight; that is, the placing of money in bank accounts and investments abroad, perceived by the rich as more secure than the risky, over-regulated and inflation-prone alternatives at home. The World Bank itself stated that much of the money being borrowed from abroad was funnelled straight out again, describing this state of affairs as a disaster. The Bank was citing information which suggested that between 1979 and 1982, $19.2 billion left Argentina, $26.5 billion left Mexico and $19.2 billion left Venezuela. This amounted to 64 per cent, 48 per cent and 137 per cent respectively of the gross capital inflows into those countries. One expert calculated a figure of $180 billion – the equivalent of the total combined foreign debt of Mexico, Argentina and Venezuela – for the total assets held abroad by Latin Americans in 1985. In the same year a Mexican newspaper published the names of 537 Mexicans, each with over a million dollars deposited in foreign banks.[5]

As import restrictions were swept away in countries which were embracing monetarism and liberalising imports on the advice of the International Monetary Fund (IMF) and World Bank, the rich and the middle classes took full advantage of the easy availability of imports and the over-valuation of their own currencies. During the three-year period between 1979 and 1982, when the Chilean peso was pegged to the dollar, non-food imports increased by

1,093 per cent; perfume and cosmetic imports shot up by 19,500 per cent; alcoholic drinks and tobacco by 9,357 per cent; and cars and motor cycles by 1,248 per cent. By 1981 such increases meant that 20 per cent of total Chilean imports were made up of 'non-traditional' luxury items. This profligacy led to the collapse of several major banks in Chile in 1982 and renewed state intervention in financial institutions.

TABLE 2: Capital flight (US $ millions)*

Country	1980	1982	1987
Argentine	11,000	35,000	46,000
Brazil	6,000	8,000	31,000
Mexico	19,000	44,000	84,000
Venezuela	15,000	33,000	58,000

*Compounded value of flight-capital assets, assuming a pre-tax return of six-month LIBOR.

(Source: Morgan Guaranty Trust Company, quoted in *Financial Times*, 4 August 1989.)

In comparison with the sums that left Latin America in capital flight or that were squandered on unnecessary imports or unproductive prestige projects, the money spent on arms by Latin American countries in these years of massive borrowing was insignificant. Between 1973 and 1983 total military expenditure in Latin America, including arms imports, rose from $4.1 billion to $10.9 billion. But expressed as a percentage of the continent's total income, or gross national product (GNP), it fell from 1.6 to 1.5 per cent.

Over the same period the military expenditure of the United States rose from 5.9 to 6.6 per cent of GNP while that of the United Kingdom increased from 4.8 to 5.4 per cent. The value of Latin American arms imports (excluding Cuba) rose steadily throughout the period, from $2.3 billion in 1973-76 to $4.14 billion in 1977-80, and to $9.5 billion in 1981-84.[6]

The beneficiaries

The major beneficiaries of the loans bonanza were the banks; Western exporters, who provided two-thirds of Latin American imports; and the citizens of industrial countries, where the impact of the recession was alleviated by such export successes.

But Latin America also seemed to benefit. Latin American growth in the 1970s was 50 per cent higher than that of the developed industrial countries. The continent's major economies matched or even surpassed Asian rivals such as South Korea, Taiwan and Singapore. *The Banker* magazine promoted Brazil as at least as good an investment as the so-called 'Asian tigers'. But appearances were deceptive: the economies of Latin America were already faltering at the beginning of the 1970s. The import-substitution strategy had failed, making the economies of the region more dependent and vulnerable to external shocks. The lending boom reinforced this trend, locking Latin America into a self-perpetuating dependence on commercial finance for as long as the banks were willing to continue lending.

More shocks: oil prices and interest rates rise again

After the overthrow of the Shah of Iran in 1979, OPEC producers increased the price of oil from $13 a barrel in 1978 to $32.50 in 1981. The Latin American countries responded as they had done before – by borrowing. The banks increased their lending but the hard-pressed economies of Latin America were already burdened with repayments on earlier debts and were acquiring new interest obligations. Because of this, the net transfer of resources to the region was actually reduced and eventually turned negative. In other words, payments of principal and interest on existing loans became greater than new loans coming in.

Meanwhile, back in the industrialised countries, economics was going through a sea-change. Governments were grappling with the phenomenon of 'stagflation', the combination of recession or sluggish growth with high inflation. A 'normal' recession is not accompanied by high inflation; on the contrary, prices are held steady or reduced and profit margins are squeezed as producers compete for the diminishing income of buyers. But after 1974 the price of oil was the main cause of inflation. Prices went up but there was no growth. By 1979 inflation was running at 13.3 per cent in the United States and unemployment at 7 million. The monetarist solution for stagflation was to attack inflation first by raising interest rates, forgetting about unemployment or growth.

Interest rates had been increasing during the late 1970s, but real rates of interest based on the US prime rate (equivalent to the bank rate set by the Bank of England in the United Kingdom) were still very low or negative. This meant that interest rates were less than the rate of inflation. In October 1979 the chairman of the US Federal Reserve, Paul Volcker, adopted the monetarist solution.

Within six months the interest rate had risen to 19.5 per cent. It fluctuated throughout 1980, ending in December at 21.5 per cent.

Crushing burden: Latin America's foreign debt

Ronald Reagan (elected in November 1980) and Margaret Thatcher (elected in June 1979) were enthusiastic exponents of monetarist policies, believing that the role of the state in economic affairs should be only to control the money supply and guarantee the free market.

TABLE 3: Latin America – net transfer of resources 1978-83

Year	Net capital inflow	Net payments of profits and resources	Net transfer of resources
1978	26.1	10.2	15.9
1979	28.6	13.6	15.0
1980	30.0	18.0	12.0
1981	37.7	27.7	10.0
1982	19.2	37.6	-18.4
1983	4.4	34.5	-30.1

(Source: Economic Commission for Latin America and the Caribbean: 'Preliminary Overview of the Latin American Economy in 1984', in Stephanie Griffith-Jones and Osvaldo Sunkel, *Debt and Development Crises in Latin America: the End of an Illusion*, Clarendon Press, Oxford, 1989, Table 8.2.)

For Latin American countries these changes in policy meant massive increases in interest charges. All their commercial debt was linked to the US prime rate or the London Inter-Bank Offered Rate (LIBOR), a free market rate normally above the US prime. These rose from an average rate of 12.1 per cent and 12.7 per cent respectively in 1979 to 16.6 per cent and 18.8 per cent in 1981. The cost to Latin American debtors of a 1 per cent rise in interest rates was an additional $1.8 billion in interest payments. In three years, 1981-83, Latin American interest payments were $94.8 billion, double their total interest payments throughout the 1970s. Mexico's interest bill leapt from $2.3 billion in 1979 to $9.8 billion in 1982, while Brazil's interest payments went from $4.8 to $11.9 billion over the same period.

At the same time, the effect of these high interest rates and tight-money policies in the industrialised countries was to reduce demand for the exports of third world countries, just as these poor nations needed to export more to pay their ever higher interest bills. By 1982, as a result of increased supply and reduced demand, commodity prices (excluding oil) had fallen in real terms to levels not seen since the Great Depression of 1929-33.

chapter two

The value of Latin American exports declined sharply. Even the more developed countries of Latin America, such as Argentina, Brazil and Chile, depend heavily on the exports of commodities and raw materials: in 1981-82 soya beans, coffee and iron ore accounted for 83 per cent of Brazilian exports; copper accounted for around 50 per cent of Chilean exports; and wheat, maize and beans made up about 30 per cent of all Argentina's exports.

Moreover, throughout the 1970s the developed world had been erecting obstacles to free trade in the form of 'non-tariff barriers' (NTBs). These are regulations and agreements drawn up by developed countries to protect their higher-cost industries by limiting access of goods produced in developing countries to the markets of the developed world. They can be overt quantitative restrictions, limiting the imports of a particular good to a specific number of units; 'voluntary' export restraints agreed by the exporting country for fear of something worse; or bogus 'safety' and 'technical' standards.[7] In 1984, according to the United Nations Commission on Trade and Development (UNCTAD), 27.7 per cent of the European Community's imports from Latin America were protected in this way.

TABLE 4: Percentage of Latin American exports subject to NTBs (by importing market)

United States	7.3
Japan	18.5
European Community	27.7
Switzerland	36.3
Sweden	32.2
Norway	21.7
Austria	37.7

(Source: UNCTAD, *Trade and Development Report, 1984* [TDR/4, Vol II], Part 2, 17 July 1984. Cited in Harold Lever and Christopher Huhne, *The Third World Financial Crisis*, Penguin Books, 1985, p92.)

At the beginning of the 1980s, therefore, the economic and financial policies of the developed world seemed designed perversely to make a debt crisis inevitable. Latin America – together with the poor countries of sub-Saharan Africa which were even less able to pay their debts – was faced with mounting interest bills, dramatically lower prices for its major exports and diminished access to the markets of developed countries.

Crushing burden: Latin America's foreign debt

The crisis

The debt crisis became official on 13 August 1982 when the Mexican authorities informed the country's creditor banks, Paul Volcker, chairman of the US Federal Reserve, and Jacques de Larosière, managing director of the IMF, that the country was going to suspend payment on the interest and principal of its $80 billion debt, most of it owed to US commercial banks. Such an announcement was inevitable: the increasingly large sums that Mexico and other Latin American countries were being asked to pay in interest were sooner or later going to prove impossible. But what precipitated the crisis was the refusal of creditor banks to extend further credit to enable Mexico to make payments on outstanding loans. Although Mexico had been able to borrow $6.4 billion in the six months preceding the August announcement, the banks had decided that the country was no longer creditworthy.

The Mexican decision threatened the stability of both the world financial system and, in particular, the United States, since nine of the largest US banks had 44 per cent of their capital tied up in loans to Mexico alone. The financial establishment reacted quickly. A deal was hammered out, involving commitments by the international financial institutions (the IMF, the World Bank and regional development banks), the commercial banks and the Mexican government.

The United States agreed to lend Mexico a series of bridging loans while the IMF, which did not have the resources to provide significant help on its own, organised further lending from the commercial banks. This lending was 'involuntary'; in other words, it was the result of arm-twisting by the IMF, which eventually produced a further $8 billion in 'new money'. Together with some rescheduling of repayments of principal, these loans enabled Mexico to renew interest payments on the debt. The price paid by Mexico was high. In return for this assistance the Mexican authorities had to agree to a structural adjustment package described by one expert as 'involving strong measures'.[8] Structural adjustment means adjusting the structure of an economy to address the central problem of the debt; in other words, to reduce imports, boost exports and make the country attractive to foreign investors. The measures included drastic cuts in public spending; privatisation in every area of the Mexican economy; tax increases; higher prices for public services; and a contraction of domestic demand achieved by the intentional reduction of the incomes of ordinary people. The aim was to reduce inflation and generate a balance of payments surplus.

Default was never really considered. The Mexican negotiators were part of the financial establishment. They feared that default would invite immediate sanctions which would paralyse the Mexican economy and bring down the government. Other similar packages followed. Argentina's adjustment programme, which included a reduction of the balance of payments deficit from $6.5 billion in 1982 to $0.5 billion in 1983, was approved in January of that year. The first Brazilian programme – there were six in all between 1982 and 1985 – was agreed in February 1983. As in Mexico, the programme included new tax measures and restraint on government expenditure. Cheap credit, with rates of interest lower than the rate of inflation, was to be substantially reduced. The cruzeiro (the Brazilian unit of currency) was devalued by 23 per cent in February 1983 and there- after was kept in line with inflation by daily mini-devaluations. Wage increases were kept below the level of inflation.

From 1982 to 1985, known in debt jargon as the 'Band-Aid' (i.e. 'Elastoplast') years, the IMF had a central role in staving off the debt crisis. The main aim was to preserve the international banking system by forcing debtor countries to meet their obligations, and by providing barely-adequate additional finance and rescheduling to help them achieve this. In these narrow terms, at least, stabilisation was successful: Latin American trade went from a small deficit of $1.7 billion in 1981 to an accumulated surplus of $113.6 billion over the next four years.

The main beneficiaries were the Western banks which, according to Britain's All Party Group on Overseas Development (APGOOD), 'were able to reduce their overall exposure and build up their capital base. The international financial system did not collapse ... nor were the debtor countries tempted to form an effective cartel withholding all service payments.' The APGOOD report, however, also noted that, '... a set of policy responses which left the developing countries with higher debt-service burdens in 1985 than in 1982 can hardly be judged a success.'

Whereas in 1982 new loans to the debtor developing countries exceeded interest payments by $16 billion, in 1985 interest payments exceeded loans by $26 billion, so sharp was the contraction in new lending. The IMF knew beforehand that for the programme to be judged a success by the debtors, the commercial banks would have to make new loans over and above those required merely to maintain interest payments on existing loans. Success for the debtors would have meant, first of all, a return to economic growth and then a readjustment of their economies to allow them to service their debts without the across-the-board cuts in government expenditure that pushed millions of Latin Americans from poverty to destitution. But for the IMF to expect the banks to lend voluntarily at such a level was simply to ignore the post-1982 reality and the banks' own role in precipitating the crisis. In the 1970s the herd instinct had pushed the banks into the loans race; after 1982 it made them withdraw from sovereign lending. In this situation, voluntary lending on an adequate scale was highly improbable.

TABLE 5: The importance of Latin American interest payments to the four major UK banks 1982-85*

	1982	1983	1984	1985
Total loans ($ millions)	17,400	17,600	18,883	19,494
Estimated interest rate (%)	13.60	9.50	10.80	9.40
Estimated Latin American earnings ($ millions)	2,366	1,672	2,039	1,833
As % net interest income	25.6	18.4	25.5	17.1
As % pre-tax profits	98.1	69.1	92.1	49.3

* Barclays, Lloyds, Midland, National Westminster

(Source: S. Griffiths-Jones, M. Marcel & G. Palma, *Third World Debt and British Banks,* Fabian Society, London, 1987.)

The most likely explanation for this apparently wilful misjudgment on the part of the IMF is that there was simply a lack of funds both on the part of the banks and official sources. The IMF-engendered stabilisation programmes were intended, accordingly, to be short, sharp shocks which would provide effective once-and-for-all adjustments. Indeed, IMF officials responded to mounting criticism of its policies by arguing that these short, drastic adjustment programmes were the only possible solution to the debt crisis because longer-term programmes would not be politically sustainable, since the 'pain' associated with them would be too prolonged.

Adjustment without a human face

The World Council of Churches, reporting on the 1983-85 experience in Brazil, said that, 'three years of recessive adjustment aggravated unemployment, poverty and social inequality.'[9] Average child mortality, which had fallen throughout the 1970s, 'bounced back to 25 per cent between 1982 and 1984.' Perhaps for the first time in Brazilian history all social classes, with the exception of the tiny minority producing for export or those speculating on the money market, were adversely affected. But the poorest were most severely affected. Their purchasing power, already abysmally low, slumped 30 per cent between 1979 and 1983. In part, this reflected the doubling of unemployment in 1983 following the IMF agreement. In 1984 it was estimated officially that one in five Brazilian workers was unemployed.

The Brazilian experience was not unique. Costa Rica, for example, implemented an IMF-type programme in mid-1982, six months before entering into formal agreement with the IMF in January 1983. Costa Rica's adjustment programme included an increase in electricity prices of 70 per cent. Six months later, immediately after the signing of the agreement with the IMF, prices were raised again – this time by 90 per cent. The price increases over the sixteen months to April 1983 totalled 227 per cent. These increases sparked widespread grass-roots opposition, led by 52 trade unions and 140 local organisations. So intense was the opposition that the government was forced to back-track and repudiate all the 1983 rises in the price of electricity.

Costa Rica, which did away with its armed forces in 1948, was celebrated for the quality and extent of its social services. In 1978, for example, 52 per cent of government expenditure was allocated to social services; 24.8 per cent was spent on the health budget; and 16 per cent on education. By 1984, the proportion of government expenditure spent on social services had been cut to 41.5 per cent. Health spending had fallen to 17.6 per cent and education to 12.6 per cent.

Such cuts might have been justifiable if they had brought about improvements in employment and income for the majority of the population. Real wages, however, declined by 25 per cent over five years. In accordance with the January 1983 agreement with the IMF, wage increases were determined every six months by reference to increases in the price of a 'basic wage basket' of eighteen essential goods. So wage increases were adjusted only after their value had been eroded by inflation over six months. In addition, the price of the 'basic wage basket' lagged behind that of an established basket of thirty-nine nutritional necessities, only eleven of which were represented in the 'basic wage basket'. It is also possible that financial pressure was used at this time to persuade the Costa Rican government to support US policy in Central America – namely the destabilisation of the revolutionary Sandinista government in Nicaragua.

No such pressures were applied to Peru under the Belaúnde government (1980-85). President Belaúnde took office committed to reforming the Peruvian economy along liberal economic lines. The negative effects of the 1981 early repayment of part of the debt and the economy's liberalisation were exacerbated by

Crushing burden: Latin America's foreign debt

adverse international market conditions for Peru's exports. Consequently, in 1982 Peru was unable to meet the conditions agreed with the IMF. The economy contracted sharply the following year. Production fell by 12 per cent. In the face of this crisis the Finance Ministry negotiated a new IMF loan in March 1984.

The new programme ignored the freak climatic conditions (a reversal of normal weather patterns caused by the *El Niño* phenomenon in the Pacific Ocean), which were a major factor behind the economic crisis, and concentrated on reducing economic demand.

In this, at least, the programme was successful. Per capita incomes fell from $1,232 in 1980 to $1,055 in 1985. Unemployment rose from 7 per cent in 1980 to 10.9 per cent in 1984. Underemployment, as in much of Latin America in 1980, was already very high, at 51.2 per cent. By 1984, this had risen still further to 54.2 per cent. At the end of 1984, only 35 per cent of the workforce was fully employed, down from 42 per cent at the start of the decade. Those workers who managed to keep their jobs saw the real value of their wages fall sharply.

This economic decline was dramatically reflected in other indicators. The incidence of tuberculosis rose by one-third from 1979-83; gastro-enteritis and dysentery multiplied almost three-fold; and bronchitis and other severe respiratory diseases were twice as common in 1984 as in 1981. The average calorie intake of Peru-vians, which had been 97 per cent of UN standards in 1979, fell to 85 per cent in 1985. The average daily protein intake fell by 9 grams to 50 grams over the same period. The proportion of the budget allocated to health spending fell from 6 per cent in 1970 to 4.3 per cent in 1984. The cutbacks affected both the number of doctors per 1,000 people (from 1.7 in 1972 to 1.1 in 1984), the number of nurses per 1,000 people (from 2.9 in 1972 to 1.4 in 1984), and the number of hospital beds per head of population (down by 20 per cent over the same period).

By the mid-1980s popular organisations were calling for the repudiation of the debt. In the Peruvian elections of mid-1985 the APRA (American Popular Revolutionary Alliance) candidate, Alan García, won a landslide victory because he promised to limit the service of the debt to what the country could afford, placing Peruvian interests before those of its creditors. *Acción Popular*, the ruling party responsible for the adjustment programme, won only 6 per cent of the vote compared with 46 per cent five years earlier. In Brazil, too, the unpopularity of the IMF-dictated measures was one factor which hastened the demise of the military government.

chapter two

The Baker Plan: recognising failure

At the beginning of his presidency, Alan García announced his decision to limit Peru's foreign-debt service payment to 10 per cent of the country's annual earnings from exports. He also repeated his campaign pledges to renegotiate the country's debt directly with its foreign creditors, thereby cutting out the IMF. Other Latin American debtors, such as Bolivia and Nicaragua, had failed to pay their debts, but the very public nature of the Peruvian announcement represented a new threat. Although the Peruvian debt was small compared to those of major debtors (such as Argentina, Brazil or Mexico), bankers, the IMF and creditor governments feared that the Peruvian strategy might be exported. And whatever their public statements, other Latin American debtors were clearly interested in the policy. Latin American delegations queued to discuss the debt-service cap with the Peruvians at the annual meetings of the IMF and World Bank in Seoul, South Korea, in 1985. Action had to be taken to prevent the formation of a debtors' cartel which would act unilaterally. At these meetings, the other members of the 'Group of Seven' (or G7, the richest industrialised countries: the United States, United Kingdom, Japan, West Germany, France, Italy and Canada), made it very clear that any debt initiative was the responsibility of the United States.

Before arriving in Seoul, US Treasury Secretary James Baker had already agreed with France, Germany, Japan and the UK to reduce the over-valuation of the dollar. The effect of devaluing the dollar would be to reduce imports into the United States, thereby easing the pressure from US producers for protectionist measures, and force exporting countries to divert their exports to other markets. In Seoul, Baker dealt with the debt problem itself. He proposed that the fifteen (later seventeen) largest developing-country debtors, ten of whom were Latin American (Argentina, Bolivia, Brazil, Chile, Colombia, Ecuador, Mexico, Peru, Uruguay and Venezuela) would be eligible to receive $29 billion in further credits over 1986-88. Of this, $9 billion would be supplied by the international financial institutions (IFIs). The World Bank, rather than the IMF, was accorded the central co-ordinating role. The balance of $20 billion was to be new commercial bank lending. In return, the fifteen countries would undertake structural economic reforms to place more emphasis on market mechanisms and private-sector initiatives.

The chances of success were not good from the outset. Under the plan, commercial banks were expected to make available $7 billion annually in new money; that is, over and above loans made specifically for the purpose of rescheduling existing debts. By

September 1986 only $2 billion in new money had been paid over by the banks. Yet, by the end of 1986, they had rescheduled $75 billion of debt, over 25 per cent of the fifteen countries' total commercial bank debt. By this time, new loans worth $6 billion had been agreed with, though not paid over to, Mexico.

The Mexican agreement, which has to be set against the background of the enormous damage – estimated at $3 billion – caused by the September 1985 earthquake, contained specific additional conditions. It included a clear link between growth targets and export earnings on the one hand, and available additional finance on the other. In the event of failure to achieve a prescribed growth rate or a further significant fall in the price of oil, new finance would automatically be provided by both multilateral and commercial lenders. Some banks opposed this automatic linking and disbursed the new loans reluctantly and with some delay, underlining publicly what they had been saying in private, at least since 1983: that they would reschedule the debts if forced to do so but they would not willingly risk any more of their shareholders' capital. Only in February 1987 did enough of Mexico's creditor banks subscribe to this agreement to release the new loans.

Baker was able to claim success in some areas. His report to the US Congress in December 1986 noted that nine of the fifteen had agreed formal IMF programmes or signed letters of intent, although both Peru and Brazil had chosen to avoid any IMF involvement. The World Bank had co-ordinated $3.7 billion worth of adjustment loans to ten countries and an additional $5 billion was under negotiation.

Despite their public support for the Baker Plan, however, the commercial banks' actions were clear indications of their misgivings. The plan provided for $20 billion in new lending from the commercial banks. At the time there was criticism that this sum would do no more than paper over the cracks revealed by the debt crisis. On the other hand the banks considered it a risky extravagance, as their actual lending shows (see Table 6 overleaf).

Regardless of the actual sums needed, the commercial banks were clearly not willing to make available anywhere near the sum envisaged under the Baker Plan. Furthermore, the situation of Latin American debtor countries did not alter significantly. The ratio of their total debt to their export earnings increased substantially over 1985 figures and only began to decline – but not below 1985 figures – in 1989. This means that the growth of the debt outstripped the ability of countries to repay it during the years of the plan. Total debt as a percentage of regional income (GNP) remained above 50 per cent for all years but 1988. Debt service as a percentage of export earnings was relatively constant around 40 per cent throughout the period but international reserves as a percentage of total debt actually show a steady decline.

TABLE 6: Commercial bank disbursements 1985-89*

Country	Amount disbursed ($ millions)					TOTAL
	1985	1986	1987	1988	1989	
Argentina	2,671	1,208	976	556	0	5,411
Brazil	0	0	0	4,000	600	4,600
Chile	0	217	0	0	0	217
Colombia	0	957	0	0	0	957
Costa Rica	75	0	0	0	0	75
Ecuador	200	0	0	0	0	200
Jamaica	0	0	0	0	0	0
Mexico	995	0	4,312	1,188	0	6,495
Peru	0	0	0	0	0	0
Uruguay	0	0	0	0	0	0
Venezuela	0	0	0	0	100	100
TOTAL	3,941	2,382	5,288	5,744	700	18,055

* NB The Baker Plan proposals covered the period 1986-88

(Source: *World Debt Tables, 1989-90*, Vol 1, Table VI.5, World Bank, 1990.)

Two years after the Baker Plan was launched it was pronounced a failure: in February 1987, President Sarney of Brazil declared a moratorium on the payment of interest on his country's debt.
The moratorium, which might have been economically sustainable a year earlier when Brazil's foreign reserves were high, was doomed to failure. It meant, too, that any future plan that relied on significant new lending by commercial banks was also bound to fail.

From now on the commercial banks concentrated on increasing their level of provisions against bad debts at the expense of new lending to the Third World, which they saw as throwing good money after bad.

The debt crisis of the banks

In April 1987, Citicorp, Citibank's parent corporation, announced that it was raising the level of its loan-loss reserves by $3 billion to $5 billion, equivalent to 25 per cent of the debt owed to it by third world countries. As a result, the bank accepted a second-quarter operating loss of $2.5 billion. This announcement sent tremors through the financial world. Other commercial banks quickly followed suit. Five of the next six biggest US banks added at least $1 billion to their reserves. The four largest British clearing banks – Barclays, Lloyds, Midland and National Westminster – together added £3.4 billion to their reserves. Lloyds and Midland, the most exposed in Latin America, added the largest amounts, amounting to £1,066 million and £916 million respectively. As a result, these two banks reported losses of £248 million and £505 million respectively in 1987, the first ever reported by the British clearing banks in modern times.

The knock-on effects were soon felt. Stock market nervousness about the profitability of the banking sector in the United States was aggravated by the virtual bankruptcy of the Savings and Loan Corporations (the equivalent of building societies in the United Kingdom). Then the Federal Reserve Board had to rescue the largest Texan bank, First City Bank Corporation. Nervousness on Wall Street spread rapidly around the world's markets, fuelling the decline of the dollar and further undermining foreign investors' confidence in Wall Street. Crisis came on 19 October 1987, known as Black Monday. Foreign investors pulled out of US dollar investments; the value of shares traded on Wall Street fell 22.6 per cent on a single day, more than double the fall which sparked the crash in 1929. Then, as a result of financial deregulation, twenty-four-hour trading and instant dealing through computer links, the collapse of markets in Tokyo, Hong Kong, Sydney, Frankfurt, Paris and London automatically followed.

The G7 governments acted quickly to restore investor confidence, cutting interest rates and agreeing measures to prevent the recurrence of such panic-selling in the future. Confidence returned quickly: early in 1988 the Tokyo stock exchange was registering record highs. But Black Monday drew attention to the fragility of the world's stock markets and spotlighted the seemingly ever-widening US budget and trade deficits.

Towards debt reduction

Debts are reduced as a last resort by lenders anxious to recover at least a proportion of their original loans. Banks can auction off the house of a defaulting buyer or put a bankrupt business in the

chapter two

hands of the receiver but they cannot treat countries in the same way. The expectation that most third world debt will never be paid back in full is recognised in the price at which banks and financial institutions will sell this debt to each other. This is the 'secondary market', on which debts are traded at a fraction of their face value. The size of the discount reflects the degree of pessimism of the financial establishment about the ability of borrowing countries to repay their debts. For instance, in 1987 Bolivian bonds were changing hands on the secondary market at 8 per cent of their face value and Mexican bonds at 58 per cent. This pessimism was zealously hidden from shareholders, however, to whom the Third World's debts were presented as assets that continued to produce a healthy return. For this reason the 1987 Brazilian moratorium sent shock waves through the system.

The secondary market gave rise to a number of transactions in which discounted debt was sold for assets in the country concerned. These are known as debt-for-equity swaps. In 1986, for example, the Japanese car company Nissan wanted to expand its operations in Mexico. It paid $40 million for Mexican bonds with a face value of $60 million. It sold these to the government for $54 million worth of Mexican pesos, which it then invested in its Mexican subsidiary.[10] In another transaction the Dutch football team PSV Eindhoven bought $5 million worth of discounted Brazilian debt and exchanged it for cruzados to buy a brilliant Rio de Janeiro footballer.[11] The problem with such deals is that they release large amounts of local currency, thus fuelling inflation. And they are also a subsidy to foreign investment which, sooner or later, will start to generate outflows of funds in the form of profits being sent back to parent companies in Japan, the United States or Europe. This, however, did not deter the Chilean military government from using debt-for-equity swaps to reduce the total Chilean debt by 36 per cent in its last four years (1986 to 1990). Some countries have been able to buy back a small proportion of their debt at discounted rates (debt-for-debt swaps). But this is hardly a solution for indebted, poverty-stricken countries which already have difficulty paying for essential imports. It is a solution, however, in which the entire value of the discount accrues to the debtor country.

Table 7 lists the value of transactions which converted external debt claims on selected Latin American and Caribbean countries (debt conversions) through debt-for-equity and debt-for-debt swaps from 1984-89. The table shows that overall there was little real interest in the region amongst investors and that debt conversions were concentrated on three countries: Brazil, Chile and Mexico. The increased pace and value of debt conversions from 1987 is attributable to legislative and administrative changes in debtor countries and, more importantly, to the sea-change in the commercial banks' perspectives. One indication of this has already been mentioned – the increase in loan-loss provisions. Banks with only a small commitment to Latin America, particularly the smaller US regional banks, chose to cut their losses and sell-out through debt conversions. Banks which had invested heavily in third world debt had little choice but to spread their geographical risk by exchanging debts with other banks and selling debt to third parties. In other words, the banks accepted the possibility of debt reduction provided it was voluntary and market-related.

TABLE 7: Debt conversions 1984-89 ($ millions)

Country	1984	1985	1986	1987	1988	1989
Argentina	31	469	-	35	1,330	500
Bolivia	-	-	-	1	349	20
Brazil	731	537	176	1,800	9,175	4,000
Chile	11	313	987	1,983	2,905	2,000
Costa Rica	-	-	7	146	17	10
Ecuador	-	-	-	125	258	-
Honduras	-	-	-	6	11	-
Jamaica	-	-	-	2	100	-
Mexico	-	769	1,023	3,804	6,670	6,000
Peru	-	-	-	-	1	-
Uruguay	-	-	-	-	9	-
Venezuela	-	-	-	-	47	-

(Source: *World Debt Tables, 1989-90*, Table V, World Bank, 1990.)

The G7 countries had accepted the principle of reduction of debt owed to governments at the Toronto economic summit in June 1988. Although initially restricted to the poorest qualifying sub-Saharan African countries, it was extended to two comparable Latin American countries – Bolivia and Guyana.

The Brady Plan[12]

The Brady Plan, formulated in 1989, takes its name from President Bush's Treasury Secretary, Nicholas Brady. It was an advance on

chapter two

the Baker Plan in that it clearly recognised that the face value of the debts had to be reduced and that G7 governments had a responsibility to encourage this. The plan responded to the Bush administration's growing concern about its Latin American neighbours: their economies were stagnating; commodity prices were still low; and debt repayments were at their highest ever. In 1988 the fifteen largest debtor countries paid $31 billion to their creditors, while their national income per head was 7 per cent below what it had been in 1980. The possible consequences – the destabilisation of friendly Latin American governments, including the 'fledgling democracies' nurtured by the Reagan administration – posed a serious threat to US economic and political interests in the region. In Mexico, with its shared border with the United States, the Institutional Revolutionary Party (PRI), which for seventy years had ruled the country as virtually a one-party state, came close to defeat in the 1988 elections despite its immense powers of political patronage and the considerable fraud and corruption exercised in its favour. Venezuela, one of the most stable democratic countries of Latin America, experienced massive urban rioting in February 1989 as a direct result of the implementation of IMF-inspired austerity policies. Hundreds were killed as police and troops fought to control the rioters. In 1989 Venezuela experienced an unprecedented 8 per cent drop in gross domestic product.

Brady proposed that:

• The overall debt had to be reduced and, implicitly, the cost had to be borne by the banks.

• Public money, via the funds of the IMF and the World Bank, should be used to encourage the banks to accept a reduction in the face value of the debt. This was a public recognition that part of the burden of the debt should be switched from private banks to public institutions. But it also meant that, in future, the debtors could benefit from discounted market valuation of their debts.

• Changes had to be made in US and other banking regulations to remove existing disincentives to debt reduction.

• A country's ability to pay must be reflected in new negotiations on debt. The proposals referred to the role of the market in deciding a proper level of discount on the debt.

• Large amounts of Japanese aid were to be encouraged and accepted into the process of bolstering the plan.

At the same time, Brady maintained the insistence of previous plans on policy reform in debtor countries, including greater liberalisation of markets, the elimination of subsidies and greater freedom for foreign competition and investment. The purpose was to encourage new investment flows, strengthen domestic savings, and promote the return of flight-capital, which was, Brady observed, 'roughly comparable to [most debtors'] total debt'. This in effect meant strengthening the implementation of existing IMF-World Bank policies. Brady emphasised that the international financial institutions (IFIs) would continue to promote 'sound policies in debtor countries through advice and support'.

Assessing the Brady Plan

By the end of 1990, four Brady-style debt-reduction agreements had been reached. Of these, three were with Latin American countries (Mexico, Costa Rica and Venezuela). The fourth was with the Aquino government in the Philippines. Possible candidates for the future included Argentina, Brazil, Chile, Ecuador, and Uruguay in Latin America, and Morocco and Nigeria in Africa, as well as some Eastern European countries.

Mexico. Mexico has occupied an enviable position in the story of the debt crisis. Having precipitated the onset of the crisis, Mexico established a number of precedents in debt-management strategy. It was the first country to win commercial bank agreement to multi-year rescheduling of debt (1984), the linking of a rescheduling agreement to economic performance (1986), and a pioneering debt reduction strategy (1988). In keeping with this record, Mexico was also the first country to seek to negotiate with its commercial creditors under the aegis of the Brady proposals.

The Mexican government, consciously taking the lead among debtor countries, was enthusiastic about the new proposals.[13] The banks, however, were divided in their views. The chairman of American Express saw the plan as a justification of his bank's decision to sell its debt on the secondary market and withdraw from third world lending. Other banks which had chosen, voluntarily or involuntarily, to maintain their third world business, including the Midland and Lloyds in the United Kingdom, were scornful of the plan. A senior Barclays Bank executive, Jolylyn Larkman, argued that it was ridiculous to ask commercial banks to accept the losses arising from debt reduction at the same time as expecting them to make new loans to debtor countries.

The negotiations with Mexico were crucial for the Brady Plan and, indeed, for the newly elected Mexican president, Carlos Salinas, who had pledged to renegotiate his country's crippling debt in the elections of 1988. Negotiations between the Mexican authorities and the fifteen-member advisory committee of creditors began in April 1989. The final agreement was signed on 30 March 1990, a year after the start of negotiations.[14]

chapter two

The agreement covered $48,500 million of Mexico's $102,700 million (1989) total foreign debt. The banks were given two options by the agreement: (i) to make new loans over a four-year period equivalent to 25 per cent of their existing exposure in the country, or (ii) to exchange their loans for thirty-year bonds backed by $7 billion borrowed mainly from international financial institutions and the Japanese Export-Import Bank.

In the event, new lending by the commercial banks fell short of expectations, with the result that the US Treasury reluctantly had to issue its own bonds to the value of $3.5 billion to rescue the agreement.[15] This effective US subsidy was severely criticised by bankers on the grounds that it meant that the agreement would not be transferable to other countries, because similar official subsidies would not be available. In the United Kingdom the Midland and Lloyds calculated that the net saving to Mexico was 'less than $1,000 million each year', equal to 10 per cent of the annual foreign interest bill.[16] The Mexican government was more optimistic in its assessment of the agreement, estimating that average annual savings over 1990-94 would be $4,040 million.[17]

Although the real value of the agreement to Mexico is disputed, the value of the reduction was calculated at $7,280 million in November 1990.[18] Creditors and the Mexican officials together agreed that these arrangements alone were insufficient to pull the country's economy around. Economic success depended not only on the oil price but also on the government's ability to continue economic reform without provoking social upheaval. In mid-1990 the economic prospects of the Salinas government were still uncertain. *The Economist* commented:

'A new foreign debt agreement in late 1990 brought some relief from the burden of repayment but not enough to provide the resources for new growth. The president's team of overseas-trained technocrats has reduced inflation by shrinking the deficit and liberalising trade but the squeeze on wages continues. A quarter of the way through his six-year term, Salinas has yet to make life better for ordinary Mexicans.'[19]

This failure is due, at least in part, to the Mexican government's commitment, required under the country's adjustment programme, to reduce further the economic role of the state and maintain strict control of public finances. Under the previous president, Enrique de la Madrid (1983-88), privatisations raised only $500 million. In the three years since Carlos Salinas took office, the government has sold 160 companies for $13 billion. By the end of 1991 eight banks had been privatised, raising $8 million, and a 20 per cent share in the state-owned telephone company was sold to international investors for $2 billion. The state-owned steel industry is now scheduled for privatisation. By the end of 1991 there were fewer than 280 state-owned enterprises, compared with 1,155 in 1982.

Strict control of public finances, however, has seen the gap between rich and poor, widen still more. Incomes remain below levels achieved in the 1970s and 41 million people survive precariously on or beneath the poverty line. An estimated 17 million Mexicans (approximately 20 per cent of the population) live almost wholly outside the modern economy in conditions of extreme poverty. The poorest 30 per cent of the population consume only 13 per cent of the foodstuffs, while the richest 10 per cent consume 21 per cent. The government is attempting to alleviate poverty through the National Solidarity Programme (set up in 1989) with a budget of $1,000 million to fund agricultural loans, emergency school-building, food kitchens, housing and improving water supplies. The programme's budget increased by 60 per cent in 1991. At the same time, the low priority given to social spending was clearly evident in the 1991 budget: while overall spending by the government was set to go up in real terms by 9.4 per cent, social spending was reduced 16.1 per cent.

Mexico's structural adjustment programme affected the poor disproportionately. The argument regularly deployed by finance ministers in these situations, however, is that such measures, although painful, are necessary to ensure future growth and, ultimately, a better life for all. Since growth depends on investment, the Mexican government took steps to boost investor confidence and, in particular, to attract flight-capital back to Mexico. According to the estimates shown in Table 2 (see page 75), capital held by Mexicans outside the country totalled $84,000 million in 1987.

As soon as its August 1989 debt-reduction agreement was completed, the Mexican government took measures to attract money that Mexicans had deposited abroad, virtually declaring an amnesty for such funds in return for the payment of a small once-and-for-all tax. Around $2,000 million was repatriated to Mexico in 1989 and $3,000 million in 1990. At least $1,500 million was invested productively in shares in Mexican businesses.

Clearly the rich are regaining confidence in the Mexican economy. The measures taken to entice capital back into the country, debt reduction and the accompanying structural adjustment programme have played a part in building this confidence. But so has Mexico's expected entry into the North American free-trade area, along with the United States and Canada. Mexico also benefited from the increase in the price of oil after the Iraqi invasion of Kuwait in August 1990. Although there had been an 80 per cent

chapter two

fall in exploration and development since 1982 because of spending cuts, Mexico was still able to increase oil exports by 150,000 barrels a day, bringing in extra income of between $1,500 million and $3,000 million in 1990 alone. All these factors helped produce 3.9 per cent growth in GNP in 1990 and about the same in 1991. Mexico is attractive to investors, however, precisely because the structural adjustment programme has reduced production costs, including wages. The poor also suffer in other ways: for instance, Mexico's pollution laws and industrial safety laws, comparable in principle to US laws, are less zealously enforced. It is far from certain, therefore, that this economic growth will adequately compensate the poor for the decline in their incomes and quality of life during the 1980s.

Costa Rica and Venezuela. After Mexico, deals with Costa Rica and Venezuela followed. Costa Rica, in particular, was able to reach an agreement quickly, because the banks were not asked to make any new loans. The deal reduced its existing commercial debt, accounting for one-third of its total foreign debt, by two-thirds. The Costa Rican agreement strongly suggested that the creditor banks had no objection in principle to reducing debt and debt service. But commercial banks still resisted the (to them) illogical requirement of the Brady Plan that they should not only reduce the debt owed to them but also make new loans.

The commercial banks also pointed out that while they were expected to accept the losses arising from debt reduction, official creditors – governments and IFIs – continued to insist that the debts owed to them were paid in full. According to the World Bank, total outstanding debt owed to commercial creditors went up from $450 billion in 1984 to $522 billion in 1990, an increase of around 16 per cent. Over the same period, total outstanding debt owed to official creditors rose from $234 billion to almost $522 billion, an increase of 123 per cent. As a result, payments owed to official creditors significantly worsened the debt problem in subsequent years. The explanation for this increase in official debt, at least in part, is that governments and IFIs were forced to lend more and reschedule debts in order to enable debtors to maintain payments to their commercial debtors, in other words, to use their taxpayer's money to bale out the banks.

The 'Enterprise for the Americas' initiative

By the middle of 1990, the Bush administration in the United States had acknowledged that by itself the Brady Plan could not provide the solution to Latin America's debt crisis. Announcing his 'Enterprise for the Americas' initiative on 27 June 1990, President Bush clearly identified US interests with those of Latin

Crushing burden: Latin America's foreign debt

America. It was already evident that the Latin American debt was a domestic political issue in the United States. Democrat Senator Bill Bradley had repeatedly drawn attention to the negative effects of the Latin American debt. He pointed to over a million jobs lost in US farms and industry as a result of the collapse of the Latin American market; the threat posed by the debt burden to newly emergent Latin American democracies; and the waves of illegal Latin American immigrants into the United States.[20] President Bush admitted that, 'While the Brady Plan has helped countries reduce commercial bank debt, for nations with high levels of official debt ... the burden remains heavy.'

The reduction of official debt, though still a relatively small proportion of total debt, was, accordingly, a significant element in the 'Enterprise for the Americas' initiative. Of almost $12 billion owed to the United States by Latin American countries, $7 billion is long-term, concessional-aid debt. The remaining $5 billion is short-term debt at commercial rates owed to, among others, the US Export-Import Bank and the Commodity Credit Corporation, which provide credit to foreign buyers to import US goods. So much official debt is owed by Latin American countries to the United States (amounting to 80 per cent of the official debt of some Latin American countries) that unilateral action by the United States could make a substantial difference to the debt-service burden.

Under the president's proposal, official debt (mostly owed by the smaller countries in the region) would be treated differently to commercial debt (mainly owed by the region's larger countries). According to the US Treasury, the amount of reduction would be decided on a case by case basis. Nonetheless, the level of reduction would be 'substantial, in some cases more than 50 per cent'. The reduced principal would be repaid in US dollars over several years in annual instalments determined by the circumstances of each qualifying country. Interest payments, however, would be made at an agreed concessional rate in the local currency and placed in special trust funds by the United States to support mutually agreed environmental programmes and other projects.

The plan also proposes to sell to private buyers a portion of commercial-rate US government loans at a discount on the secondary debt market. Having bought the bonds at a discount, the purchaser would then negotiate with the central bank of the country concerned to obtain a sum in local currency greater than the price in dollars paid for the discounted bonds, but less than the face value of the bonds. The purchaser would make use of the debt acquired in this way to conclude either debt-for-equity or debt-for-nature conversions, the latter being an agreement to use

chapter two

local currency to buy land that is set aside for environmental purposes. Eligibility for this official-debt reduction, restricted to Latin American and Caribbean countries, is limited in three ways. First, only those countries which have negotiated a comprehensive IMF-World Bank economic reform programme will qualify. Second, only those countries which have adopted major investment reforms in conjunction with the IADB will be considered. Finally, those countries that have large commercial-debt burdens must already have negotiated a debt-reduction agreement on the outstanding commercial debt.

The Gulf War and wrangles between the White House and the US Congress over the federal budget delayed the necessary legislation to put the 'Enterprise for the Americas' into practice. The US government, however, is concerned to strengthen its own links with Latin America in the face of the trading blocs of East Asia and the European Community and is highly unlikely to let the initiative drop.

Prospects for the 1990s

Some progress has been made. The Toronto agreement in 1988 and the Brady Plan were a clear recognition that debtor countries were not suffering from a temporary shortage of cash but were simply unable to service and pay off their debts. The process of debt reduction, initiated in 1987, is still continuing. In December 1991, Nicaragua, one of the poorest and most heavily indebted countries in Latin America, obtained agreement from the Paris Club of creditor governments to wipe out half the $735 million of debt due for repayment in the eighteen months up to March 1993. The creditors also agreed that in three years' time they would consider further measures to reduce the debt owed to them – $5.7 billion of Nicaragua's total debt of $10.4 billion. This agreement sets a precedent for debt reduction concessions for other countries. The measures, welcome as they are, have been criticised by debt campaigners for three reasons. First, they fall short of the concessions proposed in Trinidad in 1990 by Britain's John Major, then Chancellor of the Exchequer, who called for two-thirds of the debt owed to governments to be written off. Second, the Trinidad proposals were intended to reduce the entire stock of debt, not selected maturities, as in this agreement with Nicaragua. Third, Australia and the United States, to which Nicaragua is a substantial debtor, refused to offer debt relief, agreeing only to a rescheduling over twenty-five years.

The premise of the 'Band-Aid' schemes and the Baker Plan right up to 1987, however, was that debtor countries merely needed new credit to buy time while the IMF-designed structural adjustment programmes took effect. The purpose of these programmes

Crushing burden: Latin America's foreign debt

was to force countries to live within their means, by cutting domestic demand and boosting exports to the point where once again they could pay interest on the debt. The secondary debt market, now a respectable and lucrative source of income for commercial banks, has declared these policies successful. Between April 1990 and June 1991 the secondary market valuation of the debts of almost all Latin American countries rose in price. Chile's debt rose from 65 to 86 cents in the dollar; Venezuela's from 45 to 66 cents; Mexico's from 42 to 56 cents; and Ecuador's from 15 to 32 cents. The trend for other countries, however, while positive, still reflects considerable gloom about their prospects: Brazil's debt moved from 28 to 30 cents and Argentina's from 14 to 24 cents.[21]

Structural adjustment has not been abandoned. Indeed, it is a condition of all the debt reduction deals agreed since 1987. It is now understood, however, that the entire burden of the debt crisis cannot be borne by structural adjustment alone. Had the governments and banks of creditor nations reached this conclusion six years earlier, it is possible that the adjustment programmes initiated in the early 1980s could have taken greater account of the social costs involved. Latin America might not have entered the 1990s with a per capita income level at least 10 per cent below that of a decade earlier. For the poorest Latin Americans this cost, expressed here in matter-of-fact terms of income, meant premature death, the destruction of families and blighted lives. The prolonged refusal on the part of the banks and governments of the industrialised countries to acknowledge the real nature of the debt crisis was the product of greed and incompetence.

The political and economic realities of the 1990s are very different from those of 1980. Today, every Latin American government accepts the necessity for structural adjustment: this new economic realism is shared by socialists, Christian Democrats and conservatives alike. Those politicians who promised, as presidential candidates, to reject the dictates of the IMF (such as Carlos Menem in Argentina and Alberto Fujimori in Peru) ended up inflicting drastic adjustment programmes on their peoples once they had been elected.

Any assessment of the impact of the debt crisis and its consequences on Latin America must in the end look at each country individually. Prospects of recovery do not depend only on the Brady Plan but on other economic factors, including (for Mexico and Venezuela) the price of oil; the expected inclusion of Mexico in the North American free-trade area; and, in the case of Chile, the orderly retreat from power of a ruthless dictatorship which had crushed organised labour and created an economy led by its export potential. In these three countries, debt reduction and

chapter two

structural adjustment reinforce other trends. Peru, Bolivia and the poor countries of Central America have no such advantages. They need further debt reduction, sweeping social and economic reforms and substantial flows of aid and new investment. Nor is it sufficient to talk only in terms of countries, for within each country – even the most successful – there are still winners and losers. Chile, widely seen as the most successful Latin American economy, still depends on an army of extremely low-paid workers who tend and cut the trees and pick and pack the fruit which, after copper, are Chile's most important exports.

While one effect of the adjustment programmes has been to boost exports, another has been to force most Latin American countries to abandon the dreams of 'development' which they nurtured until the end of the 1970s. To succeed as exporting countries, the Latin Americans have to concentrate on those products in which they have an international economic advantage. For most countries this means concentrating on natural resources, mining or agricultural products in which they have some climatic advantage. In manufacturing their advantage consists of cheap labour and low taxes, as illustrated by the *maquiladoras*, the 1,800 assembly industries strung-out along the 2,400-kilometre Mexico-United States border, employing some 500,000 people.

This solution to the debt *crisis*, which is far from being a solution to Latin America's debt *burden*, has been bought at an enormous cost. First, in some countries it will be many years before the poor recover even the inadequate standard of living which they enjoyed in the 1970s. And this, in itself, depends on a return to sustained growth which, with few exceptions, has not been achieved. Second, it has accentuated Latin American dependence on foreign capital, an unreliable ally that in the past has consistently sided with the rich and powerful, undermining democratic governments and supporting military dictatorships. Third, it is increasing the technological gap between the industrialised countries and Latin America, as the US government seeks to prise open protected Latin American markets for its own high-technology products at the expense of nascent, domestic industries. Fourth, it will impose still greater pressure on the environment, as exporters and governments do all they can to reduce costs and to open up more land for the cultivation of exportable cash-crops. Fifth, it has reinforced the reliance on exports of commodities such as coffee, cocoa, grain, soya beans and minerals – a situation in which Latin American countries are forced to compete fiercely with each other and with other third world countries, and sometimes with the United States or subsidised European producers. If this trend continues, world prices will remain low, with the industrialised importing countries again reaping the benefit.

Economic policy choices for Latin American governments will be severely limited in the 1990s. Denied access to adequate investment, with little control over their economies and vulnerable to US pressure, any attempts by Latin American governments to protect the environment, to promote popular well-being and to direct investment so that it benefits primarily their own nationals, will be beset by difficulties. Yet these efforts are necessary if their peoples are to have a chance of a better life and the struggling democratic governments which replaced military regimes in the 1980s are to have a chance of success. Far from being assured, Latin American development is hedged around by as many challenges as ever.

Seamus Cleary *is an independent development consultant, retained by a number of British and international non-governmental organisations. His specialities include debt, structural adjustment and the international financial institutions. He was formerly CAFOD's research officer.*

References

1. World Bank, *World Debt Tables 1990-91*, The World Bank, Washington DC, 1990.

2. Roddick, Jackie, *The Dance of the Millions: Latin America and the Debt Crisis*, Latin America Bureau, London, 1988, p64.

3. Lever, Harold & Huhne, Christopher, *The Third World Financial Crisis*, Penguin Books, Harmondsworth, Middlesex, 1985, p44.

4. Roddick, *op. cit.*, p64.

5. *ibid.*, p65.

6. US Arms Control and Disarmament Agency, *World Military Expenditures and Arms Transfers, 1985*, Washington DC, pp44 & 101.

7. Lever & Huhne, *op. cit.*, p92.

8. de Vries, Margaret Garritsen, *Balance of Payments Adjustment 1945-86: the IMF Experience*, International Monetary Fund, Washington DC, 1986.

9. World Council of Churches, *The Debt Crisis and Brazil: a Case Study*, CCPD Documents on Justice and Development, WCC, Geneva.

10. Vallely, Paul, *Bad Samaritans: First World Ethics and Third World Debt*, Hodder & Stoughton, London, 1990, p300.

11. *ibid.*, p301.

12. See speech by Nicholas Brady in Fried, Edward R. & Tresize, Philip H. (eds.), *Third World Debt: the Next Phase*, report of a conference held in Washington DC on 10 March 1989, sponsored by the Bretton Woods Committee and the Brookings Institute, Washington DC, 1989.

chapter two

13. Silva Herzog, Jesus, quoted in Fried & Tresize, *op. cit.*

14. *Financial Times*, London, 12 October 1989.

15. *Financial Times*, 9 January 1990. The bonds were of two types: either they carried a face value discounted by 35 per cent and close to market rates of interest or they paid a below-market, fixed rate of 6.25 per cent while maintaining their full face value. The resources borrowed from the IFIs and the Import-export Bank of Japan provided collateral for all the principal and for eighteen to twenty-four months of interest payments in case of a Mexican default. In addition to the $5,700 million Mexico borrowed from official sources, new borrowing from the commercial banks was expected to be $2,000 million. The $3.5 billion of bonds issued by the US Treasury to rescue the agreement were thirty-year zero-coupon bonds to provide collateral for the principal. A zero-coupon bond pays no interest but, being guaranteed by the US Treasury, has a secure face value. Over thirty years the real value of such bonds would shrink considerably as a result of inflation.

16. *Financial Times*, 1 February 1990.

17. *Financial Times*, 30 March 1990.

18. *Financial Times*, 26 November 1990.

19. *The Economist*, 9 June 1990.

20. See, for example, Hewitt, Adrian & Wells, Bowen (eds.), *Growing Out of Debt*, Overseas Development Institute, London, 1989, and Fried & Tresize, *op.cit.*

21. *Evening Standard*, London, 3 June 1991.

chapter three

jutta blauert
ENVIRONMENTAL DESTRUCTION AND POPULAR RESISTANCE

An awareness of the progressive destruction of the Amazon rainforest by dams, logging companies, huge mining projects and landless peasants who have nowhere else to go is part of 'green' awareness all over the world. Prince Charles spent the major part of his visit to Brazil in April 1991 promoting the cause of the rainforest. And rightly so: the remaining peoples of the Amazon, such as the Yanomami and the Kayapó, are on the verge of extinction as a result of their contact with 'civilisation'.

But how much do the campaigns for the rainforest tell us about the root causes of such destruction and how it can be halted? Do they help us to see how the Latin Americans themselves are working to save their environment and how we can support them? And what are the real environmental issues for Latin Americans?

Social injustice and the exploitation of the environment

The close links between international economic forces and unjust political structures are clearly revealed in the way the environment is abused in Latin America.

The concentration of land-ownership in the hands of a wealthy élite, the profiteering policies of powerful companies and large banks, and pressures exerted by the international financial institutions and foreign governments all push people towards short-term, predatory exploitation of the environment, rather than rational and sustainable cultivation.

The greatest of these pressures is the enormous burden of Latin America's foreign debt and the consequent need to export at any cost. The debt, together with falling prices for most of the region's exports, both agricultural and mining, has forced governments and producers to cut costs and intensify the drive for export earnings. But in some countries cost-cutting and intensification have led to bankruptcy.

Most of Bolivia's chronically underfunded tin mines have closed, forcing the miners to migrate to the tropical lowlands and seek a living as apprentice coca producers or as slash-and-burn farmers.

chapter three

For many Latin Americans, environmental problems – such as the destruction of their natural resources, the contamination of their cities and the growing threat to health – are just one part of the wider struggle for human rights and greater economic and social justice. The reason is simple. It is the poor who suffer most from pollution, erosion and the destruction of the environment. The rich escape the worst of the pollution: they move away from the affected urban and industrial areas; they take holidays; they send their children away to study; they eat a better and more varied diet; they live and work in cleaner, healthier environments; and they are able to buy safe, bottled water.

In Brazil the rubber-tappers and Indians of the Amazon have used the threatened destruction of their environment to draw attention to their plight. Their success challenges the easy view of the poor as victims, unable to demand respect for their rights. But there are many more in Latin America who have not been able to attract such attention. Other indigenous peoples, fishing communities, small farmers in the temperate and semi-arid lowlands, peasants in the mountains, industrial and plantation workers, slum-dwellers, black people, poor women and children daily suffer the effects of environmental degradation. They have been largely ignored by international campaigners.

Since the 1970s, however, environmental movements have emerged in many Latin American countries, bringing together the immediate victims of pollution and destruction with researchers, journalists and campaigners. Local initiatives have blossomed into wider movements, encompassing far-reaching issues of economic justice and survival. In Colombia, for example, the struggle by Indians to obtain compensation for pollution caused by a sulphur mine was one of a number of pressures that led to the formation of one of the most active Indian organisations in the country, the CRIC (*Confederación Regional Indígena del Valle del Cauca*).

The landscape of Latin America has changed dramatically since the origins of agriculture over five thousand years ago and the development of human settlements. The colonial period, starting in the sixteenth century, accelerated the pace of change with the introduction of new technologies and demands on natural and human resources. Before the Conquest the indigenous populations had produced merely to survive and serve the needs of local empires. Afterwards, production was restructured to meet the needs and appetites of the overseas imperial powers, Spain and Portugal, the colonial settlers and the local creole élites.

European livestock was introduced to regions unsuitable for intensive grazing, displacing both people and food crops from good agricultural land. Intensive mining led to deforestation and water pollution of fragile upland and, later, lowland environments, such as the Andes and Mexico. Both in Bolivia and Mexico the rapid development of silver mining was made possible only by the harsh exploitation of the local indigenous population and enormous demands on the rural hinterland for timber and food. These demands led to the progressive abandonment of the traditional agricultural practices which had enabled generations of Aymara- and Quechua-speaking Indians to survive in the precarious environment of the high Andes. The intricate system of terraces, drainage and irrigation ditches and the raised fields that had sustained agriculture on the steep slopes were allowed to deteriorate. It is only the tenacity and inventiveness of the descendants of the original Aymara and Quechua inhabitants that has maintained these pre-Columbian technologies, from which researchers, scientists and governments are still learning today.

Extensive tree-felling to meet the demands of the mines and the new colonial settlements, the extraction and production of goods for Europe with no heed for 'sustainability', the destruction of protective terracing systems, overgrazing and the introduction of the plough, all led to an increase in soil erosion, changes in soil structure, and falling water tables and water quality.

Independence from Spain and Portugal in the early nineteenth century brought no improvement. Mining and plantation agriculture, together with food production on large landholdings, remained the central elements of the Latin American economy. Both indigenous and non-indigenous small farmers were pushed even further onto marginal lands where the struggle to meet their own needs added to environmental problems. Mining was the main cause of environmental degradation in the mountains. Rubber-tapping, the logging of tropical woods, the trapping and export of animals, the introduction of sugar, coffee and other cash crops, as well as gold-mining, later became the problems of tropical and semi-tropical regions.

As the uplands became progressively more infertile towards the end of the nineteenth century, people migrated to more low-lying land and the urban areas, creating yet more pressure on the environment. This process continues today, for example, in Bolivia with the collapse of tin-mining in the *altiplano* and in Mexico where dramatic erosion and the effects of structural adjustment policies are forcing people to head for the cities and the new agricultural frontier of the tropical rainforest.

Environmental deterioration accelerated from the 1930s as Latin American countries, impoverished by the Great Depression, sought to build up their own industries to produce for themselves

chapter three

the goods which they had previously imported from Europe and the United States. Another factor hastening the destruction of the environment was the change in the perception of the environment by ordinary people as Western 'civilisation' and modern industrial society took root in Latin America. The dramatic contrast with indigenous societies, their world-view and their approach to the environment, is becoming clearer every day. As Ailton Krenak, President of the Forest Peoples' Alliance, has said,

'What people call reality is just one petal on a flower. There are other petals; you can pull them out endlessly and you will find others below. Each time you will find other realities. The perception we have of the world is very limited.'[1]

Although there are enormous cultural differences in the way the environment is perceived within each Latin American country and, in the continent as a whole, there are also similarities. Land is a central element: inequality in landownership is the outstanding cause of environmental deterioration. Inappropriate agricultural practices and technologies aggravate the problem.

The environmental crisis is illustrated by widespread deforestation, both in the Amazon basin and temperate mountain areas; energy policies which require ever-increasing mineral, natural and hydroelectric resources; air pollution in the cities; water pollution caused in rural areas by intensive agriculture and in urban areas by industrial effluent and lack of sewage treatment; overgrazing; unsustainable logging for timber and fuel; deterioration of land as a consequence of agricultural methods which rely on the intensive use of pesticides, herbicides, fertilizers and laboratory-produced seeds; and the inadequate nutrition levels among the poor.

We need to consider the history of the interaction between human and natural environments if we are to understand the issues from a Latin American standpoint. This is the first step towards effective support for those Latin Americans who are struggling against environmental degradation.

The rape of the forests

'Many forest dwellers have been pushed out into desert areas by powerful people who waste the forest to enrich themselves. They have displaced the indigenous Americans, forcing them to use less-fertile land or to go into the highlands and fell more trees where they try to farm small patches of poor land. These changes cause significant alterations in the natural habitats of the local species. Large logging companies exploit our natural resources and make our people poor; they thwart conservationist efforts;

they ruin our environment and make it hostile to us; they contaminate our soil, water and air and eliminate animal, plant and even human life in an unthinking and irresponsible manner. Mining operations negatively affect the environment and cause the premature death of miners ... Some workers, peasants, and indigenous peoples are fighting to improve their work conditions. But they need land to work ... They need fair prices for their products. They want to be able to use the technology that will enable them to keep from contaminating the soil and the streams.' (Declaration to the Church in Latin America by the Church and Society Workshop, Costa Rica.)[2]

Deforestation exacerbates the process of soil erosion but is not the only cause of falling soil-fertility. The permanent removal of tree-cover and intensive annual cropping have devastated shallow soils in upland areas. Today, many of the hillsides of Haiti, El Salvador, Mexico and Andean countries are barren, riddled with deep gullies and susceptible to landslides and suffering heavy loss of topsoil. In spite of (and often because of) the intensive use of agrochemicals, falling productivity and water tables force many small-scale farmers to migrate from their lands to the cities or to new agricultural frontiers.

From abroad, deforestation is sometimes seen as the consequence of simple irresponsibility. But the Latin Americans who are its victims know all too well that it is the product of political and economic pressures. These include unequal access to and control of land; international lending policies encouraging activities that lead to or rely on deforestation; unfavourable international commodity prices and trade agreements; and the refusal of governments to challenge the rich and powerful or to go against the interests of local companies and transnational corporations in livestock, timber and mining. Between 1960 and 1980, for example, the forested area of Central America fell from 400,000 to 200,000 square kilometres. One-third was used for pasture for beef production, and two-thirds were lost to road construction, export agribusiness, logging, small-scale farming or simple erosion.[3]

The chain of events that leads to environmental degradation can vary, but the general pattern is as follows: first logging or oil companies – usually with government permission – bulldoze roads into dense forests to provide easy transport for their 'harvest'. The essential infrastructure for this work is often provided by the government or the military. Natural habitats are severely disrupted. Local peoples' ownership of natural resources and land and their right to an income from the extracted materials are commonly ignored.

chapter three

The second phase usually involves landless families, who are attracted to the forests by the new roads. Sometimes they are actively encouraged to settle there by government schemes. Governments have even been known to advertise internationally to sell primary or recently cleared forestlands to foreign investors and settlers. Forest clearance then serves a double purpose: first, to open up new lands for further resource extraction by private companies, encouraged by tax exemptions and subsidies; and second, to provide land, however unsuitable, for the landless at the new agricultural frontier. This enables governments to dodge the contentious issue of genuine land reform, which would provide land where the landless were actually living.

In the final phase, settlers clear further land for subsistence production and low-level cash-crop production. After producing good harvests for one, two or three years, the plots, cleared by slash-and-burn, are left fallow and new land is cleared. From the early 1970s a third stage of deforestation was encouraged by international lenders and governments keen to encourage cattle raising. Exhausted land was no longer allowed to lie fallow – a practice which at least permitted the regrowth of secondary forest cover – but was now increasingly being seeded with pasture grasses by larger landowners who moved into cattle-raising to make use of cheap credits and subsidies. This transformation also reduced rural employment because, in contrast to the labour force needed, say, for plantation agriculture, few workers are needed to tend each herd.

In the 1970s, the World Bank and the Inter-American Development Bank (IADB) lent $4 billion for cattle-raising and meat processing on newly felled forest lands in Latin America – more than for any other type of agricultural production.[4] Ranchers in Mexico, major suppliers of the US beef market, received 49 per cent of these loans.[5]

By 1983, approximately 100 million hectares (49 per cent of Mexico's total area) were under pasture and forage-crop production, while 21 million hectares were used for food crops. Government policy, particularly since the late 1940s, has assisted logging companies with easy licensing schemes and tax incentives in order to ensure the supply of raw materials for industry and to win political support from the private sector. Logging by British and US companies in the state of Chiapas in Mexico since the middle of this century has been as damaging as it was on the Atlantic coast of Nicaragua.

For Latin American economies under pressure to service their debt, exports of frozen and fresh beef represent a much needed source of foreign exchange. In the 1960s and 1970s the export of

environmental destruction and popular resistance

frozen beef was the most dynamic sector in Central American trade, with a volume increase of 400 per cent between 1961 and 1974 alone.[6] This was achieved largely at the cost of food production for domestic consumption and of soil degradation.

Between 1960 and 1980 the number of cattle in Guatemala increased from 1 million to 2.5 million, while beef exports went up by 230 per cent. Over the same period, land under pasture increased by 4,000 square kilometres. In Costa Rica pasture accounted for over one-third of the country.[7] Ownership of this profitable export 'cash crop' is concentrated in a few hands: in the early 1980s, just 2.2 per cent of the population owned 70 per cent of the agricultural land, mostly in the form of cattle ranches.

The situation in Colombia is similar.[8] Unequal distribution of land dispossesses small farmers and turns them into migrants who then have to search for new land at the agricultural frontier: 75 per cent of farms are smaller than 10 hectares and account for 7 per cent of the total agricultural land, while 0.7 per cent of farms are larger than 800 hectares and cover 41 per cent. Small farmers and the landless are thus pushed onto poor soils and steep slopes, causing further erosion. Each year in Mexico some 100,000 hectares of tropical forest are destroyed. Of the original 22 million hectares only 1.5 million remain.[9]

In Bolivia 200,000 hectares of tropical forests are lost each year, while reforestation in the whole country (which is twice the size of France) amounts to hardly 11,000 hectares.[10] In the lowland areas of Santa Cruz, the production of sugar and cotton for export – and the accompanying increase in colonisation – has caused further deforestation and intensified soil erosion to a critical extent. Watersheds and headwaters have been deforested particularly rapidly over the last twenty years. The disastrous flooding in 1983 of the River Piraí, no longer contained between heavily wooded banks, was attributed to deforestation. The floods killed 100 people and caused $45 million in damage to the road and rail systems, crops, livestock and buildings.

In 1988, in spite of all this, the IADB financed the building of a major road to improve transport between Santa Cruz and Cochabamba without assessing in advance its likely environmental and socio-economic impact. By early 1989 it was clear that the road had already drawn in settlers and opened new land to logging activities, exposing watershed areas and threatening the two local Indian groups, the Yuquis and Yuracaré, and the Amporó National Park. Only then was an Environmental Affairs Office set up to protect the area, establish a forest-management system, survey and obtain titles to land for the Indian peoples as well as to provide health and education services for them.[11]

Deforestation is devastating to local people. Their ability to produce their own food is threatened or destroyed as erosion advances and agricultural production becomes more specialised. In addition, medicinal plants and indigenous vegetables and fruits disappear, together with local families' knowledge about how they should be cultivated and used. Diets subsequently become unbalanced. Often these forest products constitute an emergency food-reserve for poor rural families, to which they can turn in times of unemployment or bad harvests. Their disappearance is literally a threat to survival and leads to further deforestation and intensification of agricultural and livestock production.

> **Proposed extractive reserves**
>
> 'The resistance of the indigenous population of the tropical forest has not abated. On the contrary, it has swelled to the point where it is more than simple opposition. It now proposes an alternative mode of development based on a balance between human beings and nature. Our proposal is rooted in respect for tradition and the experience acquired over time by peoples who live by measured use of forest resources.
>
> 'The proposal reflects our identification with the forests. The "extractive reserve" projects are therefore based on three basic principles: (i) economic viability; (ii) ecological sustainability; and, from the societal standpoint, (iii) improved living standards for extractivist communities.
>
> 'The extractive reserves proposal, if equipped with the proper economic and social infrastructure and linked to total utilisation of the extractive and market potential, is one of the most viable solutions for the Amazon region. To stop the destruction of the Amazon and the people who live there, rubber workers, riverside dwellers, Indians and other inhabitants must join scientists, newspapermen and environmentalists to show the benefits the Amazon can offer mankind. Protection of the Amazon region and its biodiversity is in the interest of all.'
>
> *Pedro Ramos de Sousa, Vice President of the National Council of Rubber Tappers for the State of Amapá, Brazil.*[12]

The destruction of forests is one of the most visible effects of military conflict, especially counter-insurgency warfare. The aerial bombardment of forests, besides killing their inhabitants, starts forest fires and destroys the natural environment. The soil of denuded forestland erodes more easily, and with the first rains bare hillsides are prone to landslides which, in turn, pull down more trees. In the 1980s around 17,000 acres of pine forest in the departments of Chalatenango and Morazán in the tiny country of El Salvador were destroyed deliberately as part of the government's counter-insurgency war.

The use of aerial spraying of defoliants supposedly to destroy marijuana and coca plantations is particularly damaging. Such spraying not only destroys the foliage of trees and other vegetation and sometimes leads to forest fires, but also directly affects food crops, water supplies and causes physical harm to people. Herbicide spraying for military purposes (or anti-narcotic and anti-malaria campaigns) is nothing new in counter-insurgency warfare: the British army used herbicides against insurgents in Malaysia to destroy their food supplies and US forces did the same during the Vietnam War.

In Latin America spraying has been reported in the rainforest areas of Guatemala, such as the Petén, and in the coca-producing areas of Bolivia. Since 1987 the Guatemalan government and the US Drug Enforcement Agency are reported to have used aerial spraying of defoliants in places where they suspected peasants of growing food for rebel groups, rather than where marijuana may actually have been cultivated. The toxic defoliant glyphosphate, banned in the USA as a carcinogenic agent, is the chemical reported to have been used most frequently in these spraying sorties. More than twenty Guatemalans were reported to have died as a result of poisoning by aerial spraying missions in 1987 and 1988.

After continued local and international pressure, and the deaths of Chico Mendes (the charismatic founder of the Brazilian rubber tappers union) and many other lesser-known rural and indigenous activists, something appeared to change in Brazil: on 12 March 1990, as one of his last acts as Brazilian president, José Sarney decreed the creation of three extractive reserves in Amazonia after detailed plans had been submitted by the National Council of Rubber Tappers and the Institute of Amazon Studies (IEA). A total of 1.6 million hectares are to make up the reserves in Acre, Amapá and Rondonia, benefiting over 13,000 extractive workers. The land still belongs to the federal government but large-scale deforestation is prohibited and rubber tappers and others need to ensure sustainable use of the forest resources under their long-term contracts.[13]

Our Dumping Ground?

Latin America, like other areas of the Third World, has been seen as a convenient dumping ground for waste and reject products from developed countries. Consumer and environmental organi-

chapter three

> **Contaminated cargos**
>
> Exports of beef and milk from Europe continued after the explosion at Chernobyl despite radioactive contamination. Peru, Venezuela, Colombia and Brazil were all sent contaminated foodstuffs. In the autumn of 1986 the head of the radiation department of the National Institute of Nuclear Affairs in Colombia, Dr Manuel Montoya, warned that Dutch milk sold in the country contained unusual levels of caesium 137 and 140, and that precautions should be taken. In May 1987 a cargo of 500 tonnes of milk powder, with radioactive levels 2.5 times higher than the maximum permitted European Community norms, left the port of Bremen in West Germany for Venezuela.[14] And in June of that year 3,000 tonnes of radioactive beef was exported from the same country to Venezuela.[15] A shipload of some 6,000 tonnes of beef from Denmark and Northern Ireland – rejected by Venezuela because of the excessive levels of caesium – eventually toured the seas for another year in search of a 'consumer'.[16]

sations have denounced the trade in food products declared unfit for consumption in Europe, their place of origin, and 'fertilisers' or 'non-toxic landfill' wastes from Europe and the United States. While stricter environmental laws may benefit European and US citizens, they pose a threat to the environment of Latin American and Caribbean peoples. One by-product of tougher environmental regulations is the dumping of toxic and nuclear wastes, pesticides and fertilisers in countries with more loosely-drawn laws and lax enforcement. Pollution is exported. At the same time that the US government, private companies and green NGOs (non-governmental organisations) are claiming to support environmental projects in Latin America, US cities are trying to find Latin American sites to dump their mountains of waste.

Many US cities have a waste disposal crisis because some state laws prohibit the dumping of sewage. A number of cities have described their proffered exports of toxic urban and industrial wastes as 'fertiliser' and have offered to construct incineration plants, promising such benefits as electricity supply for rural areas. These waste products, which may contain unspecified toxic wastes, would add to pollution at the already over-burdened urban waste dumps in Latin America. In the spring of 1987, for example, the US Amalgamated Shipping Company attempted to persuade Honduras to accept incinerator ash as landfill. Another company, International Asphalt and Petroleum, offered to build an incinerator in the rainforest area of Gracias a Dios to dispose of municipal waste from the USA and Honduras. The Honduran

Campaigning for recycling

Puerto Rican environmentalists are fighting a plan by Westinghouse Corporation to install a domestic-waste incinerator in the capital San Juan. The company claims it is offering an environmentally-friendly waste disposal service to the city, describing it as a 'resource recovery plant'. The incinerator would be a prototype for seven more units planned throughout the island and a springboard for the promotion of this technology throughout the Caribbean and Latin America. Opponents of the plan say it will be expensive and possibly harmful. Smoke from the waste now burned in dumps would be replaced by gases and toxic emissions from the incinerators. The pollution of soil and groundwater from landfills would be increased by the burial of toxic ash; and about half the garbage would still have to be dumped as toxic ash or non-burnable items.

Incinerators contaminate the air with nitrogen oxides, sulphuric oxide, hydrogen chloride, carbon monoxide, heavy metals and the most toxic and dangerous substances ever produced – dioxins and furans. The installation of incinerators would hamper the development of more environmentally-sound alternatives (such as waste reduction and recycling) because, in order to be profitable, incinerators must burn large amounts of waste. Environmentalists fear that waste might even be imported to ensure a constant flow of raw material for the plant. Puerto Rico plans to legislate to prevent separate collections of recyclable rubbish to ensure a continuous supply of waste to incinerators. The government is considering introducing taxes for waste management. Since only large waste-management enterprises can afford incinerators, they can assume monopoly control. US firms could then push local recycling operators out of business. One of CAFOD's project partners, Misión Industrial de Puerto Rico, a church-based grassroots organisation, is campaigning for waste reduction and recycling as concrete economic and ecological strategies. They are pressing the government to offer incentives for the development of local projects which recycle the raw materials found in waste – about 80 per cent of the total volume. They are also promoting a shift in consumption patterns and encouraging industries to alter production processes and to use recycled materials. The campaign for recycling and against multinational control over waste management is part of a broader struggle in Puerto Rico, in which local control of the environment – a tangible goal which would have an immediate impact on the lives of ordinary people – has assumed greater importance than political independence from the United States.[17]

government refused the offer. At the same time, Guatemala was offered a contract for handling sewage sludge from Los Angeles and the opportunity to use waste from other US cities as 'organic fertiliser' in coastal areas. But, as in Honduras, pressure from local and international environmental groups forced the government to turn down these proposals. Panama, in a double affront to the environment, was asked to accept delivery of 250,000 tonnes of incinerator ash as building material for a road through protected wetlands to a beach resort being built to increase foreign earnings.

In March 1989 an international convention on toxic waste dumping (The Convention on the Control of Transboundary Movements of Hazardous Wastes) was drawn up in Basle by 105 countries but signed by only 34 of them. The convention's central points were that waste could be exported only when the receiving country had given prior informed consent, when it had the technical means to dispose adequately of the waste and when the waste itself was properly labelled.

The third world countries at the meeting failed to get two of their central demands adopted: that there should be a total ban of toxic waste exports and that producer countries should be responsible for the ultimate disposal of their own waste. Greenpeace believes that the convention simply legitimised the trade in toxic waste and that the financial temptations to give prior consent will be too strong for poverty-stricken third world countries. US Congressman John Conyers (Democrat), a sponsor of legislation for a total ban of toxic waste exports, declared: 'Exporting waste abroad is the export of irresponsibility, the implementation of the credo "Anywhere but my backyard"; and in the end, if it's so safe environmentally, why not do it closer to home?'[18]

With or without prior consent, many Latin Americans do not want this dangerous waste – in addition to their own (often untreated) waste. In 1989, for example, the Argentine environmental organisation Tierralerta and the Argentine Greenpeace group organised a demonstration with other NGOs in Buenos Aires to protest against the import of toxic waste. Press and television helped in publicising information hitherto kept secret. Movements like these have grown and have formed the Latin American Pesticide Action Network (PAN-AL), a continent-wide association, which held its second meeting in Ecuador in 1989.

Latin America – a nuclear free zone?

Many of the organisations active in the PAN-AL network are also lobbying against nuclear energy policies in their countries. In Argentina, which like Brazil has the necessary infrastructure to produce nuclear weapons, they lobby provincial governments

Garbage imperialism

In 1987 the Maltese ship *Lynx*, chartered by the Italian chemical company Jelly Wax, was carrying over 2,000 tonnes of innocently termed 'assorted chemical garbage' – resins, pesticides, biphenyl and polychlorides – from Italy to Venezuela after having been refused permission to discharge the cargo in Djibouti on the horn of Africa.

The Venezuelan port authorities, assuming that a local chemical disposal company was going to dispose of the poisonous waste, permitted 11,000 drums to be off-loaded. But the contractor never appeared and the drums began to leak toxic gases. Nearby residents began to complain about the stench of the chemicals and of skin sores. Finally a boy died after playing close to the drums. The resulting public outcry forced the Venezuelan government to demand that the Italian government arrange for the removal of the drums. They finally left Venezuela on board a Cypriot cargo ship. After several reloadings, two deaths and a three-and-a-half year odyssey over three continents in search of a dumping ground, part of the cargo was processed in Manchester in September 1990. Meanwhile, by late 1987, Venezuela had joined African nations in pressing the UN Environmental Programme to prepare an international convention to control toxic waste dumping, and had passed laws forbidding the import of toxic wastes.

The Liberian-flagged *Khian Sea* was equally notorious. The *Khian Sea* was chartered in the autumn of 1986 by the Philadephia-based company Paolino and Sons to dispose of 13,476 tonnes of toxic incinerator ash on behalf of the Philadelphia City Authorities. The waste had already been declared too toxic for storage in the USA. The ash contained arsenic, cadmium, mercury and lethal dioxins from municipal incinerators in Philadelphia.

The *Khian Sea* was refused entry in the Bahamas, the Dominican Republic and Honduras, but was finally permitted to berth in Haiti because the captain had signed a declaration that the cargo was 'non-toxic, non-hazardous fertilisers'. The Haitian contractor was a group called the 'Cultivators of the West', run by close relatives of Jean-Claude Paul, an army colonel with a reputation for corruption and cruelty.

In January 1988 the ship unloaded some 3,000 tonnes of ash on the beaches near Gonaives before the Haitian government was made aware of the toxic nature of the contents and demanded that the *Khian Sea* leave port. By September 1988 the ship had still not disposed of the remaining 10,000 tonnes of ash.

chapter three

which have the legal right to prohibit toxic or nuclear wastes being brought into or stored within provincial boundaries.

The finished product is not the only hazard. In Argentina, for instance, uranium mining has already led to extensive pollution: between 1982 and 1985 the uranium mine in the hills of Córdoba, Los Gigantes, discharged hundreds of thousands of cubic metres of acid and alkaline residues into the basin of the San Antonio river. Today, the mine is closed and the remaining solid wastes are left completely unprotected.

There are two nuclear plants in operation in Argentina (Atucha I and Embalse de Río Tercero) and one reprocessing plant, all based on technology supplied by West German companies, such as Kraftwerk Union. In 1986, President Raúl Alfonsín promised that a second plant, Atucha II, would be completed even though the country already possessed excess electricity-generating capacity and was in economic crisis. The Brazilian nuclear programme is also based on West German technology, although the reactor itself is a Westinghouse model. In January 1975 Brazil switched on its first nuclear power station, seven years later than planned and after costs had increased fivefold.

Laguna Verde – no thanks!

Laguna Verde, in Mexico, is a typical nuclear plant; that is, its history is one of technical and organisational failure, construction delays, nationalist rhetoric, official secrecy and contempt for local opinion. The first reactor became operational in 1989, six years after the plant was supposed to be fully operational. The threat of 'another Chernobyl' and nuclear pollution, high construction costs (over $3 billion by the end of 1987), the absence of satisfactory plans for the disposal of nuclear waste and insufficient support for the development of renewable energy sources brought people from all sectors of Mexican society into the campaign against the nuclear plant.

The government decided to go ahead with the project, planned since 1966 and under construction since 1971, in the face of widespread protest and critical scientific opinion. There was a series of accidents in the first three months of operation, including the release of radioactive gas and the direct contamination of six engineers. After an explosion in November 1988, caused by a design fault, the surrounding area was occupied by the armed forces to control local opposition groups.

The campaign against the Laguna Verde plant is supported by local people from the state of Veracruz (cattle farmers, women's organisations, students, fishing families and urban organisations) and environmentalists, academics and artists from Mexico City and the country as a whole.

The campaign bases its opposition on the massive construction costs, the growing debt of the public-sector Electricity Commission (CFE) in charge of the nuclear programme, and the plant's location – near a geological fault and just 8 kilometres from an active volcano. The government attempted to appeal to nationalism by declaring that nuclear power would strengthen Mexico's independence (although the plant would produce only 3 per cent of the country's electricity) but did not acknowledge that enriched uranium would have to be imported to keep the plant running. The plant is an old BWR/5 Mark II (boiling water reactor) from General Electric – a design that has a troubled history in the United States and elsewhere. In February 1987, almost a year after Chernobyl, the director of the CFE replied to the project's critics: 'Why are you so afraid of radio-activity? Nuclear bomb tests show that it won't harm anyone.'

The campaign against Laguna Verde has organised demonstrations, blackouts and road blocks in Veracruz, but opposition has also come from within the CFE. Isidoro Becerril, former project manager of Laguna Verde, reported in 1981 that there were large cavities in the concrete surrounding the reactor, charging the National Nuclear Security Commission with negligence. A number of geologists joined the campaign because they were aware of the earthquake-prone nature of the area. Together with other scientists they were victimised for their opposition. The office and laboratory of one prominent campaigner, José Arias Chávez, was destroyed by fire in September 1988, two days after he had debated publicly with government officials about Laguna Verde. Protests increased throughout 1988, with demands that the government hold a referendum on Laguna Verde. The campaign became a national movement in February 1989 – the National Co-ordination against Laguna Verde (CONCLAVE) – and continues to organise campaigns of non-payment of electricity bills and lobbies of central government.[21]

From 1985 onwards, despite the debt crisis, it was calculated that the Brazilian government was intending to spend $800 million per year to complete the additional planned nuclear plants. This estimate includes both the construction of the reactors Angra II and Angra III and the uranium-enrichment plant in Rezenda, 80 kilometres north of Rio de Janeiro.[19] By late 1990, Brazil was suing Westinghouse for faulty workmanship in the building of the Angra I pressurised-water reactor, which suffered from a constantly faulty steam generator. Now, owing to economic pressures, it is unlikely that the Brazilian nuclear programme will remain active or even see the completion of the Angra II plant.

Nuclear devices and waste present their own unique problems of handling and disposal. One of the worst nuclear radiation accidents in Latin America occurred in October 1987 in the Brazilian state of Goiás. It involved the leaking of caesium 137 from carelessly dumped tubs that contained an old cancer-treatment device. Three people died and 20 people were treated in hospital for radiation sickness. In total, 243 people were officially declared to have been contaminated by the caesium, which has a toxic life of thirty years. Brazilian papers revealed that the waste that caused the Goiás accident was to be dumped in the weapons-testing range in the southern Amazon, near Cachimbo. Gold prospectors, fishing families, FUNAI (the official Indian protection agency) and environmental groups protested. Over 2,000 Indians live near the region's air-base, where underground installation work was suspected of being preparation for nuclear experiments or the building of waste-storage silos, from which radioactive materials could leak into the local water table.[20] Ten days before this accident President Sarney had announced a breakthrough by military scientists in uranium enrichment. While emphasising that a nuclear bomb would not be built, he nevertheless refused to sign the nuclear non-proliferation treaty.

By the mid-1980s it was clear that Latin America was not going to be the lucrative export market for which the European and US nuclear industries had been hoping. Now it seems likely that economics, the debt crisis and the Chernobyl disaster will succeed in halting nuclear programmes in Latin America where anti-nuclear movements had achieved only limited success.

The urban labyrinth

Today most Latin Americans live in urban areas. They face a multiple environmental crisis: the absence of essential sanitation, malnutrition, air pollution, contaminated water supplies, unhealthy workplaces and open rubbish dumps. Urban transport is crowded, slow and often unsafe. Street crime is out of control.

In the past thirty years most Latin American cities have been surrounded by shanty towns. The inhabitants of these shanty towns are largely rural migrants or their children who cannot make a living from agriculture: low prices for their produce, the high cost of agricultural inputs, soil erosion and the division of small and poor quality plots of land among large families combine to make agriculture unsustainable. In El Salvador, Guatemala and Colombia counter-insurgency operations and military occupation

environmental destruction and popular resistance

have also driven peasant farmers from their land. Yet rural migrants often encounter far worse conditions in cities such as São Paulo and Mexico City, where it is calculated that some 55 per cent of the population of 20 million were originally landless peasants.

Although urban settler organisations have had some success in their struggle for better services, infant mortality rates are still higher in the shanty-town outskirts of these big cities than in some rural areas. The lack of pure drinking water, inadequate or non-existent sewage and drainage systems and open waste dumps make waterborne diseases major killers. Of those who are lucky enough to receive piped water in their houses, only 10 per cent receive water that has been treated in some way.

The 1991 cholera epidemic which started in Peru, the first serious outbreak in Latin America in a hundred years, started in the overcrowded and unhealthy *barriadas* (shanty towns) of Lima and quickly spread to other areas.

The shortage of urban land has driven squatters onto hazardous hillsides, river-banks and roadsides. The shanty towns of Río de Janeiro, built on the steep slopes above the beaches, have denuded the hillsides of vegetation: flash floods and mudslides killed over 300 people in February 1988. Government officials claimed that the real cause of the loss of life was official failure to strengthen the hillsides and provide secure housing and drainage systems. Despite plans to plant trees on the dangerous hillsides (for which an international loan had been promised) new landslides in January 1991 killed some 50 people and made thousands of others homeless.[22]

A World Health Organisation (WHO) study in 1990 reported that in the whole of Latin America and the Caribbean, 30 million children, 47 million adults and 4 million elderly are exposed to air pollution levels exceeding WHO guidelines.

The Chilean capital Santiago, like Lima, Mexico City, Bogotá and Caracas, is notorious for its smog. In May 1990 an 'Environmental State of Emergency' was declared in Santiago after pollution reached dangerous levels. The response of the Chilean government was to cut urban traffic by 20 per cent by prohibiting vehicles with number plates ending in certain numbers, say two and five, from entering the city centre on particular days of the week. The government also ordered eighteen of the major polluting industries within Santiago to cut production by 20 per cent.[23]

Mexico City is situated on a high plateau (2,260 metres above sea-level) surrounded by mountains, built on the dried-up bed of the lake which surrounded the Aztec capital, Tenochtitlán. The

chapter three

spectacular mountains and the volcano, Popacatapetl, should be visible from almost any part of the city but today they are rarely seen, being almost permanently blotted out by the blanket of smog which lies over the city.

How did the Aztec capital become today's mega-city and a byword for pollution and the sheer hell of urban living? Migrants currently arrive in Mexico City at the rate of 1,000 a day. They started coming in large numbers in the 1950s, driven from their land by population pressure and erosion. During this period Mexican governments were encouraging industrialisation, relying on cheap labour to work in new factories. Industry was subject to minimal planning controls: factories could be put up anywhere and the people who worked in them settled nearby. The inhabitants of Mexico City are now paying dearly for this haphazard development. Mexico City now contains 50 per cent of the country's industrial plant, with 30,000 factories filling the valley with pollutants. The worst offenders are the oil, cement and asbestos industries.

Altitude exacerbates the city's problems. Combined with the local wind patterns it produces frequent temperature inversions, especially in winter, when layers of cold air trap warmer, polluted air close to ground level. Mexico City is also an earthquake zone and is slowly sinking into the soft subsoil of the former lake-bed.

Mexico City produces some 14,000 tonnes of rubbish every day but only 9,000 tonnes are collected. At least 5.5 million people have no toilet of any description: they defecate wherever they can; the faeces dry and become part of the dust of the city, making Mexico City one of the few places on Earth where hepatitis can be contracted just by breathing. According to university doctors, around 100,000 deaths a year from respiratory diseases can be attributed to air pollution.

It is not surprising that Mexico City has had its share of environmental disasters. On 20 April 1979, during a temperature inversion, chlorine gas escaped from the Ciclómeros S.A. factory: thirty-five workers died, hundreds more were injured. Residents close to the factory, frightened and not knowing what had happened, ran into the street. Some were killed and many were hurt.

On 3 September 1981, in the densely populated neighbourhood of Ciudad Nezahualcóyotl, industrial waste reacted with water to produce sulphuric acid and ammonia gases. Two hundred people were injured and three women aborted.

On Monday 19 November 1984, at 5.40 a.m., seismographs at the Institute of Geophysics registered an earth tremor with its epicentre in the outskirts of Mexico City, near San Juan Ixhuatepec. The cause, however, was not an earthquake but the explosion of a storage tank at the refinery of the national oil company (Petróleos Mexicanos – PEMEX). Two minutes later, the streets of San Juan were ablaze: houses burned down, people ran in panic in the streets, many covered in flames. At 6.14 a.m. there was a second explosion which destroyed several city blocks near the plant. Police and fire-brigades meanwhile evacuated other areas. There were further explosions throughout the morning.

Some days later official figures were released: 467 people had been killed and over 2,000 injured; over 10,000 people lost their homes; and some 250,000 people had been evacuated. Local residents and researchers insisted, however, that the true death toll was more than 2,000 people.

Community groups organised silent protest marches: they were outraged at inadequate safety precautions at the plant, the government's refusal to compensate the victims and the deliberate underestimation of death and injury. They claimed that twelve hours before the disaster they had warned PEMEX about a large gas leak from the plant, but their warning had been ignored. A year later, PEMEX announced that it had finally finished paying out compensation (some $4 million in total, including rebuilding work) in a statement that depicted the company as the benefactor of the inhabitants of San Juan.

At a community meeting on 9 December 1984 one of the local residents, Telésforo Rivera Morales, denounced government repression after local demonstrations following the disaster. The day after the meeting, Rivera Morales's body was found near his home. He had been beaten to death. The local priest, Fr Abel de la Cruz, was moved to another parish after he publicly accused the government and PEMEX of negligence. A local teacher, Jesús Molina, who had helped to organise community protests after the explosion, disappeared. Police prevented journalists from entering his home, declaring that he had left the city because of the 'nervous indisposition of his wife'.

With the environment becoming a political 'hot potato', the Mexican government has tried to cut pollution in the capital. The most spectacular measure was the decision, announced by the president in March 1991, to close the *18 de marzo* (18 March) PEMEX refinery near the centre of the city. Ten days before, the capital's pollution index had exceeded 300 points, forcing seventy-one industries, including PEMEX, to cut production by half. It is estimated that the relocation of the refinery would cost $500 million. Along with two small power stations, the *18 de marzo* refinery was responsible for about 4 per cent of the pollution in the capital.

A number of industries have already been moved from the capital but this has brought no significant improvement, since experts calculate that 76 per cent of the city's air pollution is produced by its 3 million petrol-driven vehicles. December 1990 was one of the worst ever months for pollution in the city, with birds falling dead from the sky near the infamous PEMEX refinery. Like the Chilean authorities, the Mexican government has sought to cut traffic by 20 per cent by stopping car owners from coming into the city centre for one day a week. The measure did reduce pollution but it was criticised as a palliative rather than a cure. There was one inevitable consequence: increased corruption as the new motoring permits created by the measure provided fresh opportunities for illicit gain by police and officials.

Until recently, Mexican petrol had one of the highest lead contents in the world. As a result, 70 per cent of new-born children in the capital register excessive levels of lead in their blood. Magnasín, a new type of petrol introduced in early 1990, does not, however, contain any lead and is said not to cause the build-up of ozone – a contaminant when it occurs at ground level. But Magnasín currently accounts for just 5 per cent of petrol sold and can be used only in cars fitted with catalytic converters, which have been obligatory since 1991. Improvement will be slow.

Cubatão – still a valley of death

Cubatão, near São Paulo in Brazil, is the biggest industrial centre in South America. The town started as a petrochemical plant thirty years ago and is now a complex of oil refineries, steelworks, petrochemical plants, pharmaceutical factories, paper mills, quarries, and cement works. In 1983, Cubatão had the highest per capita income in the country but one-third of its population lived in *favelas* (shanty towns). In 1982 doctors found that infant mortality in Cubatão was higher than in the poor São Paulo slums; that for every forty live births, one child was born with chronic congenital defects; and that skin diseases and cancer were endemic. Official figures are an underestimate, because they include only those people with sufficient resources to seek medical assistance.

Cubatão became a key issue for environmentalists and health workers in 1985 when it was revealed that Union Carbide, the company responsible for the methyl-isocyanate (MI) accident in Bhopal, India, in late 1984, was using the same process in Cubatão. The provincial government has since prohibited the processing, storage and transporting of MI.

Cubatão is located between the Atlantic coast and the 855-metre-high escarpment that is the edge of the Great Brazilian Plateau, from which the city draws its water supply and hydroelectric energy. This special situation creates a temperature inversion, retaining polluted air close to ground level, as in Mexico City. Acid vapour used to hang almost permanently in the air and killed off most of the trees (those not already used for construction or fuel), leaving the hillsides covered by lifeless stumps. Landslides, which carry away flimsy houses and their occupants, are frequent. Electricity is expensive because the company has the additional expense of repairing pylons corroded by the acidic atmosphere. Industrial waste is a constant hazard. In 1982 it was calculated that industry in Cubatão discharged 2,600 tonnes of heavy metals per year into rivers in or near the city. In 1984 almost 100 people were killed when a shanty town built near leaking oil ducts went up in flames.

As increasing numbers of deformed babies were born in Cubatão, local people began to organise. In 1981 the Association of Victims of Pollution and Bad Living Conditions (AVPM) was formed. By 1983 some 85,000 people were involved in a wider environmental movement, targeting twenty-two petrochemical and iron-smelting plants.

The protests forced the government into action. Since the mid-1980s approximately $350 million has been invested in pollution-control equipment and factories not complying with the strict standards face stringent fines. According to official sources pollution was reduced by some 70 per cent between 1984 and 1989. Environmentalists point out, however, that there are still frequent smog alerts which force factories temporarily to shut down their operations. The open-air storage of chemical wastes continues and research shows that there are still critical levels of toxic pollutants in the air and the water.

Mining the forests and the fields

Mining provides a direct and often unwelcome link between the inhabitants of remote rural areas and their exploited resources on one side, and the urban centres of Latin America and international commodity markets on the other. The peoples of Latin America and the Caribbean have been exploited for centuries because of their mineral wealth. This exploitation continues today. Perhaps it is some small measure of progress that today mining activity can be more easily monitored and the damage it inflicts on people and the environment can be publicised at home and abroad.

Gold in the Amazon is the latest mining boom. The Yanomami Indians and other groups have protested vociferously at the presence on their lands of gold prospectors, who are literally a threat to their survival, and have denounced the damage they are doing to the Amazon. The prospectors dig the land and dredge the sediment of rivers for gold. Mercury, a poisonous heavy metal, is used as an amalgam to separate the fine gold particles from other mineral components in the sediment. Between 5 and 30 per cent of the mercury used in this process is lost or discharged directly into rivers. In another process the miners burn off the mercury, releasing 20 per cent of it into the air. Scientists calculate that for every kilogram of gold, at least 1.32 kg of mercury is released into the environment, poisoning people and the wider Amazonian ecosystems. Mercury accumulates in fish, upon which many people in the Amazon rely for essential proteins. The fish migrate along rivers, allowing mercury to enter the food chain as far as 180 kilometres away from the actual mining sites.

There is also mercury pollution in Bolivia. In 1989 LIDEMA, the Bolivian environmental federation, reported that each year gold-mining operations were releasing 100 tonnes of mercury into the rivers in the northern departments of Beni and Pando.

Other mining activities – copper, nickel, bauxite, uranium and coal mining – also cause pollution. And people have protested: in 1988 Peruvian neighbourhood and environmental groups protested against the operations of the Southern Peru Copper Corporation near the port of Ilo, 1,200 kilometres south of Lima. Children were dying and bronchial diseases were widespread as a result of sulphurous smoke belched out by the plant. At human rights meetings, organised by a Jesuit pastoral centre (San Pedro Pescador) and grassroots groups, environmental issues dominated the agenda as local people pressed for more effective environmental safeguards.

Palm-oil plantations and Indian resistance in Ecuador

There are 100,000 square kilometres of rainforest in Ecuador, around 2 per cent of the whole rainforest area of the Amazon basin. Since the turn of the century, rubber extraction has been replaced as the main economic activity by sugar-cane, rice and livestock production. New activities – such as oil exploration, road construction, logging (which started in the 1950s) and palm-oil plantations (which date from the 1960s) – have brought a large number of settlers into the Indian lands of the area, causing increased deforestation and violence. Indian lands have been reduced in area as the government grants 'empty' lands to Ecuadorean and foreign companies for oil extraction or plantations. These empty lands are those which are said not to be under cultivation or which have not been cleared or visibly used in any other way. Hunting and gathering and nomadic agriculture do not qualify as productive use in the government's eyes. These meas-

environmental destruction and popular resistance

ures are a real threat to the food security of the local indigenous people who depend on hunting, fishing and gathering as well as carefully managed and environmentally responsible cultivation.

The production of palm oil, used primarily for cooking and making soap, started in 1953 in the coastal lowlands of Ecuador with the support of the Inter-American Development Bank (IADB) and the World Bank. By 1981 over 33,000 hectares were being used for palm-oil production by 13 large firms and 216 smaller concerns. The palm oil boom brought land speculation which, in turn, led to the concentration of landownership and attracted new settlers to the coast. Then the labourers on the plantations began to organise, diseases began to ravage the monocropped palms and both yields and profits fell. The companies decided to move to the Amazon.

Two large companies, Palmoriente and Palmeras de Ecuador, set up in the Amazonian province of Napo in the late 1970s. Each had been given 10,000 hectares of rainforest land near Shushufindi by the Ecuadorean Institute for Agrarian Reform and Land Registry (IERAC). Indian land came under increasing pressure as the plantations expanded. By 1985 the two companies occupied 200,000 hectares after the government, seeing palm oil as an important foreign currency earner, had designated most of the 200,000 hectares considered suitable for palm oil production as *tierras baldías* (unused land). This decision in effect allocated any land not already cleared for palm oil, agricultural or any other purpose, to the palm-oil companies. Forests were logged, drainage ditches criss-crossed the area, roads were laid and new buildings scattered over the land. The governments of France, West Germany, Belgium and Britain (through the Commonwealth Development Corporation), along with private investors and scientists, offered loans and technical assistance. The indigenous people living near the first plantations were pressured into selling land to the companies and, in exchange, were promised roads, schools, health centres and jobs. By using *contratistas* (labour contractors) to recruit their workers, however, the companies avoided their obligations to provide housing, basic sanitation and social security. The workers were also prohibited from forming unions. In 1983 the army was brought in to quell labour unrest.

Official recognition of existing Indian or settler communities did not give them any significant rights, apart from the right to be resettled when their land was given over to palm-oil production. Often, however, Indian communities did not have legal title to their lands. The ensuing destruction of natural habitats, essential for their food and social needs, threatened their culture, intricate agricultural systems and livelihood. But by 1985 local indigenous

chapter three

organisations had built up a strong resistance movement to oppose government colonisation plans based on the simple expedient of declaring land to be 'unused'. They accused the government of avoiding the pressing need for genuine land reform in the Andean highlands, where most of the settlers came from, and protested against its deference towards the agribusiness companies involved in palm-oil production.

The Huaorani Indians, already threatened by the expansion of the palm-oil plantations, were now also facing the additional threat of oil exploration on their lands. More of their villages were placed under military control as violence between settlers and Indians grew. In May 1985 the government, responding to the pressure from organisations like CONFENIAE (Confederation of Indigenous Nations of the Ecuadorean Amazon), recognised the territorial integrity of Indian lands. But two months later, after its surveyors were refused access to land in Loreto by Indians and settlers, IERAC declared a further 13.8 million hectares in the Amazon to be *tierras baldías*, opening them up for new colonisation projects.

Indigenous organisation in the Ecuadorean Amazon is a direct response to the oil exploration, palm-oil production and colonisation schemes of the last twenty years. It started in the 1970s, beginning in the villages with the setting up of *comunas*, which reproduced the traditional organisation of Andean highland communities. Land had inevitably become the central issue of survival. Yet land for the Indian, as CONFENIAE points out, is not simply a plot of earth but 'the whole locus of their existence'. A concept of a home with *sacha pacha* (the forest) and *allpa* (the ground, earth) is the essential base of existence. Building on their long experience of sustainable management of the forests, Indian organisations, like those in CONFENIAE, have carried out their own studies of the potential for a more intensive yet sustainable use of their forests and for alternative agricultural projects. As they worked on these initiatives in the summer of 1985, national and international pressures were building up. The government's response, however, was confusion, with one ministry contradicting the decisions of another. Land insecurity increased, with more land being granted to palm-oil producers while entire indigenous communities, such as those of the Siona-Secoya Indians, were erased from the maps by IERAC.

Oil exploration, in which British Gas is a major investor, is the other major threat to the people of the Ecuadorean Amazon. Oil was found by a Texaco-Gulf consortium in the Oriente region in the 1960s. In order to secure this suddenly valuable border area, the government encouraged colonisation and posted army units to the area. The settlers and oil companies created a 'boom and bust' economy, with all the conflict and social consequences of short-term wealth creation.

New roads were built, more oil companies appeared and the Indian population was increasingly pushed off its lands. In 1987 it was reported that those unwilling to move, such as the isolated Tagairi people, were being tracked down by Huaorani Indians who had themselves been converted by fundamentalist Christian missionary groups and were being employed for this purpose by an international consortium that included Britoil, Braspetro (Brazil) and Elf (France). As Ecuador's need for foreign exchange increased, the government made further land concessions to foreign oil companies. These concessions included the territory of national parks and, of course, Indian lands like those of the Huaorani people.

There were further oil discoveries in the late 1980s. By 1990 around 241,000 square kilometres (about one-third) of Ecuador's Amazon territory was covered by oil exploration concessions. In 1989 oil revenues accounted for some 50 per cent of government income and 12 per cent of gross domestic product (GDP). The US company Conoco, meanwhile, was developing its plans for oil-wells in some 700,000 hectares in the Amazon, mostly in the Yasuni National Park, claiming that its operations were an 'environmental showcase'. After intense political pressure from Indian groups and international rainforest movements several oil companies and the government signed a detailed environmental management agreement, allowing the government to launch the 'Amazon for Life' campaign. Environmentalists and Indian groups, however, are sceptical about this initiative and are demanding a ten-year moratorium on oil and mineral production in the Huaorani territories and national parks. In the meantime, the 65,000 people of the area, the environment and the animals of the Amazon are suffering the inevitable effects of oil production: a spill in 1989 left the lakes in Cuayabena National Park covered by an oil film and killed most of their fish.

Unity is strength

While environmental issues, ecology, the land and forests are of the deepest importance to peasants, indigenous peoples and the landless, they cannot be separated from the issues of violence and the struggles of rural people. Every day there are killings. The cultural backgrounds of the landless, workers, peasants, indigenous and black peoples may differ but the questions they ask and the actions they are forced to take are the same. For the indigenous and peasant groups of Latin America the 'Five Hundred

Years' is an opportunity to co-ordinate the organisations of the oppressed in drawing up a joint agenda for change and action. The politics of the environment is a central issue linking their struggles.

Many Latin American governments, however, are busy trying to contain demands for change as the environment comes under ever greater threat. Yet the signs are contradictory: some Latin American countries have had environmental laws since the 1970s – though they are often neither effective nor enforced – and Venezuela had a ministry for the environment before some European countries. The setting up of municipal 'Green Councils' by the Colombian environmental institute INDERENA, supported by the Betancur administration between 1983 and 1986, showed what might be achieved if committed people were to receive real political support. However populist in nature, the environmental policy of the Collor government in Brazil is an advance on its predecessors. The Ministry of the Environment in Mexico launched its environmental campaign in 1984 – long before the British government acquired its green tinge. All this evidence of environmental awareness on the part of Latin American governments must be examined critically, however, for the environment regrettably is a theme which governments use to shore up their credibility while avoiding the politically difficult issues of justice, peace and real democracy.

The 1987 Brundtland Commission (WCED) report, *Our Common Future*, was readily adopted at first glance by several Latin American governments. But the report and the subsequently much-used expression 'sustainable development' are based largely on first world perceptions that view the reduction of population growth as central to any attempt to deal with the environmental crisis; that do not acknowledge the need to challenge the influence of the transnational corporations; that believe growth in the First World can continue unchecked; and that regard the 'management' and planning of environmental resources – as in the controversial Tropical Forest Action Plan (TFAP) – as the central tools for effective protection of the environment.

It is difficult to see how governments that tolerate gross social injustice in their countries can also plan and manage justly the natural and human environments of their nations. Moreover, the consequence of the massive burden of debt and the structural adjustment policies imposed by international lending organisations is that the environment and social justice become even lower priorities for such governments. Many Latin Americans – environmentally aware or not – do not see why they should heed the environmental advice emanating from those Western governments which profit from the burden of Latin American debt and inequitable trading relations. One faint hope, however, is that the search for solutions to the environmental crisis may enlighten even the most recalcitrant about the real problems of Latin America and open up new ways of resolving social conflict.

Environmentalists in Europe can learn from the different experience of Latin American people – experience that makes clear that every issue affecting oppressed groups in Latin American and Caribbean societies has an environmental dimension and that every environmental issue is part of a wider political struggle. This struggle, in turn, should involve all those who are working for change and the empowerment of the poor and oppressed, including church groups, urban and rural movements, trade unions and indigenous organisations. The environmental movements of Latin America will be effective only if they are sustained by these popular organisations. They cannot afford to make the mistake of ignoring the politics of land, race and economic markets, as environmental movements in the industrialised countries have often done. It is, perhaps, appropriate to end this discussion with the following statements:

'In Brazil from the beginning of our environmental struggle we have always emphasised that environmental protection is linked to social justice. Social justice and ecological rationality are two sides of the same coin. Wherever great environmental destruction occurs, it can be traced back to unequal power structures. This is something that is clearer in Brazil and in the Third World than in Europe. Perhaps this should be highlighted more in the European environmental movements. If we fail to do this we will not get a hearing from ordinary people, and that is fundamental ... it is essential in our struggle to expose and to combat the instruments of power ... We have to define anew the concepts of progress and development, since today's definitions are only those of the powerful.' (José Lutzenberger.)[24]

'Liberation theologians have long argued that the Church has little relevance unless it is prepared to address the issues of power and oppression. Environmentalists need to address the same agenda. That of "liberation ecology".' (Nicholas Hildyard.)[25]

Jutta Blauert is a research fellow at the Institute of Latin American studies, London University. She undertook research in Mexico for a doctorate in rural sociology and environmental studies. She has participated in community projects in southern Mexico and researched environmental destruction and popular resistance in rural Latin America.

chapter three

References

1. Quoted in *Gaia* No.2, 1990.

2. Church & Society Workshop, San José, Costa Rica, July 1988 (*IDOC*, 1/89:22-24).

3. Dilger, Robert, 'Die Kolonisation der Karibischen Tiefländer Zentralamerikas', in P. Stüben (ed.), *Kahlschlag im Paradies*, Focus, Gieen, 1985.

4. Myers, Norman, *The Primary Source: Tropical Forests and Our Future*, W.W. Norton, New York, 1984, p141.

5. *Ecología/Política/Cultura*, 3/1987.

6. Nations, J.D. & Komer, D.I., 1986, 'Latin America's Tropical Rainforests: Positive Steps for Survival', *Ambio*, 12.

7. Myers, *op. cit.*, p132.

8. Gradwohl, J. & Greenberg, R., *Saving the Tropical Forests*, Earthscan, London, 1988; p43.

9. *Ecología/Política/Cultura* 2(4)/1988.

10. *Presencia* (La Paz) 7 May 1990.

11. *IDB News*, 2/1989.

12. *Our Own Agenda*, Latin American and Caribbean Commission on Development and Environment, UNDP/IDB, 1990, p53.

13. Rainforest Action Network, 13 March 1990.

14. *Frankfurter Rundschau*, 12 May 1987.

15. *Tageszeitung*, 15 June 1987.

16. *The Guardian*, 27 July 1988.

17. Marianne Meyn, Misión Industrial de Puerto Rico, quoted in *Panoscope*, January 1991.

18. *Multinational Monitor*, 11/1988, p7.

19. *LA Times/TAZ*, 21 January 1985.

20. *Ecología/Política/Cultura* 4/88; *The Guardian*, 12 October 1987.

21. Sources: García Michel, Hugo: *Más allá de Laguna Verde*, Posada, Mexico City, 1988; *The Other Side of Mexico*, No.3, 10-12/1987; No.9, 3-4/1989; *Index on Censorship*, No.18, 1989.

22. *The Guardian*, 26 February 1988; *Daily Telegraph*, 19 January 1991; *Istoé Senhor*, No.1113, 23 January 1991.

23. *Andean Newsletter*, 6/1990.

24. José Lutzenberger, a former agricultural engineer with BASF (Germany) in Latin America, then environmental activist, now Environment Minister of Brazil, speaking at a meeting in Germany, June 1982.

25. Nicholas Hildyard, *The Ecologist*, 21 (1), January 1991, p3.

chapter four

george gelber
LAND RIGHTS AND LAND REFORM

Land is the most important political issue in Latin America today, and unequal landownership the greatest cause of poverty and inequality in the societies of the continent. Unequal distribution of land did not begin with the Conquest, but reformist governments ever since have recognised that land redistribution is a crucial key to tackling poverty. The problem has been the practical implementation of land reform, because it touches all the issues of injustice and division within Latin American societies.

The special tensions of landownership in Latin America come from the juxtaposition of two extremes: large numbers of rural people live in deep poverty, with little or no land, while ownership of huge holdings is concentrated in the hands of a tiny minority, creating a degree of inequality not matched in any other region of the world. In the great cities of Latin America, the contrast is between affluent middle- and upper-class neighbourhoods, frequently equipped with their own checkpoints and private police, and the poor in their millions, crammed into city-centre slums or teeming shanty towns with little or no security of tenure.

In 1950 the largest 9.5 per cent of agricultural landholdings in Latin America accounted for 90 per cent of the continent's total farmland. *Latifundios*, a term used generally to describe very large estates but here denoting estates employing more than twelve permanent workers, constituted only 1.3 per cent of total farms in Colombia but accounted for 49.5 per cent of all farmland. In Guatemala only 0.1 per cent of farms were in this size range, but nevertheless still held 40.8 per cent of agricultural land. *Minifundios*, defined as holdings too small to enable a family to live decently if solely dependent on their own agricultural production, accounted for 64 per cent of all landholdings in Colombia but only 5 per cent of the agricultural land, and constituted close to 90 per cent of all landholdings in Ecuador, Guatemala and Peru. In these last three countries, during the mid-1960s, less than 10 per cent of all farm units were classified as 'family' farms – large enough to enable a family to earn an income above the poverty line. That proportion was higher, though still less than a majority (between 39 and 49 per cent), in Argentina, Brazil and Chile.

chapter four

The owners of *minifundios*, together with completely landless rural labourers, provide the workforce for the large landholders and for other rural employers. The incomes of those who own small farms may often be determined more by the wages and the amount of work they can find in such employment than by their earnings from production on their own land. But employment opportunities themselves depend in part on the structure of ownership: large agricultural landholdings use much more capital-intensive methods than smaller farms and hence need much less labour per hectare.

One of the economic reasons justifying land reform is that output per hectare is usually higher on small farms than on large farms. Although some land reform has been carried out in Latin America, radical redistribution simply remains a dream in most countries. Reform is difficult when large landowners have a powerful voice in government.

Land distribution in Latin America 1492-1990

Pre-Conquest. Many of the agricultural systems in pre-Conquest Latin America were sophisticated and complex. The areas of most intense agricultural achievement (Mexico, together with part of Central America and the Andes) produced the most highly developed civilisations. Andean Indians cultivated their highland valleys and terraces year after year, without exhausting the fertility of the soil. By contrast, the Middle Americans, the inhabitants of present-day Central America and southern Mexico, were engaged in forest agriculture: the soil of farm clearings was quickly exhausted, so they abandoned villages for several months in the year and worked further afield. The Mayan peoples, for example, grew maize in specially laid-out fields. Temples and sacrifices were dedicated to assure a good crop, and the Mayan calendar was devised as a working schedule for the recurring cycle of the cornfield.

The economic base of Aztec society was agriculture, with communal ownership of land. Land was granted to men when they married, but remained tribal property - only its produce belonged to the individual. Warriors who showed particular prowess were awarded additional grants of land.

The Incas in Peru were a well-ordered agricultural society. Agricultural collectives built and maintained elaborate terraces. There was no permanent private ownership of land. All land was held by the emperor in trust for the people. In each district land was divided into three portions. The produce of one portion was allotted to a small group of families for its own use. Crops of the second portion were reserved for the worship of the sun (to provide for priests and religious ceremonies). The third share went to the emperor and the government. State storehouses also served as insurance against natural disaster. The religious and government lands were cultivated by the people *en masse*.

Post-Conquest. The Spaniards and the Portuguese brought new traditions of landownership to Latin America; namely, the traditions of large estates and slave labour. Generally speaking, the Spaniards were not interested in acquiring agricultural lands in the early years of the Conquest, as indigenous food production was sufficient to meet their needs.

After the capture of the Aztec capital, however, Hernán Cortés seized some of the best lands for himself and his officers, mainly those belonging to the state or to military or religious officials. Cortés later distributed small plots of land to his ordinary soldiers, although the first regular distributions of land were made to settlers by the judges of the second *audiencia* (1530-35). From the middle of the sixteenth century Spaniards began to petition for extensive land grants. Two periods of widespread land distribution, 1553-63 and 1585-95, were linked to the great epidemics (smallpox, measles and typhoid) of 1545-47 and 1576-80 which decimated the Indian population. As herds multiplied, the great ranching estates were formed. *Haciendas* (large estates) were established between 1560 and 1600.

The steep decline of the indigenous population in the decades after the Conquest coincided with the Spaniards' occupation of the land and the propagation of European plants and animals. As early as the sixteenth century, the valleys of Puebla-Tlaxcala and the basin around Mexico City surprised the traveller with their diversified agricultural landscape, where maize, beans, squash and peppers alternated with wheat, barley, and European vegetables and fruits. Sugar-cane also transformed the physical as well as the social environment of large areas of Latin America. Cortés himself pioneered the cultivation of sugar-cane in Mexico. European occupation of land was also stimulated by the growing demand back home for tropical products such as tobacco, cocoa, indigo, dyewood and other plants that were cultivated on a commercial scale from the second half of the sixteenth century onwards.

The introduction of European livestock had the most devastating impact on the physical and cultural landscape of 'New Spain'. In areas of Mexico densely populated by Indians using traditional farming methods, these new animals invaded and destroyed the open-field cultivation system, transformed arable land into pasture, dislocated the pattern of settlement, and reduced the Indians' sources of food.

chapter four

The growth of the large estates

The *encomienda* accompanied land grants, giving the conquerors rights to Indian tribute in the form of produce or labour. The word *encomienda* means 'trust'. The spirit, if not the practical application, of the *encomienda* was that an Indian community should be entrusted to a landowner for its 'protection'. In reality, the *encomienda* system gave rise to a régime of forced labour. Without the *encomienda* to provide labour, even the most impressive grants of land would have been useless. The Spanish Crown regarded the original *encomienda* grants as temporary expedients to ensure the occupation of newly won territory and to reward its conquerors. *Encomenderos* had no title to land and no official jurisdiction over the natives under their care. But they were entitled to receive tribute levied on the Indians under their protection during their own lives and those of their immediate heirs. The *encomenderos*, of course, campaigned to have their *encomiendas* converted into private property which they could then dispose of as they wished.

In the sixteenth century, settlers regularly occupied land without having legal title in order to establish or extend their properties. Such illegal occupation began to be officially ratified between 1591 and 1616, when the Spanish Crown laid down new procedures for acquiring land. Between 1600 and 1700 most of the great *haciendas* of arable land, the livestock estates and the large properties acquired by the Church were legalised by means of a fee paid to the treasury. Thus, in little less than a century, the Spanish Crown began and completed a vast programme of land redistribution which set the pattern for the later development of agriculture and landholding in Latin America.

The main Spanish objective at the time of the Conquest was to find precious metals, not to occupy land. The sophisticated agricultural systems of the Peruvian and Bolivian Andes and the Mexican plateau were sufficient to feed the new mining towns. The local Indians continued to control land in highland areas.

In principle, the Spanish imperial government respected Indian landholding and sought to confine Spanish lands to vacant areas or tracts, the transfer of which to Spanish ownership would not affect Indian interests. But, in practice, this principle was not adhered to. Spaniards naturally assumed possession of the valuable urban zones conquered in Tenochtitlán, the Aztec capital, and Cuzco, the Inca capital. The Indians were quite unable to resist the seizure of their property in the cities by Cortés, Pizarro and their *conquistador* followers. The authorities of the Spanish colonial government – the city councils (*cabildos*) and the viceroys and their agents – normally put Spanish interests before those of the indigenous population. Spanish colonists argued that they required more land for larger-scale agriculture and cattle grazing than the Indians did for their intensive, small-scale crop cultivation. To the Spaniards, the lands that Indians used for hunting or other community purposes seemed 'vacant' and hence available to them – a familiar argument encountered by those who now campaign to preserve the 'unused' land of the rainforest. In one sense all the lands in America that ultimately came into Spanish possession were usurped from Indians. But the question of the conflicting Spanish and Indian 'claims' to land is one of great complexity.

Historical attention has been directed in large part to alienated 'village lands' removed from indigenous ownership. These were lands that formerly fell under the jurisdiction of Indian communities and were then lost, usually to white *hacendados* or other property owners. In extreme cases, all of a community's lands might be lost, for a *hacienda* could completely surround a town, causing the community in effect to be incorporated within the *hacienda's* jurisdiction. But the more common outcome in the colonial period was the loss of a portion of the community lands. While the community could survive as an independent entity, economically it was subordinated to the *hacienda*. The relationship of political separation and economic domination served the interests of the *hacienda*, relieving the *hacendado* of any obligation to provide services for the Indian community while guaranteeing the continued availability of labour.

By end of sixteenth century, the *encomiendas* were declining in importance, partly because of the disastrous decline in the Indian population. At the same time, some *encomendero* families were succeeding in acquiring title-deeds to Indian lands. One of the first and most consistent consequences of Indian demographic decline was the take-over of abandoned lands by Spanish colonists. The process was not simple. In the Indian tradition a plot of land vacated by the death of its occupant normally reverted to the community for reassignment to a new occupant and was not, therefore, regarded as available for occupation by an outsider. If there were no candidate within the community to whom the plot could be assigned, the elders (the *cacique*) or the Indian council might hold it as community property, pending the appearance of an appropriate holder. The holder, in any case, could occupy it only so long as he used it to raise crops and support his family. The characteristic Indian concept of communal land-use and landholding conflicted with the Spaniards' understanding of private property rights and complicated any simple substitution of Spanish for Indian ownership when land became 'unoccupied' through death.

chapter four

The community's capacity to retain its land, on the other hand, was severely strained under colonial conditions. As Indian communities became weakened by depopulation and increasingly unable to provide the tribute for which they had been assessed, they were sometimes forced to rent or sell land to Spaniards to avoid imprisonment. The Indian council members might do this even if it meant withholding land from community members.

Later, new Spanish laws, at first supportive and protective of Indian landholding, provided fresh means to transfer Indian land to Spanish hands. During the late sixteenth and early seventeenth centuries the state policy in both Mexico and Peru of *congregación* or *reducción* – bringing people together, or 'congregating' them – destroyed entire Indian towns by moving their occupants to other places and confiscating their lands. The aim of the law was to make Indians live in compact units for the sake of social and political order, religious instruction and municipal control, and to speed up the process of 'civilisation'. In principle, all Indian landholders resettled in *congregaciones* were entitled to retain their land or, if the resettlements were at too great a distance, to be compensated with equivalent lands near the new location. The Spaniards always denied that *congregación* was designed as a means of land transfer, but this was its universal consequence.

The effects of *congregación* were aggravated by the legal devices of *denuncia* (denunciation) and *composición* (ordering). *Denuncia* permitted any Spanish colonist to claim vacant land and, after some formalities and the payment of a fee, to hold it as legal owner. *Composición* permitted him to gain full legal possession of any portion of land under his occupation that suffered from defective registration of its title. *Denuncia* and *composición* were much used in the seventeenth century, when the Indian population had shrunk considerably and Indian resistance was greatly weakened. Land rendered unoccupied by depopulation could be 'denounced' or simply seized, held and subsequently 'composed'.

In addition to formally legal land-transfers, falsification, threats and other illegal practices were common. Individual Indians were persuaded to 'sell' portions of the community's common land to Spaniards. Some buyers pretended to negotiate for the purchase of one property but received or took a more desirable one; others bribed or forced Indians to donate land. Often, having entered into an agreement to rent land from an Indian community, they subsequently disingenuously claimed that their payments of rent were really instalments for a purchase and demanded completion of the sale. Indian communities were unable to offer more than short-term resistance to blunt or delay the effects of such tactics.

land rights and land reform

New crops for new markets

In the late nineteenth century, industrial and urban growth in Europe increased demand for Latin American foodstuffs and raw materials. Latin American countries experienced drastic changes as lands were given over to the cultivation of export crops. In the space of a few years (1875-85) the governments of El Salvador, Nicaragua and Guatemala passed laws abolishing the communal ownership of land. The purpose was to open up to cultivation the highland areas (previously of little economic significance) in order to take advantage of the burgeoning demand for coffee in the United States and Europe.

The vast, fertile pampas of Argentina produced wool, wheat and, above all, beef for export. Cuba cultivated coffee, sugar and tobacco. Brazil became the biggest coffee exporter in the world. For a short while Ecuador led the world in the export of cocoa. Landowners growing plantation crops, such as sugar and coffee, needed a large seasonal labour force. In Central America this reinforced the polarisation between enormous plantations producing for export and plots so small that their owners were forced to spend some time each year harvesting coffee.

Export crops dominated Latin American agriculture. Rapid urbanisation also created a local market. New crops, such as cotton, made their appearance in Central America after the Second World War as part of a conscious effort to diversify the agricultural economy. Soya beans, grown for export as animal feed, were introduced in Brazil in the 1970s: in the state of Paraná the area under soya beans went from 400,000 to 2 million hectares in less than ten years.

Today, many Latin American countries are introducing 'non-traditional' export crops to satisfy the palates of 'discriminating' consumers in the industrialised countries. Chileans, for example, are growing table grapes, kiwi fruit and apples, while Guatemalan peasants are growing mange-tout peas and broccoli. With few exceptions, the introduction of new crops or livestock has been bad news for peasant farmers because they increase the value of land, along with the appetite of already established landowners to extend their properties.

The 'Alliance for Progress'

Some redistribution of land in Latin America has long been regarded as an essential prerequisite for social justice and development. Revolutionaries have insisted that land must belong to those who work it, while enlightened conservatives have advocated land redistribution as a measure to pre-empt social upheaval. Economists have argued for land reform on the grounds that it would slow the drift to the cities and spread income more evenly, thus adding to the number of consumers with some disposable income and spurring economic development.

There have indeed been numerous examples of land reforms in Latin America this century. Land was one of the crucial issues of the Mexican revolution of 1910; Guatemala instituted a land reform in 1952; Bolivia followed suit in 1953; Cuba in 1959; Chile in the late 1960s and early 1970s; Peru in the early 1970s; and Nicaragua and El Salvador in the 1980s. In some cases the reforms have been reversed – sometimes violently – by political opponents, while elsewhere they have simply withered, largely because the peasants who benefited have been given unfair prices for their produce and starved of the necessary capital, technical assistance and access to markets without which no agrarian reform can be expected to work. The lasting benefits of the most recent reforms, in Nicaragua and El Salvador, have yet to be assessed. In Cuba the agrarian reform remains intact, guaranteed for the present by the communist government.

The 'Alliance for Progress', launched in 1961 by the US government in the wake of the Cuban revolution, sought to forestall revolution in Latin America through social reforms, including the redistribution of land. As President John F. Kennedy said, 'those who make peaceful revolution impossible will make violent revolution inevitable'. While Latin American governments were quite happy to take US money to set up land-reform institutes, they deliberately avoided confrontation with the large landowners, who vehemently opposed any curtailment of their privileges and property rights.

Guatemala

In June 1952 the reforming government of Jacobo Arbenz enacted an agrarian-reform law which gave it powers to expropriate the uncultivated portions of large landholdings. The measure had been recommended by a World Bank mission in 1950 as a means to rationalise and increase agricultural production. The 1950 census clearly demonstrated the need for reform: 2 per cent of the population controlled 74 per cent of Guatemala's arable land, while 76 per cent had access to only 9 per cent. Arbenz described the reform in strictly developmental terms:

'It is not our purpose to break up all the rural property of the country that could be judged large or fallow and distribute the land of those who work it. This will be done to *latifundios*, but we will not do it to agricultural entities of the capitalist type [i.e. productive agricultural enterprises].'[1]

land rights and land reform

Over the course of two years 371,652 hectares were distributed to 87,569 families. The expropriations included 1,700 acres owned by Arbenz himself, who had become a landowner through the dowry of his wife. About two-thirds of this land, however, came from one owner, the United Fruit Company (UFCO), which kept 85 per cent of its land uncultivated as a reserve. All expropriated land was to be paid for in twenty-five-year bonds bearing a 3 per cent interest rate, and the valuation of land was to be determined according to its declared value for tax purposes in 1950. This meant that UFCO, which itself had assessed the land value at $2.99 a hectare, would receive $627,527. UFCO, however, demanded $15.8 million ($75 per hectare).[2]

UFCO's strenuous campaign against the Arbenz government in Washington culminated in an invasion organised and virtually carried out by the CIA. The new government under Colonel Castillo Armas reversed the reform and ushered in a period of domination by the extreme right, under the protection of the military. Since 1954, Guatemalan history has been characterised by fluctuating civil war, repression and gross human rights violations which continue today.

Cuba[3]

In Cuba the agrarian reform of Fidel Castro's revolutionary 26 July movement was also responsible for turning the United States against the new government. Cuba, however, was very different from Guatemala. The majority of the Cuban population was urban and the country was regarded as one of the more 'modern' countries in Latin America. The land reform was intended to do away with the great sugar and cattle estates, both Cuban- and US-owned, and to bring a measure of social and economic justice to rural areas. On 11 June 1959, one week after the promulgation of the first agrarian reform law, the United States sent an official note of protest about the agrarian reform to the Cuban government, provoking the resignation of five members of the cabinet, including the Minister of Agriculture. This was an indication of the traditional relationship between the two countries:

'US notes had always represented not merely protests or expressions of concern from one sovereign state to another, but had been clear instructions to the Cubans concerning what changes were necessary in their policies if the United States were not to be compelled to intervene to protect what it considered its interests.'[4]

As in Guatemala, Cuban agriculture presented stark inequalities: 73.3 per cent of the land was in the hands of 9.4 per cent of owners. US-owned sugar plantations and mills accounted for a

chapter four

substantial proportion of these large estates. Large tracts of land were left idle. In 1959, for instance, it was estimated that only 23.6 per cent of the cultivable land was actually being used. Small, labour-intensive tenant and sub-tenant farms operated alongside the large, modern, capital-intensive plantations and farms. Landlords rented and sub-rented their land to sharecroppers who had to hand over between a fifth and a third of the crop. Under such arrangements, all the risk in farming is borne by the tenant or sharecropper. Child labour from the age of seven on farms was common.

There were two agrarian reforms in Cuba. The first, in May 1959, established an upper size-limit for farms of 400 hectares. It affected 70 per cent of agricultural land, bringing 40 per cent under state control and leaving the remaining 30 per cent as medium-sized private farms. The second, more radical, reform of 1963 reduced the maximum size of private holdings to 67 hectares, leaving only 20 per cent of land in private hands. Today, that proportion has been reduced to 15 per cent as a result of the sale or rental of private land to the state.

The predominance of the state in agricultural production brought its own problems. The total output of Cuban agriculture fell by nearly 25 per cent over the first three years of the revolutionary government. Fourteen years after the revolution, in 1973, production was still below its 1959 level. In general, Cuban state farms have been inefficient but, unlike the capitalist enterprises they replaced, they have offered equal employment opportunities for everyone at standard rates throughout the country.

After the failure of attempts to diversify from sugar in early 1960s, the government mounted a drive to increase sugar production. This created an enormous need for labour, giving rise to great campaigns of exhortation to persuade city-dwellers to join volunteer work-brigades to cut cane. The failure, by 1.5 million tonnes, to achieve the goal of a 10-million-tonne harvest in 1970, led to greater pragmatism and the use of material incentives to supplement, if not replace, reliance on revolutionary morale and the 'new man' to raise production. In the late 1980s the productivity of private peasant farmers was greater than that of agricultural co-operatives which, in turn, were more productive than state farms. This situation was exactly the reverse of the goals of the revolution, which had hoped to demonstrate the superiority of properly managed state farms.

Cuba, however, has few lessons for other Latin American countries – except perhaps cautionary ones. Agrarian reform was not an attempt to modernise a capitalist economy by improving the distribution of income, as advocated by the economists of the UN

land rights and land reform

Economic Commission for Latin America, or to shift in some degree the balance of power towards the *campesinos* (peasants). It was, rather, part of a process that brought almost the entire economy under state control.

Despite the predominance of the state, the peasant sector, both as individual producers and co-operatives, has survived and accounted for 21 per cent of all agricultural production in 1986. Its integration within the system has often been problematic: when free markets in agricultural produce from the peasant sector were allowed to flourish, they not only led to the enrichment of the most successful producers, but they also tended to suck in produce siphoned off illicitly from the state sector. The abrupt suppression of these markets in 1986 put the onus on the state, notoriously inefficient in providing distribution networks, to provide alternative outlets for the peasant sector.

The debate about the place of private producers in the Cuban system, however, is being engulfed by the crisis which the break-up of the Soviet Union and Comecon (the Soviet and Eastern European trading bloc) has unleashed upon Cuba. By 1986 around 84 per cent of Cuba's foreign trade was with the Comecon countries. The subsidies to the Cuban economy built into its commerce with the Soviet Union are fast disappearing – subsidies that enabled Cuba to build a model welfare state on a Caribbean economy which, like its neighbours, depends largely on the export of agricultural produce.

Chile

Agriculture has never been as important in Chile as in other Latin American countries. For over a century most of Chile's export earnings have come from mining, first from nitrates and subsequently from copper. In 1970 fully 80 per cent of export earnings came from mining, while agriculture provided only 7 per cent of GNP. In 1960, however, a third of the population still lived in the rural areas. In spite of the relatively minor role of agriculture in the economy, agrarian reform had always been a very sensitive political issue in Chile. Large landowners had been able to exercise political control over their tenant farmers and workers; in effect, they had been able to tell them which way to vote, thus ensuring a substantial right-wing presence in the Congress and control over the revenue that flowed into the treasury from taxes on mining.

The Falange Nacional, which changed its name to Christian Democracy in 1960, succeeded in breaking the grip of the large landowners where the Socialist and Communist parties had failed. At Molina in 1953, the Falange organised the first successful strike

chapter four

of rural workers, defying Law 8811 which explicitly prohibited rural strikes and made rural unionisation almost impossible. As the left gained electoral strength in the 1950s, Catholic unions were encouraged by the Church itself and by US government agencies to organise in the cities and the rural areas in an attempt to block the advance of the left. In the event the new Catholic activists and Christian Democrat leaders were more independent-minded than their sponsors had imagined: it was not a case of simply replacing one *patrón* (boss) with another.

Under the Frei government's agrarian reform, finally passed by Congress in 1967, nearly 3.5 million hectares were expropriated and turned into *asentamientos*, co-operative-style farms that remained under the control of the Agrarian Reform Corporation.[5] Although this arrangement was supposed to be transitional, lasting only until the *asentamiento* members had demonstrated their ability to run and work the farm independently, very few properties were ever transferred completely, either under Frei or the Allende administration. The Frei government's agrarian reform laws and institutions, however, were unable to keep pace with the growing *campesino* demands and mobilisation, fanned by the rival parties of the left, which accompanied it. Indeed, the disenchantment of the right (for whom the Christian Democrats were pious, do-gooding Catholics who turned out to be little better than the Marxist left) and the alienation of the left (for whom the reforms were not sufficient) pushed the Christian Democrats into third place in the three-cornered presidential election of 1970.

The Allende government extended the agrarian reform, reducing the maximum size of private holdings to 40 standard hectares and involving rural day-labourers as well as the permanent estate-workers in the agrarian reform. By 1973 the total land expropriated had risen to over 10 million hectares, virtually abolishing the *latifundio*, the large landed estate.[6] By mid-1972 the reforms affected 44 per cent of all farms with more than 40 standard hectares, and 54 per cent of the land (weighted according to quality) in those farms had been expropriated, amounting to 38 per cent of the total agricultural land available.[7]

Under both Allende and Frei, rural agitation and expropriations ran ahead of the ability of the government to service and administer the reformed farm sector. After a good harvest in 1970-71, agricultural production declined at the same time as demand in the cities for foodstuffs and consumption by *campesinos* of their own produce were increasing. Rising tension, inflation and political polarisation from mid-1972 onwards did not allow the agrarian reform to 'settle', frustrating any final evaluation of its effect on Chilean society.

The military regime that took power after the coup d'état of 11 September 1973 comprehensively reversed the agrarian reform, returning expropriated land to its former owners or dividing up *asentamientos* into family plots. The farmers who benefited from these divisions were exposed to the full rigours of the free market. Many went bankrupt and had to sell their land when they were unable to pay off their loans. By 1986 only ten farms with 473 families maintained the co-operative structure they had inherited from the agrarian reform which, in its heyday, had given land to over 92,000 families.[8]

Nicaragua

The Nicaraguan agrarian reform will be much harder to reverse than the Chilean one. In October 1991, President Violeta de Chamorro vetoed a bill passed by the right-wing majority in the National Assembly reversing the agrarian reform laws passed by the previous Sandinista government. With the army and police still under Sandinista control and tens of thousands of *campesinos* benefiting from the Sandinista government's reform measures, many of them as individual owners, the present government would have provoked widespread unrest if it had attempted to implement the bill as it was passed by the National Assembly.

According to the 1970 census the 1,700 families owning more than 350 hectares, constituting 0.9 per cent of the total number of farming families, owned 1,662,000 hectares, 41.2 per cent of the total cultivated land area. At the other extreme, 60,000 families, or 32.7 per cent of the rural population, had no land at all.[9] Many of these large farms belonged to the Somoza family and its close associates: as a result of their expropriation immediately after the revolution, 1,222,681 hectares, accounting for 25 per cent of all agricultural land, were transferred to the state sector (92.6 per cent) and co-operatives (7.4 per cent).[10] The extent of these holdings, expropriated for political reasons, meant that the Sandinistas never had to use the criterion of size alone to justify expropriation. They avoided a direct clash with the landowning class and managed to fulfil their pledge to maintain a mixed economy. Other laws provided for the expropriation of farms that were not being farmed properly, that belonged to people who had fled the country or where there were serious labour disputes. In a number of cases these laws were interpreted loosely by the Ministry of Agriculture in order to make over farms to militant agricultural workers, although on some occasions such expropriations were reversed by the courts.

The problem for the Sandinista government was to make the agrarian reform work for the country, thereby increasing produc-

chapter four

tion for the domestic market and for export. Like other governments, they were pulled in different directions: price controls on foodstuffs intended to favour the wage-earners of the cities and towns worked against the *campesinos*; lax credit controls, adopted deliberately to stimulate production after the revolution, favoured *campesinos* but were inflationary; free-market policies to bring prices into line with supply and demand, implemented in 1988, favoured rural producers at the expense of townspeople.

The large export plantations and farms confiscated from Somoza and his associates were maintained as state farms because it was thought that their more modern technology and complex organisation could not be managed efficiently by *campesinos*. Over the years, however, the Ministry of Agriculture acquired an unenviable reputation for bureaucracy, waste and poor management.

By the mid-1980s, when the *contra* forces had become a serious threat, the Sandinistas had to evaluate all their policies in terms of political support. They had already seen how the collectivist spirit of the agrarian reform had alienated large numbers of more conservative *campesinos* in the cattle-raising areas of Boaco and Chontales. Government policy from 1982 onwards favoured co-operatives and individual farmers, taking land out of state control.

The future of the Nicaraguan agrarian reform is not clear. Right-wing elements in the ruling UNO coalition would like to see a root-and-branch removal of the Sandinista legacy from Nicaragua, including the reversal of the agrarian reform. Thousands of demobilised *contras* who, not without reason, see themselves as the architects of the opposition victory in the 1990 elections, have been left landless despite government pledges. The most disgruntled of them have formed new military units, known as the *recontras*. They directly threaten the land reform beneficiaries and press the government for land grants, often of the choice co-operative lands that have years of work and capital invested in them.

The stage is set for bitter conflict in the countryside between *campesinos* who supported the *contras* and pro-Sandinista *campesinos* who benefited from the agrarian reform. The large number of arms in the hands *recontras* and *recompas* (reformed Sandinista units) could rekindle war in the rural areas.

In any event, the co-operatives themselves have to adapt to the free market and the rigours of commercial credit. The banks customarily demand a mortgage on the land as surety for their loans. Co-operative members, therefore, find themselves in a cleft stick: either they accept bank credit and risk losing their land or they work with their own meagre resources and risk having their land taken away from them under the Sandinista agrarian reform law, still on the statute book, which provides for the expropriation of inadequately cultivated land.

Agrarian reform – grounds for hope?

The experience of land reform in Latin America makes clear that simple redistribution of land, whether to families, co-operatives or state farms, does not necessarily change patterns of political control and subservience or permanently raise rural incomes. Even when land has been distributed, population growth puts pressure on a limited resource, reducing the average size of family holdings as they are divided and sub-divided with every new generation. In Mexico, as a result of the land redistribution undertaken by the government of Lázaro Cárdenas between 1934 and 1940, the percentage of landless labourers initially dropped from 68 to 36 per cent of the population. By 1960, however, there were more landless families than in 1910.

Landownership may be the key to rural poverty and wealth but it cannot be considered in isolation from other factors. As an experienced practitioner of agrarian reform has commented, the pressure for reform often came from middle-class intellectuals who were,

'... moved by a moral commitment to social justice and national development, by an antipathy to the traditional élite common among intellectuals everywhere and by a strong desire to hold power and direct the national destiny ... Public debate about rural development and agriculture in Latin America in the 1960s revolved around the land reform issue. Most agricultural policies, however, were much more mundane than the expropriation of large estates. They had to do with such matters as pricing, credit, marketing, taxes, subsidies, technical assistance, labour regulations, irrigation and land settlement. While these measures generally attracted little attention, taken together they constituted each country's agricultural development strategy. The groups pressing for agrarian reform generally had little influence in shaping these unspectacular routine agricultural policies. This was because the traditional political structures automatically provided a dominant role in agricultural policy-making to the large landowners and their allies. All public policies, of course, pertain to specific institutional contexts. The totality of a country's institutions, its social structure, determines in large measure what policies are feasible and what their impacts will be. To understand agricultural policy-making in Latin America one must first analyse the social structures. It boils down to a matter of power ...'[11]

chapter four

The statistics of inequality and injustice throughout Latin America give a rough idea of the dimensions of the problems facing its peoples, but they are no guide to their solution. The percentage of the labour force engaged in agriculture in European Community countries in 1980 varied from 3 per cent in the United Kingdom to 26 per cent in Portugal, with most countries under 10 per cent. The decline in the rural labour force to such low levels has been accompanied, generally speaking, by low rates of population growth, opportunities for emigration and a corresponding increase in employment opportunities in the urban areas.

In Latin America today, however, the population is still growing at a much higher rate than in Europe; there are few opportunities for legal emigration, and the channels of illegal emigration – a traditional safety valve for Mexico and Central America – are being systematically blocked; and the cities are incapable of generating employment for the people who are already living in them, not to mention the continuing flow of new arrivals from the countryside.

At the same time, the vital role which agricultural exports play in the balance of payments of most Latin American countries and the need to provide the urban population with food make governments even more fearful of addressing the problem of rural land distribution. In 1960 only in Uruguay, Argentina, Chile and Venezuela was the urban population greater than half the total population. By 1990 only in El Salvador, Guatemala, Haiti and Honduras was more than half the total population living in the countryside; and in Latin America as a whole city dwellers accounted for about 75 per cent of the total population.

In this situation the advice of the reformers and economists of the 1960s, who saw land reform as a means to create an internal market and modernise agriculture, is obsolete. Today, market forces are modernising agriculture throughout Latin America. This does not mean that modern agricultural enterprises do not depend on the mobilisation of large numbers of low-paid agricultural workers. On the contrary, the fruit farms and packing stations of Chile and the banana and coffee plantations of Colombia, Ecuador and Central America would not be able to compete in international markets without an abundant supply of cheap labour.

Dependence on export crops and the unequal distribution of land played an important role in developing the grossly distorted patterns of wealth and income which were the basis of the power and privileges of tiny minorities. Land and the wealth it generates are still crucial to any sustained attempt to tackle poverty in Latin America. The huge and profitable plantations, ranches and estates that produce for export or for the hungry cities are defended by the immense political influence of their owners – in itself an almost insurmountable obstacle to significant reform. But they are also seen as fundamental to the ability of Latin American countries to survive and prosper in the modern world economy. At the same time, as they expand, they drive peasant farmers from their land and exacerbate the inequalities which are responsible for so many of the region's social and economic ills.

Centuries after Latin America was set on this path of extreme inequality, the problems that the region faces are more intractable than ever. Today, the solutions to these problems rely as much on the willingness of the rich countries of the world to undertake daring initiatives over debt and world trade, as on the political will of Latin American governments and political movements.

References

1. Dunkerley, James, *Power in the Isthmus*, Verso, 1988, p148.

2. *ibid.*, pp147-9.

3. Much of the material for this section has been draw from Jean Stubbs' *Cuba: the Test of Time*, Latin America Bureau, London, 1989.

4. Scheer, Robert & Zeitlin, Maurice, *Cuba: An American Tragedy*, Penguin Books, Harmondsworth, 1964, p96.

5. Loveman, Brian; *Chile: the Legacy of Hispanic Capitalism*, 2nd ed., OUP, New York, 1988, p289. It should be noted that 3.13 million hectares were unirrigated. The maximum size of private farm fixed in principle by the Frei reform was 80 irrigated or standard hectares. The maximum for unirrigated land, used for cattle-raising, could be several times the 80 standard hectares.

6. Ortega, E., 'From Agrarian Reform to Associative Enterprise', *CEPAL Review*, No.40/April 1990, p107.

7. Lehmann, David, 'Agrarian Reform in Chile 1965-72', in David Lehmann (ed.), *Agrarian Reform and Agrarian Reformism: Studies of Peru, Chile, India and China*, Faber and Faber, London, 1974, p98.

8. Ortega, E., *op. cit.*, p107.

9. CIERA (Centro de Investigación y Estudios de la Reforma Agraria), *Informe al FAO*, Managua, 1983, p4.

10. *ibid.*, p62.

11. Barraclough, Solon, *The Land Problem in Latin America*, mimeo., 1974, chapter III, p10.

Acknowledgement: *My thanks to Sarah Ross for her assistance in writing this essay.*

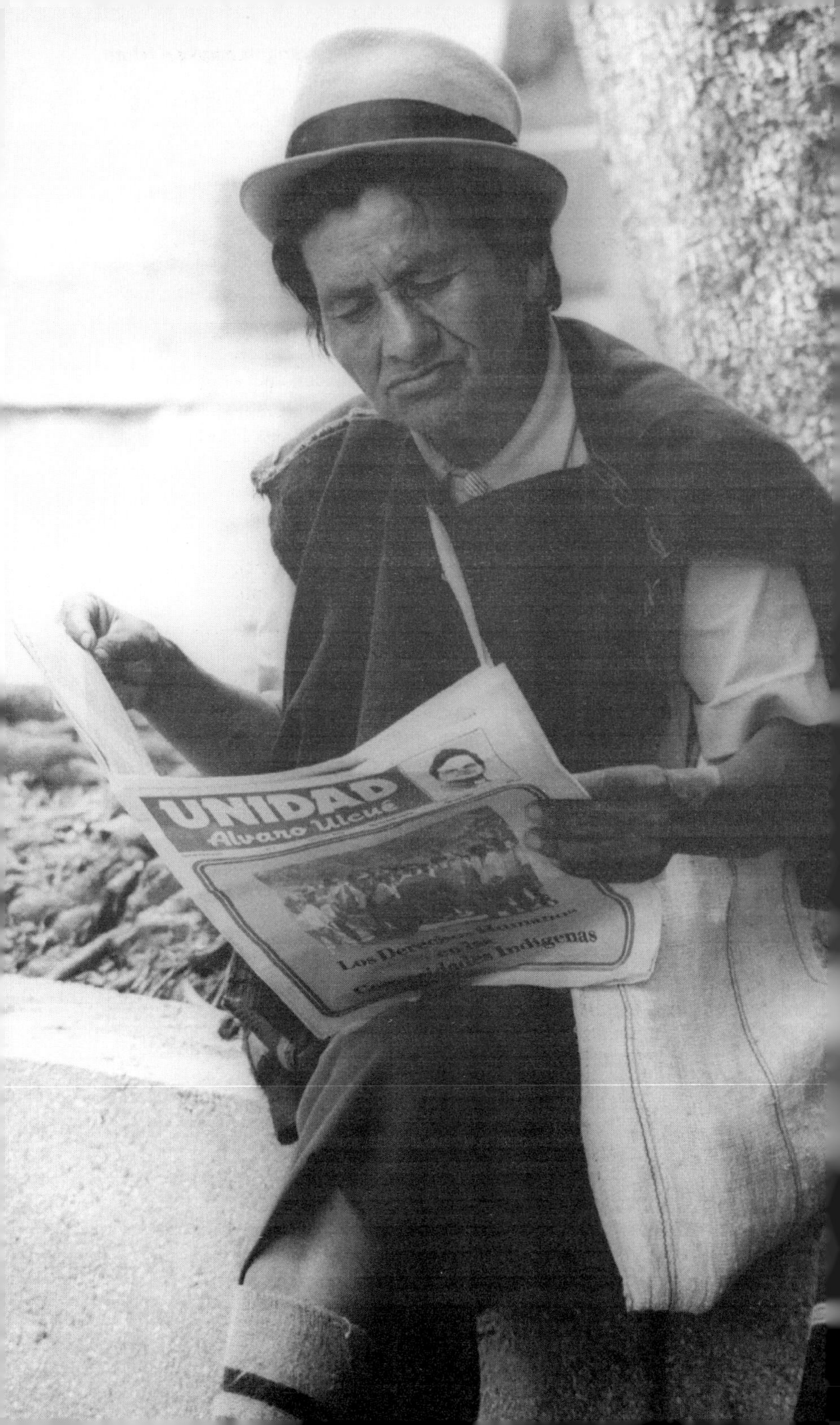
UNIDAD
Alvaro Ulcué
Indígenas

chapter five

george monbiot
AGAINST ALL ODDS: INDIGENOUS PEOPLE AND THE BATTLE FOR SURVIVAL

While the governments of Latin America prepare to celebrate the five-hundredth anniversary of Columbus's arrival in the West Indies, organisations of indigenous peoples from Mexico to Chile are planning demonstrations. Their response to the event is significant, for half a millennium of European domination has been characterised not only by the extermination of millions but also by sustained resistance on the part of many of the survivors. If in the last five hundred years the Indians have declined in numbers and been dispossessed of their territories, then it seems likely that the centuries to come will see a steady empowerment of these people, who were once the region's only inhabitants.

In the last two decades indigenous people have been recovering their pride in their heritage and social organisation. The word 'Indian' is now considered a mark of honour by the people of many indigenous groups: until recently it was felt to be a term of abuse. The pressure that Indian organisations and their supporters have applied has forced most Latin American governments to consider seriously the needs of their indigenous populations, and to grant communities more control over the course of their own development. There is still a great gulf between the demands of indigenous organisations and the responses of national governments, but the trend is positive.

At the same time, however, atrocities against indigenous people are commonplace in nations such as Guatemala, Peru and Colombia, and some Indian groups are declining precipitously in the Amazon basin. In all nations there is a failure on the part of governments to recognise indigenous peoples' rights to the ancestral territories they claim as their own. In legal disputes between Indians and corporate or individual landowners, it is most often the outsiders who win. Colonists – migrants, usually non-indigenous, from other parts of the country – continue to invade the territories of many groups and to destroy the ecosystems on which their livelihoods depend. Indigenous people in

---

The voiceless begin to speak. A Colombian Indian reads about the progress being made by his people in their efforts to regain their right to ancestral lands and protection for their language and culture. Photo by Joe Fish.

chapter five

countries such as Chile and Argentina suffer discrimination over jobs, constitutional rights and access to the law, and in almost every country in Latin America Indian representatives continue to be imprisoned or killed for defending the rights of their people.

In countries such as Argentina, Chile, Paraguay, Bolivia, Costa Rica and Mexico, Indian societies are still being destroyed by the break-up of communal landholdings, the discouragement of traditional housing, language, ritual and dress, and the actions of some insensitive missionary groups. Indigenous people in most nations are among the poorest of the inhabitants. The lack of credit, infrastructure and agricultural development that many indigenous communities desperately need is contributing to the great migrations to the towns and the lowland forests currently taking place in the Andes and Mexico.

But in the coming decades there seems likely to be an intensification of the process now evolving in Colombia and the Peruvian lowlands, whereby the indigenous people have successfully lobbied for the return of some of their lands and responsibility for their own administration. Indigenous peoples' developing awareness of their rights and the growing visibility and political strength of the Indian organisations should ensure that such positive changes, when they occur, are hard to reverse.

Indigenous peoples then and now

There is an extraordinarily wide range of opinion about the size of the Latin American population at the time of Columbus's arrival. Evidence from contemporary accounts, archaeology and land-use studies has been used to argue that there may have been as many as 100 million indigenous people in the region, or as few as 7.5 million. W.M. Denevan's figure of some 53 million is perhaps the estimate most widely accepted. If this is correct, today's indigenous population is approximately 60 per cent of that of 1492.

When European eyes first fell upon the Americas, Indian civilisation was as diverse and dynamic as that of the *conquistadores*. Social systems ranged from nomadic hunting-and-gathering communities in some parts of the lowland forests, through the stratified chiefdoms of the Amazon floodplains and the Pacific coast, to the great kingdoms of the Aztecs and the Incas. Some of the cities the Spaniards stumbled upon in the lands which are now Mexico and Peru were more populous than any in their own continent. The Aztec capital Tenochtitlán housed between 150,000 and 300,000 people, and its palaces, ceremonial centres, suburbs and markets were served by a grid of closely-planned canals and streets. The Incas, whose emperor ruled from a city of 100,000 to 200,000 inhabitants, used forced labour to build monuments which even the ravages of Spain could not destroy. In Central America the Maya, whose power was waning by the time of Columbus's arrival, had evolved systems of architecture, writing and chronometry entirely distinct from our own. Were progress to be measured not in terms of technical achievements, but by the criterion of an understanding both of the social and the physical environment, then the smaller communities of the forest lands could be said to have achieved a higher level of development than any ever reached in Europe.

Indian societies were destroyed not only by the sword but also by means of accidental biological warfare: epidemics spread ahead of the invaders, along the lattice of trade routes that covered the entire continent, and whole peoples are believed to have succumbed to smallpox, measles, typhus or the common cold before they were ever encountered by Europeans. Many of those who survived were later overwhelmed by the horrendous working conditions of the forced-labour systems imposed by the Spaniards, or perished in the famines caused by the conquerors' demands on land and labour. Others were assimilated through miscegenation.

Of the 460 million people now living in Latin America, around 30 million are considered indigenous. In some nations the Indian population has remained high and is now growing rapidly: in Mexico the indigenous community of 6 million is growing at an annual rate of 3.5 per cent; Peru's Indian population, the largest in Latin America, increases by 260,000 annually. In other places the indigenous people have gone completely, or are still declining: of the hundreds of thousands once living in the West Indies no more than 800 remain; and the Yanomami people of the Brazilian Amazon have declined by 20 per cent in three years. For them, as for many others, the Conquest is still taking place.

Land rights and survival

Indigenous peoples rely on their traditional lands not only for physical survival but also for their sense of identity. By contrast to the ease with which land can be traded or converted in industrialised societies, the loss of territories or their resources has caused both economic disaster and psychological disruption in traditional communities all over Latin America. When communal lands are divided into individual plots, an integrated community

chapter five

is transformed into a settlement in which the interests of the individual can and do diverge from those of the community as a whole. The results include the usurpation of traditional leadership, the over-exploitation of resources, and a loss of identity so severe that it has led in many cases to the assimilation or dispersal of entire ethnic groups.

Land expropriation from indigenous people is still taking place in every Latin American nation. While many countries have their own idiosyncratic means of divesting Indians of their territories, there are some features common to most. These include the disrespect with which governments treat landownership laws of their own making; the forcible eviction of indigenous people from their rightful territories by hired gunmen, police or soldiers working on behalf of landlords; and the resulting urban migration or the transformation of settled indigenous people into colonists who then invade the lands of other communities.

But there are also many positive developments, and in several nations the government has permitted the return of extensive territories to the people whose claims to the land predate the Conquest.

Disease and physical assault continue to drive communities into oblivion. International terms of trade, national economic priorities and difficult agricultural circumstances also continue to destroy some peoples. This review of land rights and survival in the Latin American nations, while considering the problems and improvements throughout the region, pays particular attention to the Andes, the Amazon and Guatemala, as it is in these places that the situation of indigenous people is perhaps the most critical.

Mexico

Mexico's six million Indians have lost 100 million hectares of ancestral lands in the last sixty years, solely by means of the government's formal confiscation of their property. This official dispossession has been augmented by the theft of traditional territories by farmers, timber companies and developers. Local political leaders continue to preside over the arrest, torture and murder of members of groups such as the Mixe, Nahua and Tzotzil, whose people are resisting the transfer of their lands. In the Chimalapas forest of the south, the 12,000 Zoque Indians have been deprived of one-third of their community woodlands by timber poachers, and are now suffering from the depredations of drug traders, who are forcing them to convert some of their remaining land to opium and marijuana fields. Already the Lacandon Indians have lost all of their forest lands and, for this and other reasons, have been reduced to penury and alcoholism in the two diminutive settlements remaining to them. Tourism is now depriving such people as the Tarascan Indians of the western highlands and the coastal Zapotec of their traditional livelihoods. Their lands are being taken, with inadequate compensation, for hotel and leisure complexes, and their fisheries are threatened by the sewage associated with these developments.[1] One result of such dispossession, as well as the problem of unemployment, is that several million indigenous people are now living as the poorest of the poor on the fringes of Mexico City.

But the campaigning work of indigenous organisations and the Mexican government's increasingly enlightened attitude have improved the situation of many rural communities. In 1988 the government granted the Triqui Indians title to 16 million hectares of their lands in Oaxaca state, and helped them and other groups to establish a radio network to broadcast in their own languages. In 1989 the president promised a commission of indigenous representatives that he would tackle their problems of land, food, health and legal protection. This, however, was quickly followed by the imprisonment of several leaders who were defending their lands in Chiapas state. More positively, an historic precedent was set in 1990 when a village 'strongman' and the gunmen he had hired were sentenced for their crimes against indigenous people.

Guatemala

Guatemala is the Latin American country in which the repression of indigenous people is most systematic. There the centuries-old burdens of discrimination, material disadvantage, cultural suppression and eviction from their lands have been supplemented by repeated military atrocities.

Guatemala, where the Maya people are believed to be in the majority, also has the worst distribution of land in Latin America. By 1988 an estimated 98 per cent of the country's 3.6 million indigenous people were reported to be either landless or with insufficient land for their subsistence.[2]

While 2.25 per cent of farmers possess 64.5 per cent of the total farmland in Guatemala, the 40 per cent of farmers with the smallest landholdings own only 1.4 per cent.[3] This is due partly to the abolition of communal land tenure in the last century to enable the local ruling classes to move into the temperate uplands where coffee grows best. The state permitted big farmers to expropriate much of the peasant land, rendering the Indian population dependent on waged labour. Elsewhere, individuals who were no longer bound to their communities either sold off their land, were tricked out of it or, if they held on to it, had to subdivide it among a growing number of sons.

chapter five

The loss of indigenous territories continues today, as landowners, with the help of the police, expel peasants from their properties, on some occasions justifying this action by accusing them of belonging to guerrilla movements. The government has seized 70 per cent of the land owned by people who have fled the country. The lack of proper government extension services and agricultural credit forces indigenous people to pledge their holdings as security for agricultural loans to commercial lenders. If they are unable to repay the loans, they forfeit their properties. Agro-industrialists, whose exports are of great importance to the Guatemalan economy, have been the main beneficiaries of the redistribution.

The cultural associations between indigenous people and their traditional lands are being severed by many things: a mass movement to the cities by the landless; flight from the country as a result of political repression; and seasonal labour. An estimated 650,000 Indians leave the highlands each year to work for several weeks on coastal plantations. On these farms the minimum wage is seldom paid, people sleep in open-sided sheds, and crops are sprayed from the air while the labourers work on them.

In the cities Indians take the humblest jobs and, as elsewhere, they find themselves subject to discrimination over health, education and access to resources. Throughout the country the life expectancy of indigenous people is sixteen years less than that of other Guatemalans. Around 82 per cent of Indian children are malnourished and only 19 per cent of Indians over the age of seven are literate.

A coup in 1954, backed by the CIA, installed a right-wing, authoritarian government. In response to increasing repression, a non-indigenous guerilla movement emerged in the 1960s. Between 1966 and 1970 around 10,000 civilians, most of them indigenous, were killed in the course of a military campaign against an estimated 350 guerrillas.[4] The armed forces continue to use the presence of small guerrilla armies to rationalise what government representatives have admitted is an attempt to eradicate indigenous culture and organisation.

The Indians of Guatemala were not involved in the armed insurrections of the 1960s, but as the fraudulent 1974 elections made it clear that there were no democratic opportunities for change in Guatemala and as the guerrillas worked hard to cultivate their support, Indians came to provide most of the revolutionary recruitment in the 1970s. As Phillip Wearne has pointed out, indigenous people joining the guerrilla armies did so on the whole because they offered the most plausible means of self-defence.[5]

At first the army responded to the guerrilla attacks with a relatively selective campaign of disappearances, torture and killings of suspected sympathisers. But this soon developed into what appears to have been an attempt to eliminate the Indian population in certain areas. The resulting slaughter was indiscriminate and vast. Between 1980 and 1984 the regular army and military death squads killed approximately 50,000 people, most of them indigenous, and bombed 350 civilian villages. The murders were accompanied by horrifying torture and mutilation. A quarter of the 4 million highlanders were displaced from their homes.

As the military campaign progressed, the armed forces began to concentrate on the integration and control of the surviving indigenous people, attempting to deny the guerrillas both economic and popular support.

All available Indian men were drafted into civil-defence patrols, in which they were forced to work with the army against the guerrillas and anyone alleged to be supporting them. The authorities forcibly rehoused Indians of different language groups in uniform prefabricated villages. These were known as *aldeas modelos* (model hamlets), and were based on the 'strategic hamlets' used in the Vietnam War. The process broke up families and removed people from their remaining lands. Surrounded by barbed wire, overlooked by watchtowers, and their movements monitored at checkpoints, the people in the *aldeas modelos* had to abandon their cultural identity. Since they are obliged to work for much of their time for the army and are confined to inadequate lands, they are becoming increasingly dependent on the non-indigenous economy.

The transition from a military to a civilian presidency in 1986 appears to have bolstered the strength of the armed forces, as it served to reopen foreign funding channels, providing money for military development projects. The army continued to control many areas of state policy. Although human rights abuses at first declined, they soon began to increase once more. The mass killings of the early 1980s were not repeated but there has been no reduction in 'extra-judicial executions', that is, murders committed by the security forces or para-military death squads: there were 653 such killings in 1990 and 101 'disappearances'. In the first six months of 1991, according to the Catholic Archdiocese of Guatemala, there were 301 killings and 91 disappearances. Despite the greatly reduced level of civil conflict, the army and the police continue to kidnap, torture and kill campaigners for agrarian reform, as well as returning refugees, people attempting to avoid service in civil-defence patrols and families requesting that the remains of their murdered relatives be disinterred for reburial.[6]

chapter five

There have been no attempts to investigate or prosecute members of the armed forces for such crimes, which the government claims are the result of common violence or anonymous terrorists. Clandestine jails operate throughout Guatemala and mass graves remain undisturbed. Around 200,000 people are in exile abroad.

Despite this, the United Nations removed Guatemala from its blacklist of nations considered to be in serious violation of human rights, a political decision which astonished human rights campaigners. In January 1991 a new civilian president, Jorge Serrano, closely associated with the most repressive of the military governments, was elected in a second round run-off against another right-wing candidate.

Today, the peasant organisations provide the only hope of fundamental change in Guatemala. They are campaigning for a redistribution of land, social and economic rights, better wages, the enforcement of constitutional provisions defending indigenous people, and an end to the disappearances which are now a favoured military means of suppressing dissent.

As the armed insurrection has been largely contained, resistance now takes the forms of strikes, demonstrations, lobbying and legal representation. In 1986, following the formation of the Association of Peasants for Land, 16,000 peasants marched from the south coast to Guatemala City. Their mobilisation has now made it possible for a few indigenous people to buy land on concessionary terms. The Council of Ethnic Communities in El Quiché province has also marched on the capital, to demand an investigation into the human rights abuses. The Mutual Support Group, formed by indigenous women whose relatives had been killed, mounted weekly demonstrations outside the presidential palace from 1985 to 1988. In the face of innumerable threats and murders, such organisation is a matter of astonishing courage.

Belize

In neighbouring Belize the 15,000 indigenous people, some of whom are refugees from Guatemala, are suffering from low crop-prices and growing rural unemployment. They are being encouraged, with the help of the International Fund for Agricultural Development, to turn away from traditional farming patterns towards cash cropping and the private ownership of land.[7]

Indian organisations are campaigning for more administrative autonomy for the indigenous people and the protection and development of their culture. The Maya of Toledo have proposed a homeland of 500,000 hectares, in which each indigenous village would be responsible for its own development.

Honduras

The Miskito communities of Honduras are racially mixed, with some black and European elements, but retain a strong sense of their Indian identity. The Miskito language, both spoken and written, is still widely used. Their long-standing contact with English-speaking outsiders and their relative isolation from the Spanish-speaking bulk of the country has enabled them to adapt without losing some of their fundamental cultural characteristics. Even so, most of the indigenous people participate in the mainstream market economy. And today, non-indigenous farmers continue to acquire the lands of Miskito and Sumo speakers, often with the help of the Honduran security forces.

El Salvador

Most of El Salvador's indigenous people lost their lands in the middle of the nineteenth century, and traditional dress and other forms of cultural expression were bloodily suppressed. The great massacre of 1932, in which between 20,000 and 30,000 mainly-Indian peasants were slaughtered in reprisals for a botched uprising (which itself caused no more than a dozen deaths) almost eliminated the last vestiges of indigenous culture from El Salvador. As a result, the 960,000 Salvadorean Indians are hard to distinguish from the general population.[8] Their cultural identity has been further threatened by the disruptions of the prolonged civil war, poverty and landlessness. In recent years members of the Indigenous Association of El Salvador have been tortured and killed by the army, and the discussion of indigenous affairs has been regarded as subversion by the authorities.

Nicaragua

In Nicaragua most of the 135,000 Indians rejected the attempts of the Sandinista government to involve them in the revolution. The Miskito communities considered the agricultural and educational programmes introduced by the revolutionary government to be unwarranted interference by the 'Spaniards'. Their leaders used the new freedoms of the revolution to press for autonomy, provoking Sandinista fears of separatism. The growing threat posed by the US-financed *contra* insurgents made the Sandinistas even more heavy-handed in their dealings with indigenous populations of the Atlantic coast. After a series of disputes followed by arrests, forcible resettlement and other human rights violations, many of the Miskito and members of other groups fled to Honduras and joined the *contra* forces. The Sandinistas admitted that this treatment of the Miskitos was a clumsy mistake and set about trying to make amends. In 1984 they initiated a process which

chapter five

culminated in 1990 – simultaneously with their own electoral defeat – with the election of regional autonomous councils on the Atlantic coast. These councils are now seeking to assert their independence against central control exercised by the new government of Violeta de Chamorro.

Costa Rica

The extensive reserves set aside for indigenous people in 1977 by the government of Costa Rica are now being invaded by colonists, timber-cutters and poachers, because of the government's failure to enforce its own relatively enlightened laws and the construction of new roads. About 40 per cent of the land in the twenty-one reserves is owned by non-indigenous people, and Indian territory continues to be bought by outsiders.

It is nearly impossible for the 25,000 Indians to obtain votes or their full constitutional rights. To qualify for identity papers, Indians have to present a certificate of good conduct, be able to speak Spanish and pass an exam in geography. As a result, the Costa Rican Guaymi have succeeded only in obtaining residency cards, of the kind normally given to foreigners. They are frequently detained by the immigration authorities. The two principal Indian organisations are now campaigning for legislative reforms.

Panama

In Panama the 100,000 indigenous people have a much stronger political presence, but are beset by unemployment and inadequate health and educational facilities. The Kuna, who have established a reputation for driving hard bargains, have succeeded in winning some control over their lands and considerable administrative autonomy. Like the Embera-Waunan they have been granted rights to a proportion of the profits deriving from minerals or timber taken from their territory. The Panamanian Guaymi are campaigning for similar entitlements, and fighting to secure one million hectares of their traditional lands, which have been heavily colonised by outsiders. As several Panamanian politicians depend on the votes of indigenous people, there has been intense public discussion of their rights. Attempts by political parties to win the support of Indian groups have left communities divided.

Colombia

The Colombian government has done more than any other in South America to uphold indigenous land rights. In 1989 the 70,000 Indians of the Colombian Amazon were granted title to 18 million hectares of their traditional territories, in which they regained much of the responsibility for their own administration, development and education, as well as the conservation of the environment. As a result, traditional leaders are re-establishing their authority and longhouses are being rebuilt. The National Indigenous Organisation of Colombia (ONIC) has pointed out, however, that there are no provisions allowing the Indians to block the exploitation of oil or minerals in these lands.[9]

Elsewhere, relations between Indians and the state have been characterised by violence. In the Cauca region in the west there is an indigenous leader killed, on average, every month, principally as a result of the people's success in regaining stolen lands. In some places both government forces and guerrillas have been working with big landowners to deprive indigenous people of their ancestral territories.[10] In response, some of the Indians have formed their own guerrilla group, the Comando Quintín Lame. Much of the land for which the 210,000 Andean Indians in Colombia have title is occupied by non-indigenous people.

In eastern Colombia colonists are invading indigenous territories made accessible by the state mining company's extraction of gold. As in Peru and Bolivia, the cocaine trade is causing serious problems, with indigenous people being attacked both by drug barons seeking to make use of their lands and the armed forces trying to stop the traffic. In the coastal rainforests, the Kuna have lost some of their lands to colonists and oil companies and are now experiencing invasions of goldminers. Like the Kuna of Panama, however, they have succeeded in retaining much of their culture.

Ecuador

In the lowlands of Ecuador the most pressing problems in indigenous territories are caused by commercial development. Twenty foreign oil-firms, working with the state oil company, are prospecting or drilling in the Ecuadorian Amazon. Operating with inadequate safeguards and out of the public eye, their actions have already led to the pollution of many of the region's rivers. Oil and the caustic chemicals used in its separation have been deliberately discharged or carelessly spilt into the rivers, thus depriving several Indian communities of the fish and riverside wildlife crucial to their subsistence.

The activities of the colonists and ranchers entering the region along the roads the oil companies have built, destroying the forest and displacing the indigenous people, are even more significant. The most vulnerable group in the Ecuadorian Amazon is the Huaorani, some of whom have had scarcely any contact with outsiders. In the last few years the population has declined

chapter five

dramatically; now the American company Conoco has been granted permission to drill for oil in the heart of their territory, the Yasuni National Park. While the government and the company claim to be taking precautions to prevent the invasion of colonists, critics consider the precautions to be inadequate, and believe that the access road likely to be built with World Bank money will allow timber-cutters, miners and agro-industrial companies to enter the region.[11] The Confederation of Indigenous Nationalities of Ecuadorian Amazonia (CONFENIAE) is helping the Huaorani to survey and obtain legal title to their lands.

Around 5,000 Amazonian Indians are affected by the planting of oil-palms by firms with backing from companies based in Europe (including British companies). In the coastal forests, the Colorado and Cayapa people are being displaced by colonists and planters of cocoa, coffee and bananas, losing traditional lands both within and outside their reserved territories.[12]

Most of Ecuador's 3 million indigenous people live in the Andean highlands, where landlessness is the principal problem. Much of their land was taken in the nineteenth century and they were forced to work for the new owners. It is still difficult for indigenous communities to regain adequate farming land. The Indian organisation, Ecuaruni, claims that 90 per cent of the cases in which the courts have intervened to settle land disputes between Indians and landlords or invaders have been resolved in favour of the newcomers. Indigenous organisations, having lost faith in government promises to improve land distribution, have attempted to purchase titles and have organised land invasions, occupying land they regard as rightfully theirs. The Otovala, by means of the effective marketing of their handicrafts and the sale of farm produce, have bought back some of their traditional territory. Few other groups have been able to follow this example.

In 1990 highland Indians launched a 'National Uprising of Indigenous Peoples', cutting off food supplies to towns, occupying public buildings and preventing access to some provinces. They demanded that the government attend to their economic and territorial problems, recognise their indigenous nations and expel missionaries belonging to the Summer Institute of Linguistics, who were supposedly operating covertly in Ecuador. The government agreed to monthly meetings with the Confederation of Indian Nationalities of Ecuador (CONAIE), to hear its demands.

The shortage of land in the highlands has led to migration both to the towns and to the Amazon, with, in the latter case, government encouragement. In response to this, the Shuar Indians of the Ecuadorean Amazon established in 1964 a federation which was to become the example followed by many other Indian organisations. The successes of the Shuar Federation led in 1989 to their recovery of 320,000 hectares, despite the government's attempts in the same year to divide the group by establishing an alternative organisation. The lowland confederation CONFENIAE has persuaded the government to grant the Secoya and Siona legal title to their lands.

Peru

The nine million Quechua-speaking indigenous people of Peru, most of whom live in the highlands, are caught between the twin terrors of the *Sendero Luminoso* ('Shining Path') guerrillas and the security forces. Since 1982 – when *Sendero Luminoso* became an acknowledged threat to national security – many thousands of Andean peasants have been kidnapped, imprisoned and killed.

Disappearances characterise the conflict: in the seven years to 1989 at least 3,000 people held by government forces have been lost; many are believed to have filled the mass graves which are now commonplace in parts of the highlands. The looting, political repression, mass arrests, torture and extrajudicial executions carried out by the security forces are mirrored by the show trials, torture and killings perpetrated by the guerrillas.[13]

Army officers have been granted powers of arrest without accountability to the civilian government. Holding villagers collectively responsible for guerilla attacks, the army has carried out reprisal killings, almost wiping out entire communities. Suspecting peasants in some places of sympathising with the army, the *Senderistas* have committed similar atrocities.

Trying to force its rigid political doctrines on the peasant economy of the Andes, *Sendero Luminoso* has attempted to ban local markets, cutting off the exchange of produce between the higher and lower slopes which is fundamental to traditional social organisation.

On the eastern side of the Andes, MRTA (Movimiento Revolucionario Tupac Amaru) guerrillas contribute to the chaos, sabotaging the infrastructure and disrupting both the economy and traditional leadership. The great majority of the victims of these troubles are non-Spanish speaking peasants. Whether by accident or design, all sides are effectively waging war against indigenous people.

While such abuses mounted during the last years of Alan García's presidency, spreading from the highland emergency zones to all parts of the country, there has been a slight decline in the number of deaths and disappearances since the new president, Alberto Fujimori, came to power in 1990. There have been no satisfactory

chapter five

investigations into the behaviour of the army or civilian authorities, however, despite the discovery of mass graves, and there is no sign of an end to the conflict.[14]

The highland peoples' problems are exacerbated by their agricultural difficulties. In 1968 Peru, unlike most other Latin American nations, instituted agrarian reforms which recognised communal landholdings, breaking up big estates to favour peasant co-operatives. Although more than 60 per cent of communities received land titles, the policies of subsequent governments limited the ability of many peasants to profit from this development.[15] The support given by the government of Alan García (1985-90) to agro-industrial companies, the lack of credit and infrastructure, low crop-prices and severe droughts have together led to the partial collapse of peasant agriculture in Peru, resulting in widespread malnutrition.[16] Many have turned to the cultivation of the coca bush as one of the only remunerative alternatives to the cultivation of staple crops. The troubles of the highlands have driven people to migrate to the cities and the Amazon. In Lima, now a city of 7 million, there are several million people, most of whom speak Quechua, living in absolute poverty.

In 1980 the government initiated a project, with funding from the Inter-American Development Bank (IADB) and USAID (the official aid agency of the US government) to settle 150,000 colonists in the territories of lowland groups such as the Yanesha and Ashaninka. While some tribal territories were surveyed and titled, other communities were severely disrupted by the great influx of Andean migrants. During 1988 the government passed a law promoting further settlement in the Amazon. Critics have labelled it the 'coca law', as they point out that neither the soil nor the facilities granted to the colonists will allow them to survive by producing anything but coca. While both are victims of the chaos and injustice governing Peru, there is little but hostility between the displaced highlanders and the lowland Indians they are in turn dispossessing.

The indigenous people of the Peruvian Amazon are threatened by big business as well as colonisation. Companies exploiting timber, oil and gold, or planting sugar and oil-palms, have been granted extensive concessions in tribal territories and have contributed to the influx of settlers. The recently-contacted Nahua of the southern rainforests are believed to have lost 50 per cent of their population through encounters with oil- and timber-workers between 1984 and 1988.[17] In 1990, in Madre de Dios, 3,000 indigenous families occupied the territory granted to a gold-mining company, aiming to prevent the activities which have been destroying indigenous communities there.

Many forest people have been killed by cocaine traffickers who are collaborating with guerrillas in the north and central Peruvian Amazon. Attempts by the United States to restrict the cocaine trade include counter-insurgency training for the Peruvian armed forces, leading to suspicion of US collusion in the abuses suffered by indigenous communities. Farmers and timber companies have enslaved Ashaninka families in the central Amazon. They are unpaid and are punished by beatings and mutilation if they try to escape.[18]

The government has made few realistic attempts to curb the power of the big landowners and corporations in the Amazon. Both in the highlands and the lowlands, Indians rarely receive a fair hearing in court. Even the legal victories over land won by indigenous communities may be followed by the murder of their representatives. The large numbers of Indians in the Peruvian Amazon who do not possess identity documents are unable to participate in elections. Despite this, four indigenous mayors were elected in the Amazon in 1989.

The Amazonian Indians have mobilised with extraordinary speed. While organisations such as AIDESEP (see page 170) have, through legal channels, taken over the surveying, titling and management of many traditional territories, the Ashaninka people have forcibly expelled the guerrillas, colonists and missionaries on their lands, following the murder in 1989 of a revered Ashaninka leader by the MRTA guerrilla group. The group has imposed its own state of emergency, policing its lands with armed patrols, and has regained much of the land which had been taken from it.

Bolivia

The land reform which took place in Bolivia, unlike that of Peru, did not recognise the communal ownership which is central to the traditions of the four million Aymara- and Quechua-speaking highland Indians. The 1952-53 reforms, granting the peasants individual land titles, were instrumental in breaking up thousands of communities. They also broke up some of the big private farms in the *altiplano* and the mountains. In the lowlands in the east of Bolivia, by contrast, the reforms opened the way for the formation of enormous cattle ranches and timber concessions, reducing the territories of the indigenous people. In the department of Santa Cruz de la Sierra, 59 timber companies control 12 million hectares, while the 21,000 Indian families have been granted only 400,000. The Indian confederation working in the lowlands, CIDOB, has laid claim to 4.2 million hectares.[19]

The last group of Bolivian nomads, the Yuqui, are being forced from their lands in the east of the country by colonists taking

chapter five

advantage of new roads and railways. Posses of settlers have hunted the Yuqui: after one 1989 massacre, eleven bodies were hung by the killers from a tree, to warn the surviving Indians not to return to their lands.

In September 1990, around 800 Indians from the northern Bolivian Amazon, protesting against the government's failure to demarcate their land and the logging operations in their forests, marched 700 kilometres from the lowlands to the capital, La Paz. As they approached their destination, after thirty days on the road, they were greeted by thousands of Andean Indians.

The president and most of his cabinet left the capital to meet them but, as he failed to answer all their demands, they continued into the city, to a triumphal welcome. They celebrated mass with all the country's bishops, held a ritual with representatives of the Aymara Indians of the Andes, and mustered such widespread support that the president was forced to recognise their ownership of their traditional lands and serve the timber companies with one year's notice of expulsion. The Bolivian government is now seeking advice from Colombian lawyers about the formation of reserves similar to those recently established in the Colombian Amazon.[20]

The indigenous people of Bolivia, accounting for 54 per cent of the population, have been severely affected by the country's economic crisis. Three-quarters of the population are considered to be malnourished and life expectancy is only 48 years. Their chronic economic problems have been exacerbated by the 1985 collapse in the price of tin, which led to the redundancy of 23,000 of the 30,000 miners employed by the state-owned mining corporation; government and US programmes to stop the cultivation of coca; and drought. The government's IMF-inspired structural adjustment programme, initiated in 1985, has reduced spending on health and education and diverted agriculture towards the production of export crops. Economic pressures and the breakdown of traditional community organisation are driving peasants from the *altiplano* and the mountains to the cities and the Amazon forests.

Bolivia has never experienced the massive human rights violations for which Central America and Colombia are notorious. Nevertheless, in times of political upheaval (1974, 1979 and 1980) peasant leaders have been killed. The increasingly military nature of the anti-drugs programmes is now a major threat. The small producers, the fetchers-and-carriers, have suffered most. Bolivian prisons are full of poor peasants unjustly imprisoned under Law 1008, the anti-drugs law. Yet many of the big dealers are apparently above the law. Other aspects of the anti-drugs war also threaten peasant livelihoods: the price of the coca leaf has fallen as a result of more successful actions against distribution networks, forcing peasants to grow less profitable crops, and some crops have been damaged by the herbicides used to kill the coca plants.

Chile

The great majority of Chile's indigenous population are Mapuches. Until the middle of the nineteenth century they occupied half of the land which is now Chile and Argentina. Having failed to conquer them, the Spaniards signed treaties recognising their independence, which the new republics of Chile and Argentina ratified, only to disavow them soon afterwards. Through several decades of military operations, the Chilean and Argentinian governments succeeded in displacing the Mapuches from most of their territory, redistributing it to colonists and forcing the Indians into reservations. Between 1970 and 1973, the government of Salvador Allende tried to redress some of these injustices, giving legal recognition to communal landholdings. These measures were reversed by the Pinochet régime.

General Pinochet, equating community living and collective labour with communism, passed a decree whereby communal lands could be divided among the members of a community if just one individual living there, indigenous or not, so requested. Backed up by forcible evictions, the 1979 land laws led to the fragmentation of 1,411 of the 2,066 Mapuche communities, leaving only 1.5 per cent of their traditional lands under communal ownership. Lumber concessions and hydroelectric contracts in Mapuche lands were granted to outsiders.

As a result, the *araucaria* pines (the 'monkey puzzle' tree of the English suburban garden), which were an essential element in the traditional economy of some Mapuches, are now extinct in many places. The 1980 Constitution rendered ethnic minorities in Chile technically illegal. General Pinochet declared, 'Chile does not have Indians; we are all Chileans.' After the coup, the security forces and the secret police spread terror throughout the country. Mapuche leaders prominent during the Allende years were imprisoned, exiled or murdered. Mapuche children were punished for speaking their own language in school.

In 1990 President Aylwin announced that his government would suspend the financial transactions dividing Mapuche communities and recognise the validity of communal landholdings. Setting up a Special Commission for Indigenous People, he announced his intentions of improving the social and economic position of the Chilean Indians, strengthening their cultural traditions and establishing a more sensitive education system, in consultation with Indian organisations. The Mapuche federations, which emerged from the repressive years of the Pinochet government divided but active believe that, despite this positive turn, many of the people's problems are still being ignored by politicians.

Argentina

In Argentina, as in Chile, the culture of the Mapuches, who account for around 10 per cent of the 350,000 officially-recognised indigenous people, has been suppressed, though not with the brutality exercised by the Pinochet government. The Argentinian media, antagonistic towards Indian mobilisation, has repeated suggestions that the Mapuches are not indigenous to Argentina, paradoxically claiming that their cause was being promoted by the Chilean government in order to lay claim to Argentine territory.

Colonists continue to occupy the lands of other indigenous peoples in the north of Argentina, often with the encouragement of both federal and local governments. In 1990 a Guaraní community in the north of Argentina was forcibly evicted from its traditional lands and relocated on an urban rubbish dump. Its own territory was requisitioned for the construction of a leisure complex.[21] In Tierra del Fuego, the southern tip of South America, Indian communities on both the Argentinian and Chilean sides of the border are on the verge of extinction.

After being evicted from their land, many indigenous people have moved to the cities, where they have to disguise their ethnic identity to qualify for even the lowest paid jobs. The Constitution, while recognising Indian rights, still charges Congress with the duty of promoting the conversion of indigenous people to Catholicism. Indian representatives and non-governmental organisations (NGOs) persuaded the government to sign a declaration in 1990 acknowledging the need to change the Constitution, to grant indigenous communities land rights and royalties on the exploitation of natural resources and to preserve the Indians' cultural identity. This has so far brought no significant improvement.

Paraguay

In Paraguay one of the greatest threats to cultural survival is the Caazapa Regional Development Project in the south-east. Laying down a network of roads and associated infrastructure, the programme has opened Indian territories to colonists and timber companies. This has led to extensive deforestation and the dispossession of several communities. The lands of many of the Mby'a have been divided among the colonists, and most of the territory of the Aché Indians has been taken by the Paraguayan government to be sold to Brazilian soya-bean producers. The

indigenous people and the battle for survival

World Bank, however, which provided part of the funding for the project, has threatened not to renew its loan if the lands of the Mby'a are not titled. The Mby'a have also been in conflict with the Mennonite communities which, with the collusion of the government, have appropriated their lands and using the dispossessed as cheap labour. The Indian communities, however, now appear to be winning the battle to recover some of their property.

Throughout the east of Paraguay, timber-cutters and other large landowners have been harassing and evicting such groups as the Pai Tavytera. The fundamentalist New Tribes Mission, conducting forays (described as 'manhunts') to make contact with and proselytise the Ayoreo of the Chaco region, have assisted the rapid settlement of most of the nation's nomadic people. Indian affairs in Paraguay are controlled by the Ministry of Defence, which has regarded organisations working on welfare and human rights issues as subversive.

Brazil

Brazil has lost over ninety indigenous groups this century, and some of the surviving peoples continue to decline dramatically. The Waimiri-Atroari, for instance, in the centre of the Brazilian Amazon, are believed to have fallen in number from 3,500 in 1974 to 374 in 1986, principally through disease and the armed forces bombing their villages. The Yanomami Indians in the far north, who, until 1987, were the largest, undisturbed indigenous group in the Americas, have recently declined by 20 per cent. Around 35 per cent of the survivors are said to be infected with malaria, as a result of the invasion of their lands by goldminers. The Uru Eu Wau Wau of the western Amazon are thought to have lost half of their number since they were first contacted by outsiders in 1981. Since 1990 they have been threatened with extinction: a large deposit of cassiterite, an ore of tin, has been discovered in their territory and the government has deregulated their reserve.

While some members of the government of President Collor, elected in 1990, have shown sensitivity towards Indian rights and difficulties, the attitude of several ministries and of the armed forces remains hostile.

A document published by the armed forces in 1990 advocated war against indigenous and environmental organisations as a means of achieving national objectives in the Amazon. The government's road-building plan in Amazonia, though now slowing down, has led to massive land invasions and epidemics among Indians in the south and west of the Amazon. Timber-cutting in Indian reserves, permitted by FUNAI, the official government Indian protection agency, during the last administration, has not abated.[22]

chapter five

As a result of lobbying by Indian representatives, the 1988 Constitution granted indigenous people rights to their traditional territories and to consultation over the use of their resources. For the most part, these rights have been disregarded. President Sarney unconstitutionally reduced the extent of Indian lands and since then even these lands have been invaded both by mining companies and freelance miners (*garimpeiros*). Mining companies control one-third of all tribal territories. Gigantic development projects, such as the Carajas programme in the south-east of the Amazon and the army's Calha Norte project around the northern frontier, have put tens of thousands of indigenous people at risk, and have contributed to the rapid advance of ranchers, timber-cutters and hydroelectric installations throughout the Amazon. Already the Brazilian Amazon's 200,000 indigenous people are outnumbered eighty times by colonists. The unequal distribution of land and economic problems elsewhere in Brazil ensure that settlers continue to arrive.[23]

Outside the Amazon there have been violent clashes, with groups such as the Pataxo Ha-Ha-Hai and the Kaingang confronting outsiders over access to land and timber. In the south-west of Brazil, seventy-two young Guaraní men committed suicide in 1989 and 1990. These deaths are considered to be a response to the reduction of their traditional territory – in one state 20,000 Guaraní are living on 16,000 hectares – and the abominable conditions in which they are forced to work in plantations and sugar mills. Since 1988, however, Indian organisations have developed rapidly, and have captured world attention by means of spectacular demonstrations, such as the meeting of 600 representatives of indigenous groups at Altamira in Amazonia in 1989, to protest about the construction of a hydroelectric dam.

French Guiana, Suriname and Guyana

The territory of the 4,500 Indians of French Guiana has also been invaded by Brazilian *garimpeiros*. Nowhere in French Guiana are traditional land rights recognised. The Indians have been forced to work for the colonists and businessmen acquiring their property. Education is in French only, and the indigenous people have to abide by a legal system which takes no account of their needs.

During the recent civil war in Suriname, Indian villages were looted by guerrillas, precipitating the flight of an estimated 8,000 indigenous people from the interior to the coast or into French Guiana. Despite the termination of the war, many indigenous communities have not recovered and several thousand Indians in the Surinamese forests have initiated a rebel movement called the Tucayanas, demanding the recognition of their land rights, more

indigenous people and the battle for survival

autonomy and aid. The rebels are said to have allied themselves to the army which, controlled by the former dictator, is at loggerheads with the civilian government.[24] Indigenous territories in Suriname are deemed to belong to the state.

Most of the 45,000 indigenous people of Guyana have been granted title to their lands, following the recommendations of the 1965 Independence Conference. But the land of those groups which did not obtain legal recognition of their territories, such as the Karina, Pemon, Kapon and Wai Wai, has been invaded by colonists and mining companies. Chronically short of money, the Guyanese government has invited foreign companies into several tribal territories. Many of the Karina have fled into Venezuela, as mining firms have moved onto their lands. The Brazilian government has been funding the construction of a road running from the border to the River Essequibo in central Guyana, thus opening up the new goldfields of the Guyanese interior. Brazilian miners leaving Yanomami territory have now moved into the lands of Guyanese Indians. And ranchers are displacing the people of the Rupununi savannahs, denying the Indians access to the best grazing land.

Venezuela

Missionaries have been entrusted with responsibility for the administration of many of the indigenous people of the Venezuelan interior. Reports suggest that in some places their work has led to the precipitous abandonment of traditional culture. Invasions of colonists, ranchers and miners have been responsible for epidemics of malaria, tuberculosis, yellow fever and hepatitis, and the accompanying ecological destruction has seriously affected the subsistence economy of some groups. The Bari and the Yukpa Indians have presented an alternative development plan to the government as an attempt to stop the destruction of their territory by miners and big farmers. The Karina's land in the eastern savannah was declared to be municipal property in 1987, favouring the oil companies working there. Since then the government has stopped providing the Karina with health, education, transport and agricultural credit. Bauxite mining threatens the Piaroa in the Amazon and tourism is beginning to affect the Venezuelan Yanomami, whose reserve has yet to be demarcated. The government's paternalistic attempts to organise Indians have hindered the formation of a national indigenous federation.

Indigenous organisation

The greatest change among the indigenous peoples of Latin America in recent years has been the astonishingly rapid growth

chapter five

of their organisations. Their achievements have been remarkable: within a decade or less, Indians in some nations have turned from being comparatively voiceless outcasts of national society into co-ordinated lobbies that politicians can no longer ignore. The six organisations considered below show something of the difficulties, determination and successes of the many forms of Indian resistance which are now becoming an important feature of the Latin American political scene.

Colombia's Regional Indigenous Council of Cauca (CRIC) came into being amid violent repression. CRIC was founded in 1971, when 2,000 representatives of the 200,000 Indians of the Cauca region converged on the town of Toribio to protest against exploitation, theft of their lands and the land tax imposed on them. The new Council resolved to recover and extend the reserved lands which had been taken from them; to refuse to pay rent for their territory; to study and demand the enforcement of Colombia's laws on indigenous people; and to promote the language, customs and indigenous education of the native Cauca communities.

Forty-five Indian councils in the Cauca region joined CRIC. The people they represented were either struggling to survive by farming on subsistence plots or working as day labourers on the ranches of the invaders. They lacked schools, health care, credit and roads and were subject to attacks by landowners, their gunmen and the police if they resisted attempts to seize their land.

As well as lobbying through legal channels for more extensive reserves, CRIC organised the non-violent reoccupation of stolen ancestral lands. By 1986 CRIC members had recovered 30,000 hectares, including some of the fertile sugar estates in the Valle del Cauca. The Council has succeeded in reducing working hours on the ranches from twelve hours a day to eight and has helped communities to escape the land tax. It has trained some members in administration, teaching and legal-assistance work, and ensured that local Indian councils are more representative. CRIC has also resisted attempts of political parties to persuade it to affiliate.

CRIC is viewed by landowners and members of the government as communist and subversive. By 1986 landlords and police had murdered 150 Indians for their association with the Council and regions such as Toribio had been placed under military control.[25] As the organisation has grown in strength, so the hostility of police and the authorities has intensified. Government forces have invaded Indian reserves and detained members of the council. In 1989, after CRIC organised a peaceful march to protest about the violence, its headquarters were destroyed by a bomb. CRIC is a member of the National Indigenous Organisation of Colombia (ONIC) which, in turn, is affiliated to the Co-ordinating

indigenous people and the battle for survival

Body for the Indigenous Peoples' Organisations of the Amazon Basin (COICA). COICA brings together Indian federations in Bolivia, Peru, Ecuador, Colombia and Brazil, with the partial involvement of groups in Venezuela and Suriname. It was founded in Lima in 1984, in response to the members' realisation that there was no multinational forum which could adequately represent their views.

They resolved to co-ordinate many of their activities, such as lobbying for land rights and cultural and administrative autonomy, and working to persuade governments in Latin America and the world at large that indigenous people should be allowed to take responsibility for their own development. This development, COICA points out, 'is not based on the accumulation of material goods nor on the greatest rates of profit, obtained at the expense of our territories and future generations ... For us development must take into account the well-being of our entire community or group, not just of a government which only lasts for five years.'[26] COICA has been instrumental in demonstrating the need and the capacity of indigenous people to establish economic systems different to those of the states to which they belong.

COICA has established an international presence with remarkable speed. Its representatives have visited several of the most powerful industrialised nations; it has made important contributions to the drafting of resolutions at the United Nations and the International Labour Organisation; and it has participated in protests about indigenous problems in several parts of the world. In 1986 its president, Evaristo Nugkuag, was awarded the Alternative Nobel Peace Prize.

In the Amazon, COICA has been assisting its member groups in schemes to bolster the independence of the indigenous economy and social organisation. Member federations have begun to demarcate and title their own lands; to remove illegal colonists and repair the environmental damage they have caused; and to research and improve traditional farming techniques and the marketing of farm and forest products. They have also endeavoured to develop traditional healing techniques and the capacity of communities to attend to their own medical problems; to train indigenous teachers, linguists and lawyers; to monitor and expose violations of indigenous rights; to establish Indian research centres and libraries; and to demonstrate to national and international society the merits of an indigenous model of environmental and social management.[27]

In the western Amazon a peaceful social revolution has been taking place over the last few years – scarcely remarked on in the northern hemisphere – in which the responsibility for develop-

chapter five

ment has been passing from the developers to the people being 'developed'. Many of COICA's demands have still not been met and many of its resources are devoted to lobbying both national governments and international organisations. COICA is pressing for freedom of movement for those peoples divided by national frontiers; the withdrawal of the armed forces from indigenous lands; for tourism in Indian territories to be controlled by the Indians themselves; for the exclusion of multinational companies from indigenous property; for consultation with and involvement of indigenous people in any development projects affecting them; and for respect for customary law and traditional leadership in indigenous territory.

COICA is persuading environmental organisations that indigenous people must be closely involved in any conservation projects on their lands. It rejects the debt-for-nature (see page 95) swaps which have taken place without the involvement of the affected inhabitants. It is pressing foreign funding agencies to set up commissions involving COICA members for consultation and joint project-design in any scheme likely to affect the inhabitants.[28] The organisation points out that the most effective defence of the Amazon is the protection of indigenous territories.

One of COICA's affiliates is AIDESEP, the Inter-ethnic Association for the Development of the Peruvian Forest. Founded in 1979, it now represents most of the indigenous communities of the Peruvian Amazon. AIDESEP's formation was a response to the growing problems of land invasion, environmental destruction and cultural suppression. In taking responsibility for their own development, its members aimed to destroy the myth of the incapacity of indigenous people, often used by outside organisations to justify intervention.[29]

AIDESEP is taking over some of the tasks for which the government is nominally responsible but is unable or unwilling to fulfil. The government claimed that it did not have the resources to survey and title the indigenous lands in Ucayali province, so AIDESEP, having raised the additional funds required from NGOs, is overseeing the project itself.

Committed to grass-roots development, it has encouraged every community in the province to determine its own borders, in order to build a contiguous indigenous territory from a patchwork of community lands.

The Aguaruna and Huambisa Council, with AIDESEP's help, has coached 150 indigenous health workers in both traditional and Western medicine. These health workers now range across an area of 200,000 square kilometres.

It has also started a marketing programme to break the monopoly enjoyed by non-indigenous middlemen and improve the transport of agricultural products by river and road.

AIDESEP's legal adviser has been training indigenous leaders in the legal defence of their rights and helping them to lobby politicians and ministries. Its agricultural specialists have designed demonstration farming plots, to help communities develop their forest resources without destroying them. All of these projects are complicated by the political instability of Peru and the conflicts in which many of the region's communities are caught up.

It is especially difficult for the Indians to affirm their rights when different interest groups – the government, the army, three guerrilla movements, drug traffickers, colonists and timber and mining companies – are vying for power in their lands. Although on most issues it finds itself in opposition to government policy, AIDESEP has been working with state institutions on certain projects. It has also received funding from NGOs in Europe.

Of the hundreds of smaller organisations represented by national federations like AIDESEP, the Tukano people's associations in north-western Brazil provide a good example of the means by which local groups are trying to protect themselves against grandiose government schemes.

The Calha Norte project, co-ordinated by the Brazilian armed forces, threatens to transform the indigenous territories around the entire northern frontier into part of the Amazon's biggest new development zone. By taking traditional territories out of the hands of indigenous people and opening them to exploitation by mineral and timber companies, cattle ranchers and colonists, Calha Norte aims to integrate Brazil's northernmost forests with the rest of the nation. The 18,000 Brazilian Tukano people have lost 63 per cent of their lands to the project. Mining companies have put forward requests to prospect in most of the remainder.[30]

In response, the people of the central Tukano territories have formed two organisations: ACITRUT, the Association of Indigenous Communities of Taracuá and the Uaupés and Tiquié Rivers, and AMITRUT, the corresponding women's group. By improving communications between the communities in their territory, the associations have enabled the Tukano of the central regions to respond to the Calha Norte initiatives as a unified body. They have encouraged the communities to study the Brazilian Constitution and, thus equipped, the people have blocked the installation of a road, two ranches and an army barracks in their territory, demonstrating to Calha Norte's administrators that these projects were illegal.

chapter five

ACITRUT and AMITRUT are now hoping to increase the speed with which they alert indigenous support groups in other parts of Brazil about new development initiatives in their territory. Without telecommunications and far from the centres of population, they often find that the armed forces have been able to complete some of their projects before they can even sound the alarm. For this reason, they are hoping to establish an office and purchase a two-way radio and a motorboat. But funding has been difficult to secure, partly because the issues in which they are involved are politically sensitive. ACITRUT and AMITRUT have now formed an alliance with a Friends of the Earth local group in Britain, most of whose fund-raising activities have been devoted to the Tukano project proposals. By improving the marketing of agricultural products and by means of the women's development of traditional handicrafts, the associations are hoping to be able to fund themselves in the future.

The Mapuche organisations of Chile, by contrast to those of many other groups in Latin America, are fragmented, principally as a result of the deliberately divisive policies of the Pinochet administration and attempts by opposition parties to win political support from parts of the indigenous community. General Pinochet established a series of regional Mapuche councils, composed of those Mapuche people willing to sell community lands and refusing to acknowledge the authority of the traditional leaders. The alignment of the Mapuche organisation Ad-Mapu with the political left has led to political conflicts within communities. But in the more benign environment created by the new Chilean government and by means of a remarkable meeting of chiefs, it appears that the Mapuche people will now be able to present a more unified response to their problems.

In April 1990 a group of 1,000 Mapuches, of whom 200 were *lonkos* (chiefs), met in the southern city of Temuco to reassert the role of the traditional leaders in defending the Mapuches' rights. They established a new national organisation, the Council of All the Lands, aiming to help the dozen or so different Mapuche organisations to unite. They demanded land rights, recognition of their leadership and a Mapuche flag and passports. Despite its historical significance – this was the first great meeting of *lonkos* for over a century – the event was largely ignored by Chile's political establishment, eliciting only criticisms of the *lonkos*' 'separatist' attitudes and suggestions that they had been provoked by the extreme left.[31]

In Mexico the Union of Indigenous Communities of the Northern Zone of the Isthmus, UCIZONI, emerged to fight the landlords and local political bosses who are destroying forests on indigenous territory, monopolising landownership and farm production, and murdering or imprisoning those indigenous leaders questioning the established order. Most of its members are drought-stricken farmers or farm-workers who are also suffering from malnutrition and a lack of education, credit and health care. In forest regions the government has enabled outside timber companies to operate freely, while restraining the indigenous people's attempts to make rational use of their timber resources. The prisons of the region are filled with indigenous people, many of whom are denied access to fair trials. According to UCIZONI, the Summer Institute of Linguistics has been helping the government to assimilate the indigenous population.[32]

UCIZONI, founded in 1983, has succeeded in regaining much of its members' stolen land, partly through legal representation and partly by recourse to physical reoccupation. It has organised the obstruction of timber companies in community forests and has worked to develop indigenous agriculture, establishing communal flour mills and marketing networks. It is lobbying the government for electricity, safe water, schools, clinics and roads, and pressing, with some success, for the release of indigenous people unfairly imprisoned. Working to restore and develop indigenous culture in the Isthmus of Tehuantepec, UCIZONI is trying to introduce education in the languages of its members, to expel missionaries from indigenous territories and reinstate the authority of traditional leaders.[33]

The Church

The treatment of indigenous people has divided the Latin American Church ever since a Dominican friar, Bartolomé de las Casas, clashed with his superiors in the sixteenth century over the atrocities committed by the *conquistadores*. Later, during the seventeenth century, the Jesuits in the Amazon and in Paraguay dissociated themselves from both the secular and ecclesiastical powers to maintain exclusive control of the Indian settlements they established.

Christians in Latin America are now divided not so much by denomination as by interpretation, as both Catholics and Protestants are split between those who consider that their most important task is conversion, and those who believe that true evangelisation cannot take place unless it acknowledges cultural differences and the reality of economic and social injustice.

In terms of indigenous policy, the two opposing poles are represented by fundamentalists, prepared to use any means to contact and proselytise the last undisturbed peoples, and those who work with Indian organisations for recognition of their political rights.

chapter five

Between the two there are many who adopt a middle-of-the-road position, dividing their energies between the spiritual and earthly welfare of their congregations.

The contradictions and difficulties faced both by the Churches and the indigenous people whose lives they attempt to change are best illustrated by the case of the last nomadic group in eastern Bolivia, the Yuqui. In the 1980s Protestant and Catholic missionaries were competing to be the first to reach the last of the Yuqui, both using what critics have described as bribery and coercion and both earning the disapproval of other Protestants and Catholics. The Yuqui were hunted by the missions, colonists and oil-workers and dragged with unseemly speed into an entirely new lifestyle by the successful Protestant evangelists. They are now said to be so profoundly disorientated that they may never again become functioning members of any community.

The fundamentalist missionaries of Latin America, many of whom have since the 1960s been associated with reactionary governments attempting to assimilate indigenous people, have attracted much adverse publicity. The insensitivity that some groups have shown towards the culture and the needs of Latin American Indians, and the brutality with which their evangelistic programmes have sometimes been pursued, has led critics to charge them with complete disregard for anything but Christian conversion. Some missions are said to be motivated by the belief that the Second Coming, in which the fundamentalists will be exalted, will not take place until the most isolated peoples have heard the Word of God. Their attempts to eliminate indigenous cultural traits have been characterised by a cartoon in which a missionary tells an Indian: 'The problem is *you*.'

But all the fundamentalist missions, while agreeing that conversion remains their first purpose, claim also to be concerned with the physical well-being of the people they proselytise. The New Tribes missionaries persuading the Bolivian Yuqui to move into mission settlements insist that they are saving them from death at the hands of invading colonists. The Summer Institute of Linguistics (SIL) has provided some groups with essential medicines.

Human rights campaigners have drawn particular attention to the ruthless methods some fundamentalist missions have used in establishing contact with isolated groups of Indians and converting them. In Paraguay and Bolivia armed Indian converts have been sent into the territories of the target populations to make contact, and this has resulted in the deaths of several of the scouts, who have later been described by the missionaries as martyrs. Baskets have been lowered from helicopters into forest clearings, containing gifts and hidden microphones, allowing the missionar-

indigenous people and the battle for survival

ies to listen to the demands of the Indians and answer them in miraculous fashion by dropping the required gifts from the sky. Low-flying aircraft have been used to broadcast messages in indigenous languages.

Once the missionaries have made contact with indigenous communities, some of them have used threats and deceit to persuade the people to convert, often with disastrous effects. New Tribes missionaries working with the Panaré in Venezuela are reported to have told them in 1987 that the Second Coming was imminent, and that they were to stop working and kill their dogs, so that they could pray for their salvation without interruption. They prayed and starved for several days before the police arrived to stop the affair. Another community was 'threatened' with an apocalypse associated with a passing comet if the people did not convert. The missionaries are reported to have told the people that if the authorities expelled them, the United States Air Force would come and bomb their villages.[34]

As a result of such methods, Indians have been driven into panic and chronic disorientation. The Ayoreo of the Paraguayan and Bolivian Chaco are reported to be dying of disease and trauma after being settled in villages by the New Tribes Mission. It is also reported that they have been made available as cheap labour for the Mennonite communities.

Critics suggest that some missions make no effort to teach the people they resettle anything but the Bible and the dominant language, with the result that when they attempt to enter mainstream society, they can find no role other than begging, prostitution or the lowest forms of labour.[35]

It is not only the Indian belief systems that are vigorously discouraged by the fundamentalists, but also much of their social organisation, their communal economy and traditional housing, dress, ritual and use of natural resources. Indigenous people are, therefore, often left with no option but to adopt the values of the foreign culture. Sadly, many of the biblical virtues are better represented in traditional indigenous societies than in those which have been successfully 'evangelised'.

The New Tribes Mission and the SIL are the two most prominent fundamentalist missions in Latin America. Both are Protestant organisations that receive most of their money from donations in the United States.

CIA documents suggest that it employed members of these missions to monitor the regions in which they were stationed until the mid-1970s. Since its involvement was exposed, the CIA has claimed that it used mission contacts only on a voluntary basis.

chapter five

Both groups are perceived to be closely associated with the US government; to regard communism and social revolution as the work of the devil; and to enjoy the support of some of Latin America's most repressive governments.

The missions claim to be apolitical, but have used Romans 13:1[36] to suggest that their host governments have been ordained by God. Latin American governments are said to have used them to further their interests in remote parts of their own nations. Some missions have encouraged communities to join the mainstream market-economy, helped the dominant classes to relieve them of their land or resources and passed the Indians on to other outsiders as cheap labour.

Despite the support it has enjoyed in the past, however, the SIL lost its contracts in Brazil, Panama, Mexico and Ecuador in 1981, though it is said by some to have returned covertly to Ecuador. The SIL continues to work in Bolivia, Suriname and Paraguay, while there are New Tribes Missions in Venezuela, Peru, Colombia, Brazil, Bolivia and Paraguay. Peru was made safe for Protestantism and the SIL by the election of Alberto Fujimori as president in April 1990. Although a Catholic, Fujimori cultivated the support of the growing Protestant Churches and appointed a Baptist as vice-president. Thirty-six of the Maya communities in Mexico are now suffering from the disruptive attentions of Mormon missionaries and Jehovah's Witnesses;[37] and in the interior of Suriname the West Indian Mission is said to have created something akin to a 'mission state'.

For five centuries the indigenous peoples of Latin America found few allies or supporters in the Church. After the Second Vatican Council and the Latin American bishops' meeting at Medellín, Colombia, in 1968, the indigenous cause became a significant theme within the Churches. This coincided approximately with changes within the fundamentalist missions in the 1960s. As the Cold War intensified, the allegiance of fundamentalist groups to reactionary governments in Latin America and elsewhere became more apparent. But at the same time other church people preaching the gospel of liberation began to work with peasant and urban union movements, as they moved towards radical change.

In 1972 representatives of Catholic orders and groups working with indigenous people produced the Document of Asunción, in which they acknowledged that missionaries had in the past been agents of oppression, racism and religious and cultural discrimination. They resolved to continue some mission work, but to dissociate themselves from any form of repression, denounce the causes of injustice and proclaim the gospel, which they described as 'essential for the full liberation of indigenous peoples'. They resolved to support the formation of the Indians' own organisations. In 1989 their position received the support of Pope John Paul II, who acknowledged that, 'When native people are robbed of their territory, they lose an element which is necessary for their own existence and are thus in danger of disappearing as a people.'

But the change in attitude of many missions – with some making drastic reforms and others even abandoning their work, on the grounds that its net effect was negative – is not simply change from above. Some missionaries, like the Salesians of northwestern Brazil, are being converted by their own congregations. This particular case illustrates some of the struggles and contradictions within the contemporary Church. By 1980, the Tukano Indians of this region were so exasperated by the continued suppression of their traditional values by the Salesians, by the repeated threats of hell if they did not adopt both the religion and the way of life of the Europeans, and by mission schools whose teaching bore no relevance to their lives, that they took their case to the Fourth Russell Tribunal on the Rights of the Indians of the Americas, and won.

Since then the Salesian missionaries have remained on sufferance. Education has been rapidly revised, following the recommendations of the Indian leaders, and now emphasises the teaching of the Tukano language, traditional stories, crafts, dancing and music, and has attempted to incorporate the Tukano world view into the study of the Western sciences. The mission itself is now deeply divided between radicals and conservatives. Some priests insist on retaining all the traditions of the Church, even on leading some prayers in Latin, while some of their opponents refuse to participate in any prayer that mentions hell.

There are several mission organisations, such as the Indigenist Missionary Council (CIMI) – the official body of the Brazilian bishops' conference for indigenous affairs – and the Amazonian Centre for Anthropology and Applied Practice in Peru, which are now working actively to defend the political rights of Indian communities. CIMI, for instance, assists indigenous groups in lobbying Congress, organising demonstrations, securing legal support and publicising their demands. It publishes a journal, *Porantim*, which reports abuses of indigenous rights and describes the traditions of the Brazilian Indians.

In Guatemala, the orthodox evangelisation campaign initiated in the countryside by the Catholic Church after the 1954 coup was quickly transformed by radical missionaries into a movement for the defence and restoration of indigenous communities. Catholic priests and lay-workers helped the Indians to establish co-operatives. While these enhanced the strength and confidence of some

chapter five

groups, the changes caused villages to divide, breaking up the traditional power structure and setting Christians against animists. Some of the Protestant missionaries working in the highlands in the late 1970s also worked to promote communal organisation, in opposition to the Protestant fundamentalists preaching deference to the state authorities.[38]

In the late 1970s, when non-violent resistance in Guatemala gave way to open guerrilla warfare, some church activists, despairing of the possibility of peaceful change, saw the guerrilla movements as the most likely means of achieving social justice and gave them considerable support. In the savage counter-insurgency campaign of 1979-82 many catechists, delegates of the word and lay-workers were killed.

The responses of indigenous people to the Protestants, Catholics and numerous minor sects in Latin America (in Bolivia alone there are said to be 170) have ranged from total conversion to total rejection. Syncretic belief systems have emerged, in which spirits become saints and God becomes the master of a pantheon. There have been attempts by some peoples to appease missionaries with a nominal acceptance of Christianity, while retaining as many of their traditional values as they can. But, increasingly, Indian organisations are coming to express their view that however sympathetic missionaries might be, however much they might assist in their health, education and political mobilisation, attempts by both fundamentalists and progressives to evangelise indigenous people threaten the very foundations of their society.

George Monbiot *worked as a radio producer with the BBC's natural history unit, before moving on to the World Service to cover current affairs. He left to concentrate on his writing, his most recent book being* Amazon Watershed: the New Environmental Investigation, *published in 1991. He has also written for the* Independent, The Times *and the* Observer.

References

1. *Latinamerica Press,* 21 January 1988.

2. Wearne, P. & Calvert, C., *The Maya of Guatemala*, Minority Rights Group, Report No. 62, 1989.

3. Pastoral letter from the bishops of Guatemala, *Guatemala's Land Crisis,* Church in the World 25, 1988.

4. Wearne and Calvert, *op. cit.*

5. *ibid.*

6. Amnesty International, *Guatemala – Human Rights Violations Under the Civilian Government*, Amnesty International, 1989.

7. IWGIA, *Yearbook 1988,* IWGIA, Copenhagen, 1989.

8. Stephen, D. & Wearne, P., *Central America's Indians,* Minority Rights Group, 1984.

9. *Survival International Newsletter,* No. 9, 1990.

10. Gray, A., *The Amerindians of South America,* Minority Rights Group, Report No.15, 1987.

11. World Rainforest Movement, *World Rainforest Report,* VI (4), 1990.

12. Gray, *op. cit.*

13. Amnesty International, *Peru – Human Rights in a State of Emergency,* Amnesty International Publications, 1989.

14. *Cambio* (Peru), No. 147, 27 December 1990.

15. Gray, *op. cit.*

16. *Cambio,* 27 December 1990, *op. cit.*

17. IWGIA, *op. cit.*

18. COICA, *To the International Community,* (Circular), COICA, 1989.

19. Arambiza, E., 'Indigenous Peoples, Indigenous Organisation and the Problems Facing Ethnodevelopment in Eastern Bolivia', in *Indigenous Self-Development in the Americas,* IWGIA document No. 63, 1989.

20. Bunyard, P., 'Good News from Colombia', *Resurgence,* No.142, 1989.

21. *Latinamerica Press,* 4 October 1990.

22. Monbiot, G., *Amazon Watershed: the New Environmental Investigation,* Michael Joseph, London, 1991.

23. *ibid.*

24. *Latinamerica Press,* 4 October 1990.

25. Pearce, J., *Colombia – Inside the Labyrinth,* Latin American Bureau, 1990.

26. COICA, *op. cit.*

27. COICA, *Our Agenda for the Bilateral and Multilateral Funders of Amazon Development,* (Circular), 1989.

28. *ibid.*

29. Nugkuag, E., 'Analysis and Proposals Concerning Development Assistance and Ethnodevelopment', in *Indigenous Self-Development in the Americas, op. cit.*

30. Monbiot, *op. cit.*

31. *Crónica de Hoy* (Chile), 3 May 1990.

32. The Summer Institute of Linguistics presents itself as an academic institution but is widely known as a fundamentalist missionary foundation which has received money from USAID. See Stoll, D., *Fishers of Men or Founders of Empire? The Wycliffe Bible Translators in Latin America,* Zed Press and Cultural Survival, 1982.

chapter five

33. Ballesteros, M., 'Indigenous Resistance and Self-management', in *Indigenous Self-Development in the Americas, op. cit.*

34. Lewis, N., *The Missionaries*, McGraw Hill, 1988.

35. E.g. IWGIA, *Ethnocide: Mission Accomplished*, IWGIA document No.64, 1989.

36. 'You must all obey the governing authorities. Since all government comes from God, the civil authorities were appointed by God, and so anyone who resists authority is rebelling against God's decision and such an act is bound to be punished.' (Romans 13:1.)

37. IWGIA, *Yearbook 1989*, IWGIA, Copenhagen, 1990.

38. Wearne & Calvert, *op. cit.*

Acknowledgements: *My thanks to Hannah Scrase, Andrew Gray, Javier Farje, Reynaldo Mariqueo, Marcus Colchester, Elizabeth Rendell, Survival International and the Latin American Bureau for their invaluable help.*

chapter six

john king
THROUGH THE EYES OF ARTISTS

'And when we saw all those cities and villages built in the water and other great towns on dry land, and that straight and level causeway leading to Mexico, we were astounded. Those great towns and *cues* and buildings rising from the water, all made of stone, seemed like an enchanted vision from the tale of Amadis ...

'I say again that I stood looking at it, and thought that no land like it would ever be discovered in the whole world, because at that time Peru was neither known nor thought of. But today all that I then saw is overthrown and destroyed; nothing is left standing.'[1]

Bernal Díaz's *True History of the Conquest of New Spain*, was written in 1568 and recounted the first campaigns of Hernán Cortés, in which Díaz himself had fought some fifty years previously.

His is one of the most complex early accounts of the 'encounter of two worlds' which is being 'celebrated' five hundred years later. Díaz hints at two major stories that have been told and retold in the intervening centuries, neatly encapsulated here in the words of the writer Gerald Martin:

'The conquest involved the penetration of alien territories and societies, the invasion of that cultural space and the creation of a new race of people, not by consent but by violation.'[2]

The poet Octavio Paz argues, in his seminal essay 'The Labyrinth of Solitude' (1950), that Mexican development, or lack of development, is symbolised by that first 'violation', when the conqueror Cortés took by force the indigenous woman La Malinche. He sees the pattern of power in archetypal terms, between the *chingón* (the violator) and the *chingada* (the violated). Paz writes,

'The *Chingada* is the Mother forcibly opened, violated, or deceived. The *hijo de la chingada* is the offspring of violation, abduction or deceit. To the Mexican, dishonour consists of being the fruit of a violation.'[3]

Cultural violence is a dominant theme in Latin American history, from the overthrow of the Aztec temples in the sixteenth century

chapter six

('all that I then saw is overthrown and destroyed') to the more pervasive forms of late twentieth-century cultural homogenisation. In a deregulated, transnational world of signs and electronic impulses the losers, as always, will be those on the peripheries of the new technologies. Such pessimism seems to be echoed in the final sentence of Gabriel García Márquez's *One Hundred Years of Solitude*: 'everything written on them was unrepeatable since time immemorial and forever more, because races condemned to one hundred years of solitude did not have a second opportunity on earth.'[4] Eduardo Galeano, the Uruguayan writer, adds:

'To ensure the perpetuation of the current state of affairs in lands where every minute a child dies of disease or hunger, we have to be taught to see ourselves through the eyes of the oppressor. The law of the jungle, which is the law of the system, is sanctified, so that defeated peoples should accept their situation as their destiny.'[5]

The continent's other persistent theme is the impulse towards liberation. Galeano, again, states that, 'Latin America's contemporary reality does not derive from some indecipherable curse. My intention ... [is] to explore its history in order to explain it and to help to make it by opening up those spaces of liberty in which the victims and the defeated of the past might become the protagonists of the present.'[6]

Writers in society

The Latin American writer is a narrator, therefore, not just of stories relating crushing defeats but also of cultural resistance and cultural complexity. The utopian dream of national or continental liberation has beguiled many of the region's artists over the centuries. Differences of nationality, race, class and gender stand in the way of, but also fuel the desire for, the dream of liberation and the quest for cultural identity. It was put most clearly by the liberator, Simón Bolivar, in 1815:

'It is indeed a grandiose idea to form out of our New World one single nation with one single link connecting all its parts to one another and to the whole ... but this is not possible because remote climates, different situations, opposing interests and dissimilar characters divide America.'[7]

The conditions of unequal development in Latin America have also given artists a high profile and a recognised social function. The Mexican Carlos Fuentes states:

'Generally for us the main motive for writing is the weakness of the civil societies. If you don't say certain things they won't be said. It is a very powerful motivation ... and a continuing need.

When you consider that the most developed civil societies of Latin America would be Uruguay, Chile, Argentina and look what they've gone through, and are going through. You get Pinochet, *desaparecidos*, torture, generals, juntas. Think of countries that have no civil society like Nicaragua, El Salvador, Honduras, what do you expect from them? It's still a long road to be travelled. Good for novelists, bad for people.'[8]

To be such a spokesperson in society raises a number of vexed questions. What is the appropriate language with which to express particular situations? What is a 'national' reality in spaces already occupied by a multitude of cultures and invaded by transnational media? What is the relationship between artists (largely middle-class intellectuals) and the 'people' they hope to represent? And what, finally, is the true nature of 'popular' culture? The Paraguayan Augusto Roa Bastos describes one of the dilemmas for a writer brought up in a country such as Paraguay, where the majority of the indigenous population do not speak Spanish – the language of the Conquest:

'But when he writes in Spanish, the writer – and particularly the writer of fiction – feels himself to be suffering the most personal of alienations: linguistic exile. How far can he move from that part of reality and collective life that is expressed in Guaraní, from a Paraguayan culture marked indelibly with the sign of orality, or original mythic thought?'[9] Yet, for all the difficulties, few artists in the continent would disagree with Mario Vargas Llosa, who remarks that:

'In the USA, in Western Europe, to be a writer means generally ... to assume a personal responsibility ... In Peru, in Bolivia, in Nicaragua etcetera, on the contrary, to be a writer means, at the same time that you develop a personal literary work, you should serve, through your writing but also through your actions, as an active participant in the solution of the economic, political and cultural problems of your society. There is no way to escape this obligation.'[10]

Popular culture in Latin America

Mario Varga Llosa is one of Latin America's most successful writers. He reached a mass audience, however, only when he appeared on television as a presidential candidate for Peru. Colombia's Gabriel García Márquez is an internationally best-selling author, an almost unique phenomenon in the region. Across the continent his book *One Hundred Years of Solitude* has sold several million copies, although he is acutely aware that each night some 15 to 20 million Colombians tune in to an episode of a television soap-opera (*telenovela*) – more people in a single night than have read all his novels over the course of thirty-five years. As a result, García Márquez is now writing soap-operas to reach this vast and widespread audience. In his opinion, all culture is popular culture.[11]

'Popular culture' is a complex term, especially in Latin America, because it has to include both rural and urban cultures: everything from ritual, handicrafts, narratives, music, dance and iconography (in pre-capitalist or 'folk' cultures) to the mass media of radio, film, television and comics. In Brazil, for example, pre-capitalist forms of popular Catholicism (in the form of rituals and festivities) exist happily alongside *Dallas* or *Pantanal*, the latest ecological smash-hit soap-opera. García Canclini puts it well:

'Although capitalist development tends to absorb and standardise the forms of material and cultural production that preceded it, the subordination of traditional communities cannot be total, given the inability of industrial capitalism itself to give work, culture and medical attention to all, and given the resistance of the ethnic groups who defend their identity.'[12]

Oral popular poetry and song, whether as *folhetos* (broadsheets) or sung by *cantadores* (the direct descendants of the troubadours of medieval literature), help people to structure and make sense of everyday experience. For millions of Brazilians this is a far more meaningful cultural medium than, for example, the sprawling novels of Jorge Amado, Brazil's most popular novelist.

Nevertheless, it is difficult and to a great extent wrong to attempt strict definitions of the terms 'rural' and 'urban', for, as Rowe and Schelling point out, 'to see the city as a corrupting and contaminating force, in opposition to a pure and authentic culture rooted in the rural areas, is to indulge in nostalgia.'[13] Today, 75 per cent of the population of Latin America now live in cities. But, more importantly, the city is the centre of power and information; the point of transmission of cultures, be they urban or rural in origin; the site of the modern and the postmodern, of satellite and cable television, of transnational culture and comic strips – in short, of the culture industry, together with the technologies on which it depends, reaching electronically into the most remote hinterlands and between social groups and classes. All cultures in Latin America, therefore, are now mediated to some extent by the city.

An earlier essay in this book [chapter five] has pointed to the cultural death but also the cultural resistance of indigenous communities. The same points can be made about urban cultures. The 'culture industry' tends to iron out differences. It has been argued that, unlike great works of art, industrial culture creates mass deception and a single national market for all cultural products. Yet there are also countless examples of popular culture resisting or working through the gaps and spaces of this homogenising process, from popular radio stations in local *barrios* and *favelas*, to alternative video, the subversive use of genre (such as soap-opera) and the appropriation of well-known ficticious characters to serve a local context – *Superbarrio*, for example, is an adaption of the comic-strip/film character Superman, and has become an important symbol of popular resistance for Mexican social movements.

Popular culture is, therefore, transformative and can adapt to new situations, showing that the people are not merely passive recipients of alien or distorted values. If the oft-used term 'acculturation' suggests the one way movement of culture (that the dominant culture will always swamp native cultures) then more flexible terms such as 'transculturation' (the mutual transformation of cultures) should be used in the Latin American context. The Brazilian anthropophagous movement made the point well in the 1920s. Rather than assuming that the colonisers would always absorb the riches of their defeated enemies, the Brazilians suggested that their cannibal ancestors, the Tupy Indians, could 'cannibalise' the culture of their European conquerors, digesting the positive aspects and spitting out the negative points. This points to a more positive way of viewing the transformative functions of popular culture.

Fiction and poetry

In the mid-1960s, Latin American fiction began both to reach an expanding Latin American audience and receive greater international attention. Today, it is widely regarded in the English speaking-world and beyond (especially in France and Italy) as perhaps the most dynamic of all modern literatures. It has greatly influenced writers from a variety of different cultures: penetrate the surface of writers such as Italo Calvino, Milan Kundera, George Perec, Pvic, Paul Auster, Umberto Eco and Salman Rushdie and you can feel Borges and García Márquez in the bones. Hispanic Americans are currently leading a major assault on Anglo-Saxon culture. The recent success of the Cuban-American Oscar Hijuelos, with *The Mambo King Sings Songs of Love,* is one of many examples that can be given across the cultural spectrum.

This success was firmly rooted in the novelists' increasing ability to fuse European forms with Latin American contents, to learn the lessons of modernism, but also to apply them to a complex political and social reality. The process began in the 1920s, with writers such as Miguel Angel Asturias, Mário de Andrade, Alejo Carpentier and Jorge Luis Borges, and was completed with the writers of the 1960s, the most visible of whom were Mario Vargas Llosa (Peru), Julio Cortázar (Argentina), Carlos Fuentes (Mexico) and Gabriel García Márquez (Colombia). The 'boom' period of Latin American fiction during the 1960s had a number of important, lasting effects in the continent which are still felt today. It created for itself an increased reading public both in Latin America and abroad. It also allowed for the 'professionalisation' of the writer. Before the 1960s, most writers needed another source of income to supplement earnings from their writing. Many found employment in areas such as diplomacy, education and journalism. But during the 1960s the better-known writers began to reach a point where they were able to live off the financial fruits of their writing.

The professional writer also became something of a media star and an increasingly important political figure who was ambiguously related to the state (that 'philanthropic ogre', to use Octavio Paz's evocative phrase). This higher social profile has placed writers firmly in the cultural market-place, which exerts constant pressure to produce new work and has led, on occasion, to a drop in quality. The 'boom' years also helped to create a sense of community among Latin American writers that had not really existed before the 1960s. Even though a number of them have now fallen out ideologically, the 'community spirit' still remains. The 'boom' also signalled a great upsurge of self-confidence among the writers, an awareness that they need no longer be bogged down in regionalism or exoticism, or stand in awe of North American or European models. They were, as Vargas Llosa said, 'creators' not 'primitives'; and, in the words of Paz, they were 'contemporary with the rest of the world'. The continent's writers still possess this self-confidence – and with good reason, for Latin American fiction is now as good as anything currently being written elsewhere in the world.

Although the key figures of the 'boom' period were male, women writers have been receiving considerable attention in recent years, following the growth of feminism and the establishment of a number of women's presses. Important precursor figures were rediscovered, like the brilliant seventeenth-century poet, intellectual and nun Sor Juana Inés de la Cruz. A number of talented writers – including Clarice Lispector, Silvina Ocampo, Elena Poniatowska, Luisa Valenzuela and Margo Glantz – have at last received deserved recognition. The status of women's writing in Latin America will certainly continue to grow over the course of the next ten years.

Despite the confidence of the last thirty years, it is not clear that subsequent generations of writers will have such an impact. After all, the likes of Fuentes, García Márquez, Vargas Llosa, Cortázar, Borges, Puig and Roa Bastos are a difficult act to follow. It is likely that we will still be reading the works of these writers during the next decade, but it is difficult to predict another 'mini-boom' of younger authors successfully toppling these father-figures.

Latin American poets have not had the same international profile as their counterparts in fiction, although Octavio Paz recently won the Nobel Prize for literature (a prize that has been bestowed on other Latin American poets, such as Gabriela Mistral and Pablo Neruda).

But to measure success merely in terms of access to the great traditions of international modernism is largely to miss the point. The relationship of Latin American poets to the cultures of Europe and North America has always been ambiguous: a relationship of strong attraction tempered by the powerful lure of the vision of an autonomous, self-confident and independent Latin America. While some Latin American poets (such as Rubén Darío of Nicaragua) clearly owed much to European traditions, often living there for years, there is another tradition which the critics Mike Gonzalez and David Treece have called,

'... an echo of public dissent, of common language ... [which] has broken its isolation not by occupying a subordinate place at the Elysian fields of cultural tradition, but rather in the rediscovery of a collective voice and a collective experience found at times in popular culture, at times in shared ritual or song, at times in folk memory.'[14]

It has sought, in the words of the Nicaraguan poet-priest Ernesto Cardenal, 'the community of the shadows to be its voice'. 'Conversational' or 'public poetry' draws on the specific circumstances of Latin America, and has found important exponents in the recent literatures of, for example, Cuba and Nicaragua.

Central America, with its low literacy levels and the weakness of the middle classes ensured the persistence of an oral culture: it was poetry, therefore, rather than the novel, that became an appropriate form for the beginnings of a new awareness and identity. Poetry and song can also be useful instruments of mobilisation and propaganda. In such situations the gap between private desires and public needs narrows or disappears altogether.

Poetry in Latin America, therefore, covers a range of writing, from the anonymous troubadours of north-eastern Brazil to hermetic private utterance, from what has been called 'the secrecy of private language to a gathering of voices'. Juan Gelman, an Argentine poet, writes:

'With this poem, you won't take power,' he says
'With these verses you will not make the Revolution,' he says
'You will not make the Revolution with thousands of verses,'
                                                   he says
He sits at the table and writes.

Art and *artesanía*

In 1989 the Hayward Gallery in London organised the most extensive retrospective of Latin American art yet seen. It surprised and disconcerted many critics who could not find the vocabulary to deal with the different styles of painting or the popular arts and crafts on show like basket-weaving, textiles, ceramics, metal- and feather-work, and masks. Conventional divisions between 'high' and 'popular' art seemed to be challenged both by the artists themselves and by the unusual layout of the gallery.

In a stereotypical vision of the world (echoed by many of the critics), Latin American art has been reduced to Western notions of primitivism – from Madonna's colourful appropriation of the great radical painter Frida Kahlo, Breton's designation of Mexico as the 'surrealist continent', to the tourist industry's ready assimilation of folk art. It is against such stereotypes that artists have fought to mark out a distinctive set of images for the continent. The Uruguayan painter Torres García drew a famous sketch which reverses the map of South America so that the South Pole is at the top and the Equator at the bottom. 'Our north', he said, 'is the south', and that by reversing the globe 'we have a true idea of our position, not how the rest of the world would like it.'[15]

But museums or galleries are far from ideal showcases for indigenous artefacts or *artesanía,* which have now become an integral part of folklore and which modern states in Latin America have used to project and amplify their own nationalist identity. This can be seen in the extraordinary anthropological museums in Mexico City or the 'Monumento a América Latina', a massive cultural complex housing a permanent exhibition of Latin American folklore in São Paulo, Brazil.

However well-planned they may be, such centres tend to present the 'indigenous' and *artesanía* as artefacts of disappearing, dying cultures, or as part of a living museum rather than manifestations of vibrant, living cultures. There is the danger that indigenous cultures just become spectacle, enabling the tourists who encounter them to be rejuvenated and seduced into thinking that, 'poverty does not need to be eradicated, and that ancient tools may fit in well with modern cookery'.[16]

Within the realm of 'high art', the museum or gallery has also tended to highlight the cultural power of the metropolis. Few Latin American artists have international reputations because the art market is centred on a small number of galleries, mainly in New York. In the art world, internationalism is largely a one-way marketing strategy, reaching out from the centre of cultural power to other parts of the world. Movements like abstract expressionism and pop art, for instance, were largely created by New York art dealers such as Leo Castelli.

Latin American art, however, lives in a continual dialogue with the metropolis. Painters such as Alberto Gironella constantly debate with the colonial past, as shown by his obsessive, fragmented versions of Velázquez's portraits of the Spanish royal family. Botero from Colombia also borrows from Velázquez and Goya and, in his own words, 'puffs up' his characters so that they are no more than empty caricatures, parodies of colonial grandeur.[17]

The region's artists have also worked seriously with the debates and mythologies of surrealism: the work of Matta (Chile) and Tamayo (Mexico) has explored the world of the unconscious, investigating dislocation and isolation. Traditional landscape painting has also been infused with specifically Latin American contents, though as Valerie Fraser has pointed out, the artists are aware of contradictions: the land has been colonised by so many different forces, such as anthropologists, US mining companies, travellers and missionaries. For example, the Uruguayan artist Gamarra creates an atmosphere of exotic jungle fantasy which is broken by small but very discordant elements – a distant aeroplane, a savage colonial encounter or a Toyota Land Cruiser aboard a raft on an Amazonian river.

Artists have also succeeded in taking the debate out of the galleries and into the street. The great Mexican muralists Orozco, Siqueiros and Rivera created a new form of public art with their massive paintings on the sides of public buildings. They also led some of the most sophisticated debates in the 1920s concerning art and revolution and pioneered a number of innovatory techniques which were taken up – and emptied of their political content – by North American modernists in the 1930s and 1940s. Latin Americans helped to pioneer kinetic art and were in the forefront of 1960s movements to disrupt the complacency of the dealer/gallery system.

Many practitioners have also resisted official definitions of art. An important aspect of resistance against this cultural pigeonholing is the way in which the traditional skills of women have been used to create entirely new art forms, such as the Chilean

chapter six

arpilleras – patchwork pictures often with sharply expressed political content.[18] As Dawn Ades has pointed out, the main problem for the artists in Latin America is, 'on the one hand, resisting marginalisation and entering an international artistic discourse without losing a sense of his or her own identity and, on the other, of avoiding the further marginalisation of native culture.'[19]

Music

Latin American music draws on three main sources: indigenous Amerindian sources, the colonising Hispanic music and the transported African music. Any comprehensive survey – and as yet there is no one study that offers such an overview – would have to look at rural contexts: the function of music, for example, in religious festivals and pilgrimages; the combination of Catholic and indigenous elements in music, dance and instrumentation (in particular in carnival festivals); and the transformations wrought by the migrations to the cities. For example, *samba* grew out of traditional African cultures in which music did not have an existence that was separate to the religious life of the community – a life in which music, dance, ritual and myth were all essential elements.

In the cities of Brazil, black popular culture developed the world of *samba* out of these traditional forms and was strongly allied with religious cults such as Candomblé. *Samba* drew on a counter-culture of play and leisure (the culture of the outsider) and was collective, as a combination of music and dance based on a syncopated rhythm. It became an integral part of carnival but later lost some of its critical and radical thrust as the middle classes and the state gradually turned it into a national symbol of exoticism.[20]

Another music/dance form which began in the urban slums and later became gentrified on cosmopolitan dance floors was the *tango* from Argentina. Originally seen as a dance so provocative that it could only be performed by men, it developed a song form in the 1910s which was popularised by Latin America's greatest musical superstar, Carlos Gardel. The pessimistic lyrics of loss and nostalgia as well as the tightly choreographed dance are still an integral part of Argentinian culture and have wider regional resonances. Together with the *tango*, other rhythms invaded the world at large. In the 1930s and 1940s the *son cubano* – which included *bolero, mambo, rumba, conga* and *chachacha* – became the basis of big-band rhythms throughout the world. The most recent additions are *salsa* and *lambada*. *Salsa* is mainly known as a dance, but Willie Colón and Rubén Blades have sharpened it

through the eyes of artists

by adding biting lyrics. Blades' song *El padre Antonio y su monaguillo Andrés* ('Father Anthony and his altar-boy Andrés'), which deals with the death squads in El Salvador and is a homage to Archbishop Romero, recently topped the music charts in many Latin American countries.

The 1960s brought innovations in music and song which have loosely been termed the 'New Song' movement. Jan Fairley attempts a definition:

'The ties that bind the movement are predominantly ideological as regards a struggle for socialism and self-determination at both national and continental levels and the struggle for both a national and continental popular music, with right of access to an audience denied it by both particular governments and commercial policies of national and multinational companies. The argument espoused to date by those involved is one of cultural imperialism and hegemony.'[21]

The main exponents of 'New Song' included Silvio Rodríguez and Pablo Milanés (Cuba), the Parras, Inti Illimani and Quilapayún (Chile), Daniel Viglietti (Uruguay), Amparo Ochoa (Mexico) and Chico Buarque (Brazil). The music reflected the optimism of the 1960s and early 1970s, the imaginative proximity of social revolution and the shared horizons of experience and desire.

It was also crucial when these dreams were shattered under the brutal dictatorships of the 1970s and early 1980s, as the 'New Song' musicians became an important part of exile culture, with the need to proclaim solidarity and resistance. Today, they are playing an important role in consolidating the new democracies.

Cultural resistance has also been expressed through rock music, which has so often been seen as a form of English-speaking domination. In Argentina under the dictatorship, for example, 'national rock' was a form of underground culture in the harsh years of the repression. When the dictatorship began to crumble, open-air concerts drew massive crowds hostile to the government. The lyrics of Charly García spoke for a generation of young people who had been savagely repressed.

Given the vast numbers of young people in Latin America, music will continue to be a vital element of cultural development.

Cinema

Latin America has always had to compete on unequal terms with the high-cost technological advances of Western cinema. Many national film industries took years, for example, to convert to making sound movies; and whole industries today work with

chapter six

annual funds equivalent to the budget of a single Hollywood feature film.[22] Financial constraints make film-making a high-risk business. The situation is well analysed in Carlos Sorin's *La pelicula del rey* ('A King and His Movie') of 1985. This film recounts a young man's desperate attempt to make a film about Orelie Antoine de Tounens, a Frenchman who in 1861 founded the kingdom of Araucania and Patagonia in southern Argentina. The Frenchman's deranged quest is mirrored by that of the young film-maker, struggling with no money, a dwindling cast and an inhospitable terrain.

The dominant Hollywood film model soon succeeded in universalising a 'correct' way of filming, a 'correct' way of seeing. Film-makers in Latin America consistently work within or against this set of values, in a market-place geared to the production, distribution and exhibition of the Hollywood product. In a recent interview Miguel Littín, a prolific Chilean film-maker both at home and abroad, asked why Latin American cinema had not had the impact abroad of the continent's novelists, many of whom are now recognised as among the world's most influential writers. At one level, the answer is simple: cinema (as an industrial and a technological form) is more conditioned than literature by the economics of the culture industry. Latin American films are rarely distributed and exhibited in British cinemas, for example, and are given late-night slots on television.

When discussing popular cinema in Latin America it must be acknowledged that the term 'popular' is not a neutral one. While it is true that the major audiences in Latin America, at the outset, were working-class people in the expanding cities of the region, this did not make cinema inherently democratic or make it reflect their own lives and struggles. In fact, commercial entrepreneurs saw that their own profit lay in the new technologies and the rapid distribution of a standard product across wide areas. From the early years of the twentieth century in Latin America, with very few exceptions, cinema did not reproduce real, lived environments, but rather particular forms of spectacle, based mainly on imported genres. Since the 1910s, when the big US feature films such as *Civilisation* and *Birth of a Nation* first achieved remarkable success in Latin America, US cinema has captured roughly 95 per cent of the region's screen time. The *Moving Picture World* journal of 1916 was remarkably prescient when it stated that, 'The Yankee invasion of the Latin American film-market shows unmistakable signs of growing serious. It may, before long, develop into a rush as to a New Eldorado.'

Cinema in Latin America, therefore, constantly redefined the 'popular'. Local producers had to acknowledge the impact of

Hollywood in forming popular taste. This does not mean that they had slavishly to reproduce the Hollywood formula: for some it was a question of using this imposed formula to say what they wanted. The earlier producers found a space in the market-place, especially with the advent of sound, by drawing on the strong traditions of popular theatre, such as theatrical spectacle or vaudeville and tent shows.[23] Many of the most enduring screen actors and actresses came from this background.

Music, comedy and melodrama, often combined in one film, were the successful formulae on offer. Carlos Gardel, Argentina's *tango* superstar, became a popular screen presence. Cinemas on numerous occasions had to stop the film to rerun his most famous songs. Cantinflas, the leering Mexican comedian, and the Brazilian comic Oscarito had a huge following throughout Latin America. Some of these early films did, however, have a raw energy which was diluted as the laws of the market-place demanded rapid reproduction and a steady supply of a standard product. The Mexican industry of the 1940s became a mini-Hollywood within Latin America by successfully exploiting two or three fixed genres. Among its most popular stars were the 'Edenic' couple Dolores del Río and Pedro Armendáriz, the haughty María Félix and the macho crooner Jorge Negrete.

A reaction to cinema's growing commercialisation occurred in the 1950s. It sought to oppose the idealisation formed by and in a foreign culture, by portraying the experience and actions of Latin American men and women in real environments and acknowledging that histories are made up of the aspirations, victories and often crushing defeats of real people, who do not necessarily follow the plangent rhythms of singing *charros* (Mexican cowboys). The film-maker could draw on this experience in a variety of roles: as teacher, prophet, ethnographer or dispassionate observer. Most prominent film-makers of this period were fired by some sort of socialist principle, putting their cameras at the service of social criticism or revolutionary social change. This period produced a body of remarkable films and generated complex theoretical debates which are still relevant today.

These 'new cinemas' grew up throughout the continent, powered by film-makers such as Nelson Pereira dos Santos, Glauber Rocha and Ruy Guerra (Brazil), Fernando Birri and Fernando Solanas (Argentina), Miguel Littín and Raúl Ruiz (Chile), Jorge Sanjinés (Bolivia) and the revolutionary Cuban cinema of Santiago Alvárez, Tomás Gutiérrez Alea and Humberto Solás. All sought to regenerate national cinemas and seek pan-American solutions to problems of underdevelopment and cultural colonialism. The dreams and illusions of the 1960s are clearly demonstrated in the endur-

chapter six

ing films of the period, such as Rocha's 1963 *Deus e o diablo na terra do sol* ('Black God, White Devil), Gutiérrez Alea's *Memorias del subdesarrollo* ('Memories of Underdevelopment'), Solanas's *La hora de los hornos* ('The Hour of the Furnaces') and Jorge Sanjinés's *Yawar Mallku* ('Blood of the Condor') – all three made in 1968.

The military dictatorships of the 1970s generated an important culture of resistance – demonstrated in particular by the remarkable work of Chilean film-makers in exile – but also a reappraisal of the limits of what was possible during the slow transition to democracy. The films that in Argentina most successfully spoke of the traumas of the military dictatorship (1976-82) and the painful readjustment to the present – María Luisa Bemberg's 1984 *Camila* and Luis Puenzo's 1985 *La historia oficial* ('The Official Version') – both worked within the well-loved genre of melodrama. There seemed no longer a space for radical films outside the mainstream. Today, the popular is once again viewed in terms of what is successful, but it is now a far more precarious marketplace than that of the 1940s. Cinema screens are fighting a losing battle against other more dominant players in the culture industry, such as television and, in particular, the new technologies of satellite, cable and video.

Cinema in Latin America has always had to contend with the stop-go nature of the continent's weak economies and the continual shadow of censorship. The state has played the role of both short-term saviour and censor, sometimes (as in the case of Brazil) actually banning films that it had helped to finance. One such example was Roberto Farias's 1982 *Pra frente Brasil* ('Onward Brazil'), which was banned for several months despite its rather bland analysis of state repression.

Censorship can vary from subtle forms of internal persuasion, such as the control of financial patronage, to outright violence and brutality. Governments pay particular attention to those media that reach the widest public or least educated members of society: radio, television and cinema. The history of Latin American cinema has lurched between libertarian and authoritarian views concerning freedom of expression. Self-censorship is obviously prevalent where film-making or distribution depend on funding by commercial advertisers or governments, falling uncomfortably under the shadow of the 'philanthropic ogre' state.

While there have been countless examples of the ogre in action, there have also been a number of significant examples of 'philanthropy' – where the state has developed the market for cinema or even protected cinema from market forces. Most national film industries have, at some point, needed financial aid from the state in order to guard them, in some small way, against the power of Hollywood. In the case of Latin America, virtually no protection was given to the weak, underdeveloped industries during the early years of cinema. But from the 1930s to the 1950s the three big cinema industries – Argentina, Brazil and Mexico – received varied amounts of state assistance.

Now, with a deepening economic crisis throughout the continent, state subsidies are declining everywhere. While film-makers have constantly questioned the limitations imposed by working with the state, they realise only too well the further limitations imposed by working without it. The state has maintained Cuban cinema over the last thirty years and the brief flourish of Argentine cinema in the mid-1980s was also aided by government institutes. Currently the only buoyant cinema in Latin America is that of Mexico, where the state is offering major incentives to film-makers.

The future, therefore, seems particularly uncertain. We have seen that the history of Latin American cinema has been an uneasy relationship with Hollywood that has constantly wavered between attraction and rejection. Today, Hollywood itself is losing ground to television, and to an increasingly powerful international media order which is fighting for control of cable and video.

Latin America has produced its own media conglomerates, in particular the extremely powerful Televisa in Mexico and TV Globo in Brazil. Some lucid critics realise that compromise will have to be made with this new order. García Márquez, for example, is currently engaged in making a progressive TV soap-opera. More contact with television, the production of films for a wider Latin American market, rather than for just one country, are possible strategies for survival.

It is encouraging that, in spite of economic difficulties and the new political climate, there are still film-makers with an idea in their heads and a camera in their hands, to paraphrase the Brazilian director Glauber Rocha's famous dictum. García Márquez captured this mood of optimism in a speech to celebrate the inauguration of the Latin American Film Foundation in 1985. His remarks offer a suitable conclusion to this brief overview of Latin American culture.

'Between 1952 and 1955, four of us who are now on board this boat studied at the Centro Sperimentale in Rome: Julio García Espinosa, Vice Minister of Culture for Cinema, Fernando Birri, the great pope of the New Latin American cinema, Tomás Gutiérrez Alea, one of its most notable craftsmen and I, who wanted nothing more in life than to become the film-maker I never became ... The fact that this evening we are still talking like madmen about the

chapter six

same thing, after thirty years, and that there are with us so many Latin Americans from all parts and from different generations, also talking about the same thing, I take as one further proof of an indestructible idea.'[24]

John King is a senior lecturer in Latin American cultural history at the University of Warwick. He has written a number of books, the most recent being Magical Reels: A History of Cinema in Latin America, *published in 1991 by Verso.*

References

1. Díaz, Bernal, *The True History of the Conquest of New Spain*, Penguin, Harmondsworth, 1963, pp214-15.

2. Martin, Gerald, *Journeys Through the Labyrinth: Latin American Fiction in the Twentieth Century*, Verso, London, 1989, p15.

3. Paz, Octavio, *The Labyrinth of Solitude: Life and Thought in Mexico*, Grove Press, New York, 1961, p79. Recently issued in Britain by Penguin Books.

4. García Márquez, Gabriel, *One Hundred Years of Solitude*, Penguin, Harmondsworth, 1972, p383.

5. Eduardo Galeano, in George Theiner (ed.), *They Shoot Writers Don't They*, Faber and Faber, London, 1984, p191.

6. Galeano, Eduardo, 'Notes Towards a Self-Portrait', quoted in Martin, *op. cit.*, p359.

7. Bolivar, Simón, 'The Jamaica Letter', 1815, quoted in Martin, *op. cit.*, p30.

8. Carlos Fuentes, interview with John King in John King (ed.), *Latin American Fiction: A Survey*, Faber and Faber, London, 1987, p150-1.

9. Augusto Roa Bastos, *ibid.*, p302.

10. Mario Vargas Llosa, in *They Shoot Writers Don't They?*, *op. cit.*, p162.

11. See the *South Bank Show* television documentary directed by Holly Aylett, 'Tales After Solitude', London, 1989.

12. Néstor García Canclini, quoted in W. Rowe & V. Schelling, *Memory and Modernity: Popular Culture in Latin America*, Verso, London, 1991.

13. *ibid.*

14. Mike Gonzalez & David Treece, introduction to *The Gathering of Voices: Latin American Poetry*, Verso, London, 1992.

15. Quoted in Dawn Ades, *Art in Latin America*, Catalogue, Hayward Gallery, London, 1989, p285.

16. Néstor García Canclini, quoted in Rowe & Schelling, *op. cit.*

17. This paragraph is based on Oriana Baddeley and Valerie Fraser, *Drawing the Line: Art and Identity in Latin America*, Verso, London, 1989, especially Fraser's analyses of Gironella, Botero and Gamarra.

18. *ibid.*, chapter VI.
19. Ades, *op. cit.*, p300.
20. See Schelling's analysis of Brazilian urban culture in Rowe & Schelling, *op. cit.*
21. Jan Fairley in 'Folk and Popular Music', S. Collier, H. Blakemore & T. Skidmore (eds.), *The Cambridge Encylopedia of Latin America and the Caribbean*, Cambridge, 1985, pp379-82.
22. For an analysis of Latin American cinema, see John King, *Magical Reels: A History of Cinema in Latin America,* Verso, London, 1991.
23. It will be noted that this chapter does not contain a separate section on theatre. Although many readers will be acquainted with novels, poetry, cinema, painting and even soap-opera from Latin America, very few will have had access to the region's theatre, although the recent LIFT international theatre festival in London (July-August 1991) did contain original work by Ariel Dorfman (Chile) and Griselda Gámbaro (Argentina). Until now, no Latin American dramatist has succeeded in building up an international following and work travels very infrequently outside the region. Recognition of this work is long overdue, as indeed is a general book in English on Latin American theatre. Partial accounts include L.F. Lyday and G.W. Woodyards, *Dramatists in Revolt: the New Latin American Theatre* (University of Texas Press, Austin and London, 1976) and *The Latin American Theatre Review,* (University of Kansas). The work of Catherine Boyle at King's College, London, is beginning to fill this gap. See, for example, her 'Griselda Gámbaro and the female dramatist', in Susan Bassnett (ed.), *Knives and Angels: Women Writers in Latin America* (Zed, London, 1990, pp145-57). Such a history would need to include the strong tradition of music hall and vaudeville in the late nineteenth and early twentieth centuries. It would examine the development of professional dramatists in Argentina (Eichelbaum, Arlt, Nalé Roxlo) and Mexico (Villaurrutia, Gorostiza and Usigli) during the 1930s who produced original works and introduced Pirandello, Chekhov, O'Neill and other influential playwrights to the region. It would also look at the growth of radical theatre in the 1960s and 1970s, which were often closely aligned to the developing movements for social change of that period. Perhaps the best known theoretician of the time was the Brazilian Augusto Boal, who used theatre as a form of 'conscientisation' (consciousness-raising) in rural areas. Other examples are the Chilean university theatre groups of the 1960s and under the government of the Popular Unity party, and the pioneering Cuban Escambray theatre group that worked in Cuban rural areas. Theatre also became important under the dictatorships in many Latin American countries in the 1970s, as a form of social protest. Censors looked closely at newspapers, television and the cinema: they often did not perceive the radical thrust of theatre.
24. Gabriel García Marquez, quoted in King, *op. cit.,* p252.

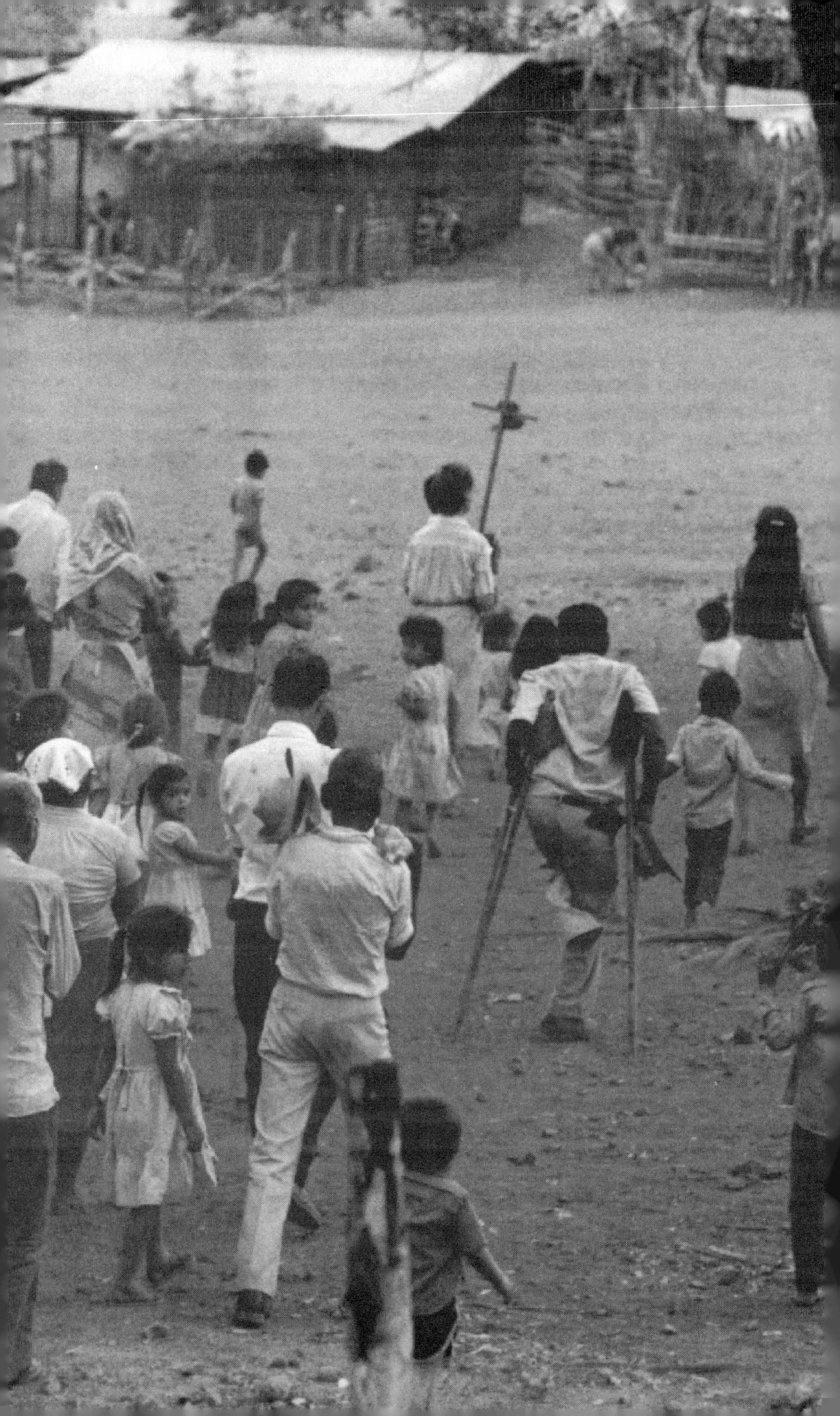

chapter seven

george gelber
THE CHURCH IN LATIN AMERICA

Christianity arrived in the Americas with Christopher Columbus in the same year that Granada, the last stronghold of the Moors in Spain, fell to the forces of Ferdinand and Isabella. Indeed, Columbus's last meeting with Queen Isabella before his first voyage to the New World took place in the Spanish camp outside Granada, which was then still in the hands of the Moors. The centuries-long war against the Moors had been a crusade as well as a battle for territory. The methods and the attitudes with which it was fought were carried over the seas by Columbus and those who followed him. The Conquest of America, therefore, was also regarded as a crusade.

The singular alliance between Church and state in the American colonies of Spain was brought about by the weakness of the Church. The papacy had no means with which to undertake independent evangelisation and, as it were, sub-contracted this task to the Spanish and Portuguese monarchs. Under this arrangement, known as the *patronato*, the monarchs appointed the bishops of Latin America.

Two years after Columbus's first voyage the Spanish and Portuguese monarchs signed the Treaty of Tordesillas under the aegis of Pope Alexander VI, dividing their western territories: the Portuguese were given all land to the east of an imaginary north-south line 370 leagues to the west of the Azores, and the Spaniards all territories to the west of this line.

Like Columbus, the *conquistadores* were obsessed by gold. The brutality of their conquest, first of the island of Hispaniola (present-day Dominican Republic and Haiti) and then of Mexico and Peru, might be seen as unexceptional in terms of the age in which they lived.

But even at the time there were critics of the violence of the *conquistadores*. On the fourth Sunday of Advent, 1511, a Dominican friar named Antonio de Montesinos, preached before a specially-invited congregation on the island of Hispaniola that

The way forward. A refugee community in El Salvador celebrates the faith which brought them through war and exile and back to thier homeland. Photo by Rhodri Jones.

chapter seven

included the governor, Diego Columbus, Christopher's son. The friar's words were a thundering denunciation of the treatment of the people of Hispaniola only nineteen years after the arrival of the Spaniards:

'You are all in mortal sin. You live and die in it, because of the cruelty and tyranny with which you treat these innocent peoples. Tell me, by what right and by what justice do you hold these poor Indians in such cruel and horrible servitude? With what authority have you waged such detestable wars against these people in their gentle and peaceful lands, where you have killed uncounted numbers with unheard-off death and destruction? How can you keep them so weary and oppressed, neither giving them food nor healing the ills which strike them down, caused by the excessive work which you give them, so they die on you. I should say, rather, you kill them to get more and more gold every day. And what care have you for teaching them so that they can come to know their God and creator, to be baptised, to attend mass, to observe feast days and Sundays? Are these not men? Do they not have rational souls? Are you not obliged to love them as yourselves? Do you not understand this? Do you not feel this? How can you be so utterly and deeply asleep?'[1]

The words of Montesinos could equally well have been used to castigate the treatment of the Andean Indians in the mines of Potosí, one of the harshest labour régimes the world has ever known, where the miners were allowed out of the mine only on Sundays to attend mass. Such denunciations by men like Antonio de Montesinos did little to impede the serious tasks of empire-building and getting rich. With a few heroic exceptions, the Catholic Church, as an institution, was the pliant companion of a colonial régime designed to extract wealth from Latin America. The preparatory document for the fourth conference of Latin American bishops to be held in Santo Domingo, in the Dominican Republic, in 1992, speaks tactfully of 'light and shade' in the record of five hundred years of evangelisation, anxious to avoid the excesses of either the 'dark' or the 'rose-tinted' versions of the history of the Church in Latin America.

The evangelisation of Latin America was carried out mainly by the religious orders, which were often unhappy at being yoked together with the military and money-making aspects of the Conquest. Jesuits and Dominicans both made strenuous efforts to work as independently as they could, because the conduct of the *conquistadores* was such a contradiction with the gospel they came to announce. Indeed, mere association with the *conquistadores* often proved fatal. On the north coast of the Spanish Main (present-day Venezuela) a number of Dominican missionaries were killed in 1513 because Spanish ships were raiding the area for slaves at the time. Six years later, the local people killed two more missionaries and burnt down their missions either, as the historian Francisco López de Gomara commented, 'because of their natural wickedness or because they were forced to labour in pearl-fishing' (pearls being the substitute for gold as a source of wealth on the coast of the Spanish Main).[2]

The Dominican, Bartolomé de las Casas, was one of the first to champion the cause of the Indians. His great history of 'The Indies' records Antonio de Montesinos's denunciation of the exploitation of the native inhabitants of Hispaniola and his own conversion from local settler to priest and defender of the Indians. As Bishop of Chiapas in Mexico, Bartolomé de las Casas prevailed upon the viceroy to let the Dominicans establish a mission – without using military force or being accompanied by settlers – in Tuzutlán, Guatemala, where the local people were still resisting the Spaniards. The Dominican missionaries christened the area Vera Paz ('True Peace'), the name it bears to this day. Even so, in 1544, twelve years after the mission was set up, the local people rose up against the missionaries, killing thirty and driving the rest away.

In recent years Vera Paz has been the scene of some of the worst atrocities by the Guatemalan army against the Mayan Indian population. The present bishop, Gerardo Flores, has been their ardent defender, giving them protection from the army in the massive colonial Dominican convent which adjoins the cathedral of Cobán.

At the time of their expulsion in 1767 the Jesuits controlled enormous extensions of land in Paraguay, called the *reducciones* ('reductions'). These were colonies of Guaraní Indians which the Jesuits administered with firmness and paternalistic loving kindness. The prosperous *reducciones* gave protection to the Guaranís against the harsh labour demands of the local landowners.

Three murdered Paraguayan Jesuits were beatified in 1934 for their evangelisation of the Indians. One of them, Roque González, came from a local aristocratic family and was called upon to resist the pressures on the *reducciones* from his own brother, who was the local representative of the Spanish Crown.

During the three hundred years of the empire the Church grew rich and amassed great privileges. In 1792, the city of Lima (in modern-day Peru) had 3,941 buildings, of which 1,135 belonged to the Catholic Church as churches, chapels, colleges, hospitals, convents, and so on. One source records the Archbishop of Lima

chapter seven

as earning a salary of 65,000 pesos a year – 4,000 more than the salary of the viceroy, the highest political authority of the colony. An ordinary priest received 250 pesos a year, an income which put him on a level with a gentleman of modest means.[3]

The Catholic Church, however, was an apparently effective instrument of conversion or evangelisation. Although many indigenous beliefs and practices survived within the practice of Catholic religion – with pre-Conquest deities being thinly disguised as Christian saints, for instance – a hundred years after the Conquest there was no other openly acknowledged religion on the continent to challenge it. The Church in Latin America, however, depended on the Spanish empire for its power and its privileges. When the Spanish empire collapsed after the Napoleonic wars, the most natural course for the Church was to strike a bargain with the new rulers of Latin America. But they, whatever their political views about the place of the Church in society, wanted to inherit the powers which the Spanish monarchs had enjoyed under the *patronato*. At the same time the papacy, under pressure from Spain, refused to recognise the new Latin American republics. This refusal was maintained until 1835, some fifteen to twenty years after most countries had won their independence. The Vatican then relented because many bishops had left the continent or died, leaving their sees vacant: Honduras, for instance, was without a resident bishop for forty-one years; the archdiocese of Mexico was vacant from 1822 to 1840; and Bolivia had not one bishop at the time of its independence.[4]

The end of the empire initiated a period of steady decline of the Church throughout Spanish America. Many who priests had played important roles in the struggles for independence in Latin America enjoyed the support of liberal forces in society. But the opposition of Rome to European liberalism, which was virulently anti-clerical in France, soon extended to the Americas. As a result 'Conservative' came to be associated with 'Catholic', and 'Liberal' with 'anti-clerical'. The Church supported the conservatives throughout Latin America, in the hope of recovering some of its lost privileges. But throughout the nineteenth century, governments chipped away at the privileges which the Church had enjoyed under the empire. In Latin America as a whole, after a century of independence, the Catholic Church was poorer, had less priests and was less distinguished intellectually.

The end of the century saw a resurgence of missionary work as governments, often appreciating the contribution that the Church could make to internal stability, opened their doors to religious orders. In Colombia the 1902 'Convention of the Missions' conceded absolute authority to the missionary orders to govern, police, educate and generally control the Indians of the interior. The missions thus came to control 75 per cent of the national territory. The largest of these orders were the Capuchins who worked in southern Colombia. They became a combination of priests, magistrates and entrepreneurs. As a result, the Capuchin missionaries were criticised as being a state-within-a-state:

'... a theocratic dictatorship which usurped the land and freedom of the Indians in exchange for a spurious civilisation. These are value-judgments reminiscent of the charges levelled against the Jesuits in Paraguay in the eighteenth century and, like them, they fail to do justice to the religious motivation of the missionaries and their need for a protective framework. They also fail to establish whether alternative and probably inevitable forms of contact – with merchants, landowners, officials, anthropologists – would have been superior to that of missionaries or provided better material prospects for the Indians.'[5]

By the 1930s the great struggles of Liberals against Conservatives about the separation of Church and state had mostly been resolved in favour of the Liberals. Nevertheless, the Catholic Church continued to be virtually the established religion of all of Latin America except Mexico, which instituted a rigorous separation of Church and state after the revolution of 1910. A solemn *Te Deum* in metropolitan cathedrals still forms part of Independence Day celebrations all over Latin America. Throughout the continent the Church was regarded as a conservative force allied with the landowning class and nervous of the rising middle class, which was given to freemasonry and radicalism. The appearance of Communist parties in Latin America in the 1920s (and, later, other parties inspired by Marxism) constituted a new challenge for the Church and provided a fresh political cause just as the Liberal-Conservative disputes were being laid to rest.

In the 1930s the groundwork was laid for policies and attitudes which are still at the centre of the Catholic Church's stance on Latin American political issues. The Great Depression of 1929-32 shattered the foundations of the Latin American economies. Military and right-wing governments suppressed protest and held down wages to maintain the status quo. Young, upper-class Catholics in Latin America began to be influenced by the ideas of the French Catholic writer Jacques Maritain, who put forward the idea of a socially-just society in which each social class would play its role with rights and responsibilities. The Chilean *Falange Nacional*, an offshoot of the Conservative Party, was formed in 1936 to put these ideas into practice. The *Falange Nacional* became the Christian Democrat Party in the 1950s, but its name shows its early kinship with the corporatist ideology of Francisco

chapter seven

Franco in Spain and Italian fascism. The leaders of the *Falange Nacional* were also members of Catholic Action, a movement transplanted from Europe, which was organised in several Latin American countries in the 1930s to train lay people in Catholic social teaching.

As the Cold War set in after the Second World War, Catholic parties, especially the Christian Democrats, began to gain momentum, breaking completely with conservatism and advocating a third way between communism and capitalism. Chile and Venezuela were the only countries where the Christian Democrats came to power with their vision intact. In Chile, Eduardo Frei's slogan in the successful election campaign of 1964 was 'Revolution in Liberty', stealing key words from both the left and the right. He won a straight fight with the socialist Salvador Allende. Frei was heavily supported by the United States and the traditional right, which reluctantly voted for him as the lesser of two evils.

The experience varied from country to country, however, and there are many examples of clerics supporting right-wing régimes from their pulpits, especially when they were justified as fighting communism. In Guatemala in the early 1950s, Archbishop Rossell organised a crusade against the reformist government of Jacobo Arbenz in the name of anti-communism. Cardinal Spellman of New York acted as an enthusiastic intermediary between the CIA and Rossell, with the result that a pastoral letter was read out in all churches demanding that '... the people of Guatemala should rise up as a man against the enemy of God and the fatherland ... in this national crusade against communism'.[6] After the successful CIA-organised invasion in 1954, the archbishop blessed Colonel Castillo Armas as a liberator. The reward for the Church came in the new constitution of 1955 which restored some of the privileges stripped from it by previous liberal governments.

Anti-communism intensified throughout Latin America after the Cuban revolution in January 1959. Within two years, driven as much by external pressures as by internal conviction, the Cuban government had declared itself to be Marxist-Leninist. But the Cuban Church had already been alarmed by the agrarian reform of May 1959, loudly denounced as communist-inspired. In March 1961, Fidel Castro publicly accused the Cuban clergy of being the 'fifth column of the counter-revolution'. The consequences for the Catholic Church of its implicit alliance with the anti-Castro forces were dramatic: in 1960 there were 745 diocesan priests and 2,225 religious in Cuba; by 1970 these numbers had fallen to 230 and 200 respectively.[7] This abrupt reduction in the number of clergy gives only a glimpse of the revolution's effect on the Church and Catholic Christian faith. Two generations of Cubans grew up without, or with only difficult access to, religious culture. As an institution involved in education, the Catholic Church simply vanished. The root-and-branch opposition of the Cuban Church to the revolution was in fact a departure from the Church's normal practice of seeking some sort of *modus vivendi* with varying political régimes to enable it to carry on its core tasks of teaching and ministering to the people through the liturgy and the sacraments. Influenced by events in Cuba, the bishops of Chile, where the Communist Party was powerful enough to elect senators and deputies, warned in 1962 that 'communism is diametrically opposed to Christianity'. In the wake of the Cuban revolution, Monseñor Agostino Casaroli (later the Secretary of State at the Vatican), speaking on behalf of Pope John XXIII at Notre Dame University in the United States, called upon bishops and religious superiors in North America and Europe to commit 10 per cent of their personnel to Latin America by 1970. In 1960 the Pontifical Commission for Latin America set up the Papal Volunteers for Apostolic Collaboration in Latin America. These calls were a response both to the threat of communism and to the perceived shortage of priests in Latin America. The result was an immense influx of foreign church-workers. The number of US Catholic missionary personnel working in Latin America increased from 2,126 in 1958 to 3,506 in 1964. Some countries benefited more than others: in the 1960s around 68 per cent of all US diocesan clergy in Latin America were working in Peru.[8] Ironically, many of these foreign missionaries were 'conscientised' by their experience of poverty and injustice in Latin America and were among the first to build bridges between the Church and movements working for social justice.

Medellín

The Second Vatican Council (1962-1965) spurred a wave of reflection and reform in Latin America. The process of reflection, carried on in fits and starts in most countries, culminated in 1968 in the second general conference of the Latin American Bishops' Council (CELAM) at Medellín, Colombia. (This conference is now known throughout Catholic circles simply as 'Medellín'.) The idea of the gospel as liberation took root at the conference, alongside 'development', as the appropriate response to the problems of Latin America. The conclusions, given added authority by the presence of Pope Paul VI at Medellín, examined every aspect of Latin American society, returning again and again to the urgent need for structural change. In the section on violence, the conclusions state:

'a situation of injustice ... can be called institutionalised violence when, because of a structural deficiency of industry and agriculture, of national and international economy, of cultural and political life, "whole towns lack necessities, live in such dependence as hinders all initiative and responsibility as well as every possibility for cultural promotion and participation in social and political life", thus violating fundamental rights. This situation demands all-embracing, courageous, urgent and profoundly renovating transformations. We should not be surprised, therefore, that the "temptation to violence" is surfacing in Latin America.'[9]

Medellín gave support to the beginnings of two parallel but interdependent movements within the Church: base communities and the theology of liberation. Gustavo Gutierrez's book, *Theology of Liberation*, was first published in 1971, three years after Medellín. The Christian base community movement gained momentum throughout the 1970s, especially in Brazil.

Liberation theology

Liberation theology is a gift given by Latin America to the world which has now been taken up by theologians in other countries where poverty and oppression go hand in hand. Liberation theologians insist that their theology is not the product of libraries and ivory towers but of the insights of the poor themselves and the base communities which they have built on and systematised. Liberation theology sees the Bible as good news for the poor, because it calls them to awareness of themselves as human beings, of their communities and of the forces of death which oppress them, and affirms the duty of all Christians to work for liberation from sin and injustice as part of the task of making the Kingdom of God visible in this world.

For the poor and landless of Latin America the biblical stories of Exodus and the promised land, along with the denunciations of the prophets, especially Isaiah and Amos, have a particular resonance. So too does the teaching of Jesus, with his own love for the poor and the outcast. Again and again among the Christian base communities one finds the idea of the 'journey' on which the people of God have embarked, a journey full of suffering which many will not complete, but which ends at the 'promised land'. This journey is mirrored in the pilgrimages and marches that play a central role in the popular religion of Latin America, through which the personal sacrifice of the participants becomes personal worth, deserving of God's favour. When such marches are undertaken by a group or community, then the worth is shared among all. Marches and pilgrimages are now frequently organised to campaign for peace, human rights, land rights and so on, and often culminate in a mass.

One of the most important changes in liberation theology in the last twenty years has been the positive re-evaluation of 'popular religiosity' – for instance, ceremonial veneration of the saints, which fell out of favour after Vatican II. This goes together with a reassessment of indigenous beliefs, which are marked by a reverence and respect for the natural world and for community, and which seem so much closer to authentic gospel values than the selfish individualism propagated by the Spanish and Portuguese invaders.

Base communities

Christian base communities are communities of the poor who meet to celebrate their faith; to read and reflect on the Bible together in the light of their own circumstances; to discuss; and to decide what needs to be done and what they can do themselves to change things. They stress the role of the laity as the 'people of God' and do not depend directly on the parish priest, although it is recognised that they function best when they are supported by the local clergy and other structures of the Church. This is clearest in Brazil, where many bishops have actively encouraged Christian base communities and value them as a thriving and vibrant part of the Church. Their contribution to the whole Church is to set out and make known the perceptions and reflections of the poor, something that is essential if the whole Church is to take seriously its 'preferential option for the poor'. In their best and most effective form, Christian base communities are territorial organisations which aim to include all the church members in a given street or area so that their discussions and decisions reflect not only the perceptions of the most committed members of a community but, by taking seriously the reservations of the more fearful or more conservative, also enable the active community to grow in size and coherence. Unlike trade unions or political parties, Christian base communities do not provide an easy avenue for personal advancement, so they bring out a different form of leadership that has to be constantly revalidated by the community: it is more difficult for base community leaders to become 'bosses'. This is one reason why so many women leaders have emerged from the base community movement. There has been, inevitably, some dilution of this strong definition of the base community. In some places base communities are little more than mass-centres, established to help hard-pressed parish priests.

The Church and human rights

With the exception of Central America, the 1970s were years of dashed hopes for would-be revolutionaries and their sympathisers throughout Latin America. By the mid-1970s no less than fifteen

chapter seven

Latin American countries were ruled by military governments. Whether traditional (like Somoza in Nicaragua or Stroessner in Paraguay) or modern (like Pinochet in Chile and the generals in Brazil), the military leaders all shared a visceral hatred of 'communism' – a label applied to social movements of all kinds – and claimed that by carrying out their ruthless oppression they were defending the values of Western Christianity. Many traditionalist Catholics shared this point of view. *Fiducia*, the Chilean branch of the right-wing Catholic organisation 'Tradition, Family and Property', which is based in Brazil, played a vociferous if minor role in the destabilisation campaign that led up to the Chilean military coup of 11 September 1973.

This period of military rule proved to be a severe test for all the Churches of Latin America, and the Catholic Church in particular. The natural institutional desire to find a *modus vivendi* with government clashed painfully with the duty to bear witness to what was happening in their countries. Even in Chile and El Salvador, where the Catholic Church is known for its defence of human rights, its involvement in these dangerous and controversial issues was the product of initiatives undertaken by individual bishops who had never dreamed that they would be called to face such a challenge. In Chile, Cardinal Raúl Silva Henríquez was supported by several like-minded bishops. In time, almost the entire Bishops' Conference closed ranks against government attacks on the Church. In Ecuador, Bishop Leonidas Proaño of Riobamba was rather a lone voice raised in favour of the poor, although he did have the constant backing of the Archbishop of Quito. El Salvador's Archbishop Romero was supported only by a single colleague, Bishop Rivera Damas.

Only in two countries – Brazil and Guatemala – could one really speak of a corporate response by the Church to dictatorship and social injustice. In Brazil the whole Catholic Church was not united around these issues, but a large and well-organised minority of the bishops' conference gradually won the support of more middle-of-the-road bishops and formed a solid majority which for nearly two decades has consistently spoken out for social justice and human rights. The Pastoral Land Commission (CPT) and the Indigenous Missionary Council (CIMI) concern themselves with the human, social and economic rights of some of the poorest Brazilians. Both are official departments of the Brazilian Bishops' Conference (CNBB), which was founded in 1952. They have played a crucial role in documenting human rights violations and supporting community and social organisations. And during the 1980s the Guatemalan Bishops' Conference quietly and consistently challenged the government on human rights and all aspects of social and economic injustice.

Solid institutions, able to stand up to governments and attract funds from abroad, may need the vigorous support of bishops but they do not tell the whole story of the Church's defence of human rights. Throughout Latin America committed lay-people, sisters and individual priests dedicated themselves to the cause of social change and human rights. In the more open 1960s they formed organisations which plainly advocated radical or socialist solutions, such as the National Office of Social Investigation (ONIS) in Peru, the Golconda group in Colombia, Priests for the Third World in Argentina and Christians for Socialism in Chile.

Under the dictatorships of the 1970s and 1980s many Christian activists paid for their commitment to the poor and to human rights with death, imprisonment or exile. Tens of thousands of members of the base communities of Central America have been murdered by security forces and death squads. They provide the great majority of the Christian martyrs of these years of repression. Three bishops – Oscar Romero in El Salvador, and Enrique Angelelli and Carlos Ponce de León in Argentina – were killed because of their opposition to military repression. In all, twenty-one priests have been killed in El Salvador, seventeen in Argentina and sixteen in Guatemala. But almost every country can point to dozens of martyrs from the grassroots of the Church as well as priests or sisters. The Protestant Churches too have provided their share of martyred activists in the struggle for human rights.

The need for an urgent humanitarian response to dictatorship and human rights violations provoked a surge in practical ecumenism – that is, Protestant Churches working together with the Catholic Church to provide assistance to the victims, rather than drawing towards each other as a result of elaborate inter-church negotiations. Ecumenical organisations for human rights and practical solidarity, such as FASIC and the Peace Committee in Chile, the Permanent Assembly for Human Rights and MEDH in Argentina, Diaconía in El Salvador, Clamor in Brazil, the Committee of the Churches in Paraguay, were all active in the 1970s and 1980s. Invariably, however, this ecumenism was a coming together of liberal protestantism and the more socially open sectors of the Catholic Church and, therefore, a limited phenomenon.

Puebla

The third conference of Latin American Bishops, attended by the newly elected Pope John Paul II, was held in 1979 at Puebla in Mexico. At Puebla there was an attempt on the part of conservative sectors of the Latin American Church to turn the clock back by modifying and neutralising the most powerful commitments of

Medellín, and thereby to rein in the most active defenders of the poor and oppressed. Indeed, some of the inconsistencies of the final Puebla documents are the product of the uneasy coexistence of the differing outlooks and aspirations represented at Puebla. In the event, however, Puebla reinforced the line taken at Medellín, unambiguously adopting the concept of the 'preferential option for the poor'.

Brazil

With 242 dioceses, 382 bishops, over 13,000 priests and about 100,000 base communities, the Brazilian Catholic Church is the largest in the world. What happens in Brazil has an influence on the rest of Latin America and on the rest of the world. The Latin American Bishop's Council (CELAM) has a special weighting system to limit the numerical influence of the Brazilian Catholic Church which has more than a third of all Latin American bishops.

Under the energetic prompting of Bishop Helder Camara, the second Secretary General of the Brazilian Bishops' Conference (CNBB), some bishops were already moving towards a radical critique of Brazilian society long before the military coup of 1964. The CNBB set up its own literacy campaign, the Basic Education Movement, in 1961 using the 'conscientisation' methodology of Paulo Freire. The motto of the movement was *Viver é Lutar* – 'To live is to struggle'.[10]

The military coup of 1964 met with different reactions in the Brazilian Church. Outright and immediate condemnation was rare because the Goulart government, notorious for its incompetence and corruption, had few defenders. Cardinal Agnelo Rossi of São Paulo, however, celebrated a mass declaring that by 'the mercy of God and the courage, piety and strength of his children, the imminent communist plot had been thwarted ... which proposed to change this nation to a zone of silence.'[11] More telling statements of disapproval came later when the real character of the military régime became apparent. In December 1967 the Executive Committee of the CNBB (twenty-two bishops who were representative of the whole country) issued a statement titled 'The Mission of the Hierarchy in Today's World' in which they said,

'Their [the government's] assertion that they are defending *Christian civilisation*, while at the same time they deny the Church's mission of defending human values, is nothing more than the defence of a disguised paganism. We are surprised by the miraculous transformation of violent liberals and agnostics into defenders of an other-worldly Christianity far removed from the gospel.'[12]

Such prophetic denunciation of the ideology of the military dictatorship and its use of repression against the Brazilian people became the consistent stance of the CNBB until the transition to civilian rule in 1985.

The first Christian base community was started in 1968 in São Paulo in Vila Yolanda, a working-class neighbourhood in the industrial suburb of Osasco. Immediately after he was appointed auxiliary bishop in São Paulo, Dom Paulo Evaristo Arns formed his first pastoral team (the first in Brazil) of three priests, three sisters and between ten and fifteen lay people. They started work in the fifty parishes of the northern region of the archdiocese. This innovation sowed the seeds of the base communities. Soon after Dom Paulo was appointed Archbishop of São Paulo in 1970, there were 5,000 base communities in the city.[13]

The base-community movement was most successful where it was supported enthusiastically by the local bishop. The pastoral teams provided the formation and training which filtered down through leaders and groups to streets, *favelas* and rural communities. Often the Church went from an almost colonial institution, sacramental and dominated entirely by the local priest, to being the Church *of* the poor, without passing through the intermediate stage of being the Church *for* the poor.[14] Finding that they had a voice in the Church, people were able to express in their own words their experience of oppression and hardship. No other institution in Brazilian society permitted this to happen, certainly not the traditional unions or political parties, which all too often were vehicles for the personal ambition of local bosses. It was no accident, therefore, that the new, genuinely representative unions, the peasant organisations and ultimately the new opposition party that were formed under the military régime were led by people who had become politically aware within the Christian base-community movement.

The Brazilian Church retains much of the openness and the critical, questioning attitudes it developed under the military dictatorship. For the four-year period of 1991-94, for instance, the CNBB prepared a consultative document backed by extensive social analysis, *Brazilian Society and Pastoral Challenges*. Its comments ranged from the political (referring to 'prolonged and authoritarian transition' and 'reforms born dead') to the challenge of human sexuality ('... the great challenge for the Church is to recover human sexuality for the salvation story'). The consultative document, with questions, was discussed by parish groups and base communities and returned to the CNBB team so that their comments could be evaluated and incorporated in a definitive plan.

chapter seven

In April 1991 the twenty-ninth annual assembly of the CNBB again chose a leadership clearly committed to the preferential option for the poor, re-electing Archbishop Luciano Mendes Almeida as president and Bishop Antonio Celso Queiroz as secretary general. Both, however, were pushed to a third ballot by a competing list of conservative candidacies, headed by Cardinal Lucas Moreira Neves of Salvador. Observers believe that this may be the last time that the so-called progressive wing of the Brazilian Church will lead the CNBB because, by the time the next elections are held, the number of newly appointed bishops, who tend to be more conservative, will throw the election the other way. It is noticeable that many of the great bishops of the Brazilian Church, who have done so much to make the option for the poor a practical reality, are now ageing. According to one observer, many of their appointments were the product of Helder Camara's friendship with Giovanni Batista Montini, first as Deputy Secretary of State at the Vatican and subsequently as Pope Paul VI.[15]

Brazil, however, presents unprecedented challenges to the Catholic Church. Although economic and social conflicts are diffused somewhat by imperfect democracy, the Church will continue to be confronted by injustice and human rights violations. At the same time, evangelical and pentecostal Churches are growing very rapidly. It is hardly a time for a renewed traditionalism that turns its back on social involvement.

Chile

The fate of the Allende government was sealed early in September 1973, when eleventh-hour negotiations between Salvador Allende and Patricio Aylwin, the leader of the Christian Democrats, broke down. The negotiations took place in the house of Cardinal Raúl Silva Henríquez, the Archbishop of Santiago. Like many Chileans at the time of the September coup, a majority of the clergy thought that social and political tension had reached such a pitch that the country was ungovernable. The military action was accepted as something inevitable, even desirable, if it succeeded in re-establishing a minimum consensus for government. This was the position of the Christian Democrats who confidently expected to be asked to form a transitional government after a period of martial law. The Chilean Bishops' Conference indicated that the Church would accept and try to make the best of the change of government brought about by the coup. Six bishops made statements thanking the military for national deliverance.

General Pinochet and the coup leaders, however, were not democrats. They were impatient with the fudging, compromise and caving-in to vested interests, which they saw as the endemic evil of Chilean democratic politics. For them the Allende government was only a symptom of a deeper malaise. Their obsessive determination to root out the 'Marxist cancer' within Chile led to the killings, disappearances, torture and imprisonment for which the Pinochet régime became notorious.

The initial response of the Churches to human rights violations by the military régime was ecumenical. The Catholic Archdiocese of Santiago, together with the Baptist, Methodist, Greek Orthodox and Lutheran Churches and the Jewish community, set up the Peace Committee (*Comité para la Cooperación para la Paz*) less than a month after the coup. By the end of December 1975, when it was dissolved, the Peace Committee had initiated legal actions on behalf of more than 7,000 people who had been arrested, tried or 'disappeared' by the security forces. A second ecumenical committee, the National Refugee Committee, was set up after the coup to assist foreigners living in Chile. It was able to help 5,000 to leave the country between September 1973 and February 1974.

After the involvement in November 1975 of some priests and nuns in helping to obtain political asylum for members of a left-wing group who had been involved in a gun battle with the security forces, Cardinal Silva agreed under severe pressure from the government to close the Peace Committee at the end of December. In January 1976, however, the cardinal set up the Vicariate of Solidarity (*Vicaría de la Solidaridad*) as an integral part of the structure of the archdiocese of Santiago. The vicariate gave the cardinal more control over human rights work, but also gave those working within it considerably greater protection than the Peace Committee, which had never had any recognised legal status.

From 1976 onwards Church-state relations deteriorated steadily as a result of attacks by the government against the Church and senior members of the Christian Democratic Party. In August 1976 three Chilean bishops were deported from Ecuador after meeting they were attending in Riobamba, the diocese of Bishop Leonidas Proaño, was broken up by the Ecuadorean military. The participants were arrested and accused of discussing 'subversive themes of a Marxist orientation'. When the deported Chilean bishops arrived in Santiago they were met by a violent and hostile demonstration of Pinochet supporters, including members of the secret police. The Permanent Committee of the Chilean Bishops Conference responded with a statement criticising the doctrine of national security, suggesting for the first time that the military régime was fundamentally illegitimate.

The attitude of the Catholic Church towards the Pinochet régime evolved throughout the 1980s, as did moderate political opinion.

chapter seven

The new archbishop of Santiago, Juan Francisco Fresno, appointed in 1983, sponsored the National Accord, a centrist coalition of parties and interests that called for a return to democracy in 1985. And as Pinochet's electoral timetable, providing for a plebiscite in 1988, came nearer, the Church supported the voter-registration drives and civic education campaigns that were fundamental to the eventual opposition victory over General Pinochet. At the same time the call for reconciliation became the dominant theme in public pronouncements.

The re-establishment of democracy under the leadership of the veteran Christian Democrat, Patricio Aylwin, has allowed the Church to redirect itself to more traditional concerns. The one issue that will not go away, however, is the question of the human rights violations during the years of the dictatorship. The Church has repeatedly called for truth and justice as a necessary part of reconciliation.

The official report on deaths and disappearances under the military régime, announced to the nation by President Aylwin in March 1991, draws extensively on the careful documentation of the *Vicaría de la Solidaridad*. It does no more than establish the facts, however, leaving the courts to decide upon prosecution.

The temptation of the politicians, daily growing stronger as the Pinochet years recede into the past, is not to push for the guilty to be brought to trial. In the Church, too, the goal of national reconciliation is gradually becoming separated from its logical prerequisites – truth and justice. On 1 December 1989, just before the presidential election, the Chilean bishops issued a pastoral letter in which they said,

'We have called upon all for reconciliation. We have spoken of forgiveness and forgetting. But there remains the right to truth and justice. Not only the victims, but the whole of society, have the right to know who are guilty of the crimes committed. It is the task of the justice system to investigate the facts, evaluate the circumstances and apply the punishments.'[16]

Six months later, after Patricio Aylwin had been inaugurated as president, the Permanent Committee of the Bishops' Conference, reacting to the discovery of more secret graves of victims of the dictatorship, still acknowledged the need for truth but barely mentioned justice. On this occasion they said,

'those who have suffered most .... can, with their pain, help to heal Chile and teach us, with their magnanimity and forgiveness, that this cannot happen again. No one more than they can open the way for the country to a future of hope where love is stronger than violence or rancour.'[17]

El Salvador

In January 1992, after eleven years of civil war and over a century of history disfigured by repression and human rights violations, the Salvadorean government and the rebel FMLN, meeting in New York at talks sponsored by the Secretary General of the United Nations, reached agreement to end the civil war and enact fundamental reforms.

The FMLN was able to obtain this settlement from the government through flexibility and sheer doggedness. The right-wing ARENA government was also more flexible than its predecessors had been, accepting that it would not be able to win a military victory over the rebels and that the US government would no longer provide the funds and military equipment to pursue such a goal. If fully implemented, the agreement will bring about some modification of the land-tenure system, a reform of the army, the police force and the judiciary, and enable the FMLN to return to politics as a civilian political grouping. It is a time of hope in El Salvador, coloured as always by the scepticism with which such breakthroughs are invariably greeted.

In El Salvador it is possible to meet people for whom the story of Exodus and the promised land describes their own lives. The refugees who fled into Honduras in the early 1980s under a hail of army bullets have now returned to found their own settlements: Ciudad Segundo Montes and Ciudad Ignacio Ellacuria (named after two of the Jesuits killed in November 1989), Nuevo Gualcho in Usulután, San José Las Flores in Chalatenango and Santa Marta in Cabañas. In Nuevo Gualcho, Sunday mass is held under an enormous *guanacaste* tree and the homily is a discussion of the week's events in the light of the Bible readings of the day. The refugees' achievements and their unfulfilled hopes both feed into the faith of the community and are themselves fed by their faith.

The civil war in El Salvador started because the rich, a tiny minority of the population, refused to countenance the smallest curtailment of their power and privilege. They dominated the media and rigged elections, relying ultimately on the security forces to cow the population into submission.

For many years the Catholic Church shored up the system by preaching a message of acceptance of authority. This began to change after Medellín. The work of relatively few diocesan clergy, together with a majority of the Jesuits in El Salvador and some Dominicans, Franciscans and Passionists, made an enormous difference. The experience of the Catholic Church as a companion of the poor brought about rapid change. In concrete terms, this

chapter seven

meant taking seriously the experience and lives of the poor and training them as catechists and 'delegates of the word' to be the presence of the Church in remote rural hamlets and the shanty towns of San Salvador. In the forcing-house atmosphere of this tiny, politically polarised country, conscientisation often led quickly to politicisation. The military and the extreme right leapt to the conclusion that the priests and sisters of this 'new' Church were responsible for the growing wave of unrest. Between 1977 and the end of 1980, fifteen priests, four American church-women and one archbishop were killed. In the late 1970s and early 1980s the discovery by the security forces of a Bible or a photograph of Archbishop Romero in the house of a *campesino* (peasant) or shanty-town dweller could be a death warrant for its owner.

After the international outcry at the murder of the American church-women in December 1980, El Salvador again became safe for clergy. Meanwhile Monseñor Rivera Damas, who spent four years as Apostolic Administrator of the Archdiocese of San Salvador before being confirmed as Archbishop, continued to use Romero's pulpit to denounce human rights violations and to call for a negotiated end to the conflict. The Jesuits, based at the UCA (*Universidad Centroamericana José Simeón Cañas*), did all they could to persuade the Salvadorean political élite that the FMLN guerrilla movement and those they represented were legitimate but excluded participants in the political process, and that there could be no lasting solution without negotiating with them.
It was this steadfast insistence, completely devoid of any starry-eyed illusions about the guerrilla leaders or the armed struggle, that caused army leaders to order the killing of the six Jesuits during the FMLN offensive against San Salvador in November 1989.

Many of the community and union organisations of El Salvador, known as 'popular organisations', have been held together by people whose faith was kindled and sustained by the Church's option for the poor. Their counterparts in the Church are the Christian base communities, which nurture the belief that organisation and solidarity of the poor can still turn their country into the promised land. It would be a mistake to assume that this is a majority movement in the Salvadorean Church: as elsewhere in Latin America, Christian base communities are in a minority. They remain strong, however, because they still see community and social organisation as effective ways of rooting the Church and Christian values in society. As the FMLN feels its way towards its new role as a civilian political party, the Christian base communities and the wider 'popular organisations' will seek to ensure that ideals of social justice are not overwhelmed by pragmatism and compromise.

'Monseñor'

Wherever Christians are resisting oppression in Latin America, they are inspired by Oscar Romero, or 'Monseñor' as he was affectionately and respectfully dubbed by the Salvadoreans. Until the cathedral in San Salvador was closed for further building work in 1990, Romero's tomb in the east transept was covered by little plaques giving thanks for his help and miracles; whatever the result of the Vatican's deliberations in the future, the people of El Salvador have already 'canonised' him.

Romero was appointed archbishop because he was seen as a safer choice than Monseñor Rivera Damas, the auxiliary bishop of San Salvador. Romero, however, was not a simple-minded conservative, nor did he seek a quiet life. It had been Romero's energetic but prudent measures to deal with a radical peasant-education centre in his diocese of Santiago de María that first attracted the attention of the papal nuncio. Romero dispersed the teachers to the parishes, thus preventing the centre becoming a hotbed of radicalism without depriving the peasants of its instruction.

Throughout his life Romero struggled sincerely to overcome negative aspects of his character. In Mexico, in 1971, Romero noted down his faults as he saw them: 'avoiding social relations with others, not getting to know people, concern about being criticised, perfectionism, disorder in his work, lack of austerity and lack of courage in speaking out and defending his opinions'. In 1972, also in Mexico, he underwent three months of psychoanalysis which he described as an instance of God's providence in his life. Thus Romero actively sought change and growth throughout his life as a bishop. The sessions with the psychoanalyst and his regular conversations with a psychiatrist friend in San Salvador – as well as his retreats and meetings with his confessor – clearly had their effect: one of the things that made Romero so beloved by the poor was his accessibility and willingness to listen and to take seriously what they told him.

Oscar Romero visibly grew in stature and self-confidence in his three years as archbishop and, at the end, refused to compromise his ministry of truth to the Salvadorean people in the face of the most serious threats. The openness and firmness of character which he deliberately encouraged in himself meant that Romero responded courageously to the events that proved to be the turning point in his life: the murder by a right-wing death squad of his friend, the Jesuit priest, Rutilio Grande, only three weeks after Romero was appointed archbishop in February 1977, and the bad faith of the government which he experienced as he tried to persuade the politicians and military to stop attacking the Church. In the year before he was murdered on 24 March 1980, Romero was repeatedly threatened. Romero took these threats seriously but did not allow them to deflect him from his mission to preach the truth and announce the good news to the people of El Salvador. In April 1978 he prayed in St Peter's in Rome '... for the courage, if need be, to die as did all these martyrs ...' Two weeks before he was killed Romero told a Mexican correspondent in an impromptu telephone interview:

'I have often been threatened with death. I must tell you, as a Christian, I do not believe in death without resurrection. If they kill me, I will rise up in the Salvadorean people. I am not boasting, I say this with the greatest humility.

'As a pastor, I am obliged by divine command to give my life for those I love – and this means all Salvadoreans, even those who are going to kill me. And if they carry out their threats, I now offer my blood to God for the redemption and resurrection of El Salvador.

'Martyrdom is a grace of God which I do not think I have earned. But if God accepts the sacrifice of my life, let my blood be the seed of freedom and a sign that hope may soon be reality. Let my death, if it is accepted by God, be for the liberation of my people and as a witness of hope in the future.

'You may say, if they succeed in killing me, that I forgive and bless those who do it. I wish they would realise that are they wasting their time. A bishop will die, but the Church of God, which is the people, will never die.'[18]

Nicaragua

The four priests in the revolutionary Sandinista government of 1979[19] were a symbol of the difference between Nicaragua and Cuba. Christians throughout the world saw Nicaragua as opening up a concrete example of how the 'preferential option for the poor' could be put into practice in a poverty-stricken third world country. Beyond noting the participation of Christians at all levels in the Nicaraguan revolution, however, it is not easy to assess what was the specifically Christian contribution. The Sandinistas abolished the death penalty; had a generally good human rights record, despite the difficulties created by the *contra* war; maintained a mixed economy; respected members of all Churches; and, during their ten years in power, introduced a genuinely pluralist political system. In all these respects the Nicaraguan revolution differed from the Cuban revolution. But to claim these qualities as the specific result of Christian influence would be to set up a non-existent dichotomy in the Sandinista revolution between 'good Christians' and 'bad atheists', as well as an insulting failure to acknowledge the vision and humanity of non-Christian Sandinista leaders and activists.

There were two sorts of conflict involving the Catholic Church during the years of the Sandinista government. First, within the Church the supporters of the Sandinistas vied with their political opponents to be acknowledged as the legitimate voice of Nicaraguan Catholics. Second, there was a less-developed struggle (often confused with the first) between those who favoured a Church founded on grassroots communities with ample space for lay initiatives and those who hankered after a hierarchical Church, responsive primarily to the needs of the middle and upper classes.

This second struggle was much less significant because, before the revolution, the base-community movement was not well developed: it was limited to a few poor neighbourhoods in Managua; the area around Rivas where Father Gaspar García Laviana, who died fighting in the southern front in 1979, had worked; the city of Estelí; and the Atlantic Coast area, where the US Capuchin friars had encouraged lay participation as a response to the shortage of priests and the enormous difficulties of effective communication in the vast area for which they were responsible. According to one estimate, by the end of the 1970s, there were three hundred base communities throughout the country – the high point for the movement in Nicaragua.[20]

The Sandinista victory in July 1979 halted the development of the grassroots Church. Many of its most active participants then devoted their energies to secular social movements, government and political organisations. For this reason the second, intra-Church conflict was often seen as part of the larger political conflict.

The protagonists were the same in both sets of conflicts: by 1982 Archbishop Miguel Obando y Bravo of Managua was being received in Washington virtually as a leader of the opposition. At the same time, he sought to restore the unquestioned authority of the Nicaraguan bishops in general and in particular his own personal authority in Managua. On the other side were the priest-ministers and the grassroots Church, the 'Church of the Poor', as it was called by its supporters. Although the ministers had agreed to a temporary suspension of their priestly duties (that is, not to say mass in private or in public) in 1981 because of their continuing political role, they still provided a focus and an inspiration to Christians in Nicaragua and abroad.

chapter seven

The conflict between Archbishop (later Cardinal) Obando y Bravo and the Sandinistas was marked by great bitterness on both sides. The Sandinistas were frustrated and angry that the Cardinal consistently refused to condemn even the worst *contra* atrocities or US support for them.

Cardinal Obando himself never accepted the olive branch extended to him at various times by the Sandinistas, always suspecting them of some underhand plan to instrumentalise the Church. Indeed Obando is known to have considered the *contra* war as a 'just war'. His overt opposition moderated after 1987, when, as part of the Central American peace process, he was appointed President of the National Reconciliation Commission by Daniel Ortega, the Sandinista president.

Today, after the electoral defeat of the Sandinistas, Cardinal Obando's position in the Nicaraguan Catholic Church and, indeed, in the country, is unrivalled. As a figure of moral authority, he is unchallenged, certainly by the victorious but continually squabbling politicians of the UNO governing coalition.

The new diocesan bishops appointed since 1990 had all worked with him as auxiliaries in Managua and are unconditionally loyal to him. After refusing all offers of help from the Sandinista government, Obando is now building a new cathedral in Managua to replace the one damaged by the earthquake of 1972. Construction is being financed by Tom Monaghan, owner of the Detroit Tigers baseball team. Monaghan himself was a prominent supporter of the *contras* and is a member of the Catholic group 'The City of God', which has several adherents in the new Nicaraguan government.

The electoral defeat of the Sandinistas in February 1990 was a triumph of reality over idealism. The Sandinistas won a respectable 44 per cent of the vote but the majority voted for Violeta de Chamorro, the opposition candidate, because a vote for the Sandinistas was seen as a vote for economic hardship and prolonged war. Few believed that the US government would ever come to terms with the Sandinistas even if they won a scrupulously clean election. Peace of a sort has been achieved, but miserly US aid for the new government and drastic anti-inflationary policies have aggravated economic hardship. For the Christian base communities, and especially their poorest members, sheer survival now takes precedence over the tasks of social transformation. Some, however, predict that the economic crisis will become so desperate that poor neighbourhoods will have to develop their own networks of social solidarity in order to survive, providing an opportunity for the 'Church of the Poor' to rediscover itself.

Protestantism, sects and the Catholic Church in Latin America

The Catholic Church in Latin America has co-existed happily with Protestantism in Latin America since the middle of the nineteenth century. This co-existence, however, was based on immense security. The Protestant Churches that set up in Latin America in the nineteenth century were the so-called 'historic' Churches, established to minister primarily to European expatriates and settlers or invited by liberal governments to counter-balance the influence of conservative Catholicism. Although they won some converts among Latin Americans, they were not a threat to the Catholic Church.

The expansion of the evangelical and especially pentecostal Churches in Latin America since the 1950s is quite different. They originate in the United States rather than Europe. The scale and speed of this expansion and their ability to put down roots in Latin America is dramatic. In the late 1960s there were some 5 million Protestants, excluding children, in Latin America. Twenty years later this number had grown to at least 40 million.[21] The estimates of numbers and proportions vary: the number of evangelical and pentecostal church attenders, a much larger number than official members, is said to be between 24 million[22] and 32 million.[23] In 1985 there were 15,000 full-time Protestant pastors in Brazil compared to 13,176 Catholic priests.[24] The other countries with a high proportion of Protestants are Guatemala (30 per cent), Chile (20 per cent), Nicaragua (20 per cent) and Costa Rica (16 per cent).[25]

The proselytising efforts of United States-based Churches are clearly responsible in part for this expansion but, equally clearly, the highest growth rates are being achieved in those countries where such Churches depend least on foreign mission-personnel. For instance, in Brazil the Assemblies of God, the largest pentecostal Church, now claims 68,300 groups or places of worship with only twenty-five US mission personnel in the country.[26] At the same time, money raised in the United States continues to be of importance: before he was disgraced in February 1988, Jimmy Swaggart was reported to have supplied 40 per cent of the funds used by the medical and educational programmes of the Assemblies of God in Honduras and to have provided $6 million to the Assemblies of God in El Salvador.[27] In 1988, US Protestant Churches, including more liberal denominations, raised $1.7 billion for their development and evangelisation church work outside the United States.[28]

The evangelical and pentecostal Churches have often been contemptuously labelled as 'sects' and the Latin American political left has been quick to identify the evangelical and

chapter seven

pentecostal Churches as part of the onslaught of US imperialism. Their uncritical acquiescence with the political status quo is seen as evidence of a plan to undermine the socially and politically active wing of the Catholic Church which, as early as 1969, was identified as a danger to US interests in Latin America by Nelson Rockefeller. The notorious Santa Fé document, drawn up in 1980 by right-wing academics as a primer on Latin America for the Reagan administration, identified liberation theology and its supporters as an enemy of US policy. Finally, Central America in the 1980s provided plentiful evidence of attempts by the Reagan White House and the right to use evangelical and pentecostal Churches to combat the influence of the socially-active wing of the Catholic Church. At the same time, however, the Reagan administration assiduously cultivated conservative Catholic clerics to whom it gave equal if not greater prominence.

It is true that huge sums of money have been raised in the United States for aggressive proselytisation in Latin America. It is also true that some Churches – such as the California-based Church of the Word to which the former military ruler of Guatemala, General Ríos Montt, belongs – have been used as an adjunct to counter-insurgency, providing the 'beans' component of the Guatemalan military's 'beans or bullets' programme. The perception of otherwise defenceless Mayan Indians that such Churches were approved by the government, and therefore a haven from the terrifying violence of the armed forces, undoubtedly helped them to gain converts. Fundamentalist US Churches and groups (as well as some Catholic groups) lent themselves eagerly to Colonel Oliver North's campaign to keep the Nicaraguan contras supplied when the US Congress had prohibited official aid.

The connection with the United States, however, is only a minor part of the runaway success of pentecostalism in Latin America. One Central American writer observes,

'With its clapping hands, guitars and cheerful choirs, this new form of popular religion is taking the ground away from an inadequate and arthritic Catholicism, and also from other more traditional forms of Protestantism. It is taking the pulpits, the streets and consciences away from the two rivals.'[29]

It is not surprising that pentecostalism should have been gathering momentum in Latin America since the 1970s at a time when Latin Americans have been embracing the goal of development – the American dream – with increasing enthusiasm but when, as a result of international debt, structural adjustment and the implantation of neo-liberal economic models, they are faced with diminishing possibilities of ever making it a reality. One of the most successful pentecostal Churches in Brazil, the Universal Church of the Kingdom of God, claiming 5 million adherents, was founded by Edir Macedo, a former lottery ticket vendor, who is now a millionaire. He owns fourteen radio and two television stations on which he claims to have cured people of AIDS and brought them fortune. A Catholic theologian explained,

'Sects are successful because they promise miracles. For a person living in misery who feels morally lost they seem to offer a way out ... the problem is the Catholic Church can never do what the sects are doing – promising miracles – and that's what the people want.'[30]

But it is not only miracles. Pentecostalism, with its cathartic modes of worship, offers an escape, however temporary, from the drab grind of poverty and the realities of everyday life. At the same time, with its moral precepts and inward-looking, sectarian solidarity, it attacks the problems (alcohol, family break-up, despair) that compound the enormous hardships of living in a shanty town or rural slum. Because of their strict codes of personal behaviour, evangelicals and pentecostals are frequently seen as 'good' people. Their pastors are themselves poor and are present in the street, the rural community or the *barrio* in a way that Catholic priests, by virtue of their education and, frequently, middle-class background, can never be. In recognition of the honesty and personal commitment of many pentecostal pastors, it must be noted that there are glimmers of ecumenical activity between them and the Catholic Church in such places as the vast *favelas* of the Baixada Fluminense in Rio de Janeiro.

Their success has been aided by intensive use of radio and, increasingly, television, as well as barn-storming evangelistic campaigns undertaken by Latin American preachers such as Luis Palau (Argentina) and Yiyi Avila (Puerto Rico), as well as Americans such as Jimmy Swaggart. These methods and their faith in a personal, redemptive God make some pentecostal and evangelical church people easy prey for unscrupulous 'evangelists' who fill vast stadiums with enthusiastic crowds and promise miracles, while raising enormous sums of money for themselves.

Another explanation advanced for the success of pentecostalism is the change it often produces in the machismo of the traditional Latin American male. On the one hand, these Churches appear to reinforce patriarchal male roles by supporting the traditional male-led household and giving prominence to male leadership (the voices the passer-by hears coming out of their *templos* are almost always male). On the other hand, the pentecostal Church offers a safe haven where men may pour their hearts out and weep before others without shame. One observer has noted that there are more women than men in the Protestant Churches and that women clearly benefit from the behavioural changes in men which pentecostalism can bring about, suggesting that the household may be the key to evangelical expansion in Latin America.[31]

Liberation theology and the base-community movement belong to an entirely different tradition – one that values shared goals derived from rational analysis, so apparent in the Medellín documents. Faith in this kind of Church goes together with belief that people, even the poorest, can change their circumstances by working together and, ultimately, by social and political action.

The way ahead

It is too early to make any considered judgment about the eventual impact of the pentecostal and evangelical Churches on Latin America. The speed of their expansion means that, for the majority of pentecostals and evangelicals, membership of these Churches is a first generation phenomenon. Whether the evangelical and pentecostal Churches will remain so politically and socially passive in the future is less clear. Much will depend on the possibilities of social and economic progress for the poor. The degree of influence of parent Churches in the United States will also be relevant. A few pentecostal Churches (in Chile under Pinochet and in Nicaragua under the Sandinistas, for example) have shown that their faith is not incompatible with ecumenism, social activism and the defence of human rights.

The advance of the pentecostal and evangelical Churches constitutes a challenge for the Catholic Church. Although the majority of the population in Latin America is still nominally Catholic, practice is very low, between 3 and 10 per cent in the cities and perhaps reaching 30 per cent in some rural areas. Migration to the cities, the widening gap between the rich and the poor and the continuing deterioration of the living conditions of the poor together with the closing-off of economic opportunities are the conditions under which evangelisation must take place. In October 1991, Pope John Paul II bitterly criticised the injustices of Brazilian society and the activities of the 'sects' but gave no clear indication of how the Catholic Church should challenge them. One headline reduced his advice to 'Fight harder, Pope tells clergy'.[32]

The Catholic Church, from the Vatican downwards, is committed to the pursuit of social justice as a constituent element of the Christian faith, as the impressive accumulation of encyclicals since the 1960s makes clear, not to mention the numerous pastoral letters produced by bishops' conferences throughout Latin America. At issue is the speed, the methods and the energy with which social justice should be pursued.

A return to an 'other-worldly' Catholicism, in which injustice and the status quo were tolerated because they were of no ultimate significance compared to the riches of eternal life, seems unthinkable. The prediction, therefore, of more widespread and severe poverty and greater economic and social polarisation in Latin America is, quite apart from its ethical implications, a problem for the Catholic Church. It aims to bring the good news of the gospels to all but, in purely secular terms, the good news for the poor is often seen as essentially bad news for the rich. Exhortations to the uncaring rich to mend their ways are unlikely to be successful while a wholehearted 'option for the poor' may simply alienate more of the rich and middle classes. Today, the poor of Latin America are more urban, less obsequious and more open to outside influences than ever before. While it seems inevitable that Latin America will become more religiously pluralist, the most durable presence will belong to those Churches which sustain the Christian vision of the 'integral person' at the centre of their faith, that is, the vision of each and every person having access by right to the material and spiritual goods that make her or him whole.

One way for the Catholic Church to move in this direction would be to encourage those within the Latin American Catholic Church who are seeking to bring together the insights of liberation theology with the commitment of the base communities and the celebratory traditions of popular religiosity. But this is only one option. Opinions are clearly divided, for there are senior clerics who are theologically and politically conservative and who reject the direction the Latin American Church has taken since Medellín. For them, liberation theology has gone too far towards secular ideology, base communities can threaten the central role of the priest and popular religiosity, especially if tinged with indigenous rites, can undermine doctrinal purity. This attitude finds a favourable response among middle- and upper-class Catholics, many of whom dislike the practical application of the preferential option for the poor which they see as 'the Church meddling in politics', and a threat to their own position in society.

There is a danger for the Church, despite its official commitments to social justice, that in seeking to down-play the social content of the gospels and Catholic teaching, and to replace the more open and participatory Church of the past twenty years with a more hierarchical and authoritarian approach, these conservative forces will limit even further its ability to appeal to and evangelise the poor. This would create the conditions for even faster growth of the rival pentecostal and evangelical Churches. Indeed, some Protestant observers see the success of the pentecostal Churches in Latin America as part of the expanding wave of nonconformity which originated in Britain in the seventeenth century, but which was stifled there by the aristocratic, authoritarian traditions of the Anglican Church. For them, though it lacks the immense social power which the Anglican Church enjoyed in Britain during that period, the aristocratic, authoritarian Church in Latin America today is the Catholic Church.[33] Given the rapid pace of change in Latin America and the at least partial accuracy of this perception, it becomes clear that the Catholic Church cannot rely on its historical heritage or its questionable status as the 'established' Church to meet the new challenges. These will require all the commitment and creativity of which the Latin American Church has given such abundant witness since Vatican II.

References

1. Quoted in Gustavo Gutiérrez, *Dios o el oro en las Indias, Siglo XVI*, Instituto Bartolomé de las Casas/CEP, Lima, 1989, p29.

2. Clissold, Stephen, *The Saints of Latin America*, Charles Knight, London, 1972, p18.

3. Klaiber SJ, Jeffrey, *La Iglesia en el Peru*, Fondo Editorial Pontificia, Universidad Católica del Peru, 1988.

4. Lynch, John, 'The Catholic Church in Latin America, 1830-1930', in Leslie Bethell (ed.), *Cambridge History of Latin America – Vol. IV*, Cambridge, p529.

5. Lynch, *ibid.*, p548.

6. Cardenal SJ, Rodolfo, 'The Challenge of the Gospel in Guatemala', in Dermot Keogh (ed.), *Church and Politics in Latin America*, Macmillan, London, 1990, p208.

7. Dussel, Enrique, *A History of the Church in Latin America: Colonialism to Liberation*, William B. Eerdmans Publishing Company, Grand Rapids, Michigan, 1981, p162.

8. Klaiber, *op. cit.*, p359.

9. Second General Conference of Latin American Bishops, *The Church in the Present-Day Transformation of Latin America in the Light of the Council: Conclusions II*, Secretariat for Latin America, National Council of Catholic Bishops, Washington DC, 1979, p53.

10. Dussel, *op. cit.*, p148.

11. *ibid.*, p150.

12. *ibid.*, p153.

13. Ana Flora Anderson, *The History and Nature of the Base Communities*, mimeo, São Paulo, 1987.

14. Martin CSsR, Leonard, 'The Call to Justice: Conflict in the Brazilian Catholic Church, 1968-79', in Dermot Keogh (ed.) *Church and Politics in Latin America*, Macmillan, London, 1990, p309.

the church in Latin America

15. See Scrutator, 'Pope John Paul's New Bishops: Look Over Your Shoulder', *The Tablet*, 26 October 1991, pp1306-7.

16. 'Certainty, Coherence and Confidence: Message to Catholics at a Time of Transition', working document of the Chilean Bishops' Conference, Santiago, 1 December 1989,

17. *'Facing the truth'*, Permanent Committee of the Bishops' Conference, Santiago, 13 June 1990.

18. Material for this profile was largely taken from *Romero: a life*, James R Brockman, Orbis Books, Maryknoll, New York, 1989.

19. Miguel D'Escoto, Maryknoll, Foreign Minister 1979-1990; Fernando Cardenal SJ, Minister of Education 1984-1990; Father Ernesto Cardenal, Minister of Culture 1979-1989; Fr Edgar Parrales, Minister of Social Welfare 1979-1981.

20. Foroohar, Manzar, *The Catholic Church and Social Change in Nicaragua*, State University of New York Press, Albany, 1989, p68.

21. Martin, David, *Tongues of Fire: the Explosion of Protestantism in Latin America*; Blackwell, Oxford, 1990, p50.

22. *New York Times*, 25 October 1987.

23. Mr & Mrs P.J. Johnstone, International Research Office – Worldwide Evangelisation Crusade, quoted in David Stoll, *Is Latin America Turning Protestant?*, University of California Press, Berkeley, 1990.

24. Martin, David, *op. cit.*, p50.

25. *ibid.*, p51.

26. Roberts, W. Dayton & Siewert, John A. (eds.), *Mission Handbook – 14th Edition, USA/Canada Protestant Ministries Overseas,* Marc & Zondervan, Monrovia, California, 1989.

27. Stoll, *op. cit.*, p322.

28. Roberts & Siewert, *op. cit.*, p53.

29. Martínez, Abelino, *Las Sectas en Nicaragua*, Departamento Ecuménico de Investigaciones, San José, Costa Rica, 1989, p1.

30. Lamb, Christina, 'Church Falls Foul of Changing Times', *Financial Times*, 15 October 1991.

31. Stoll, *op. cit.*, pp317-18.

32. *The Tablet*, 19 October 1991.

33. See Martin, David, *op. cit.*

Latin America

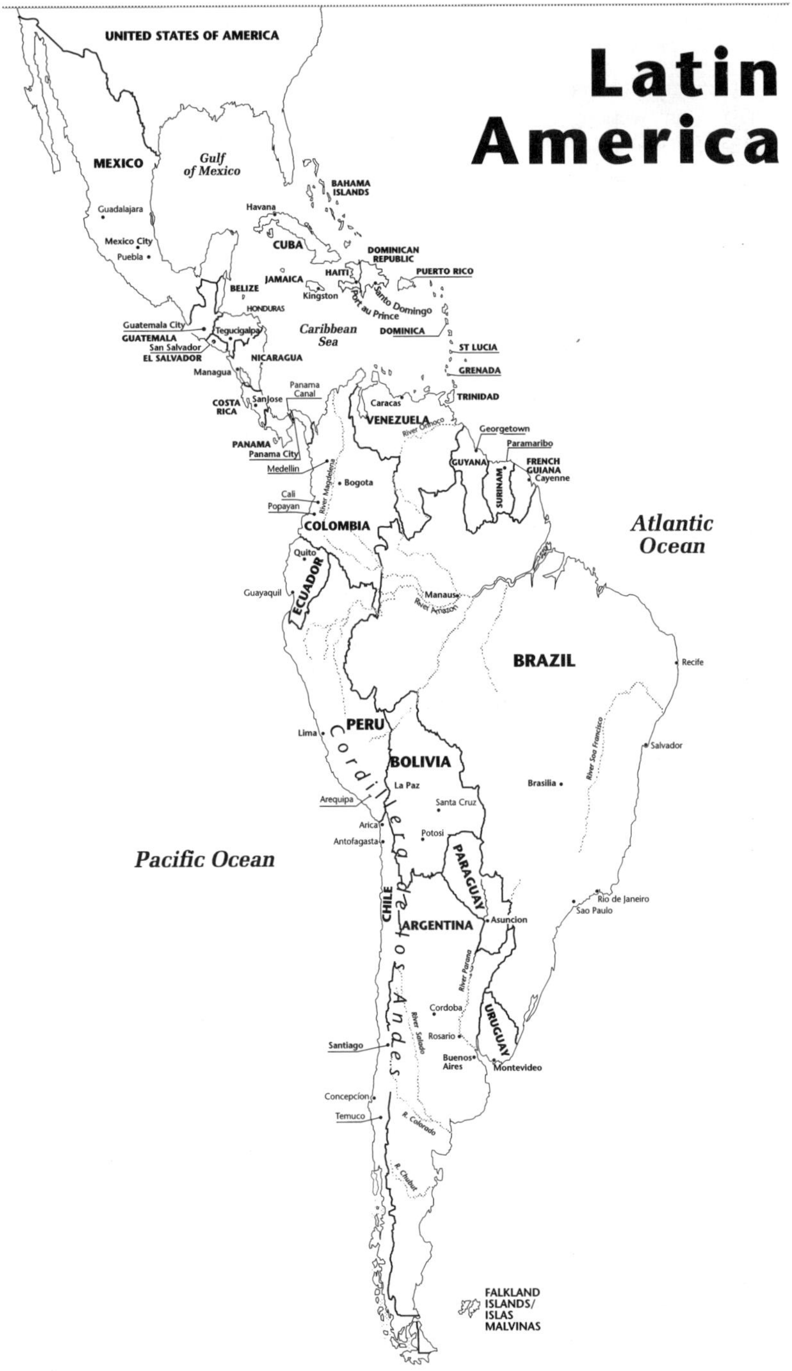

IN PROFILE: THE COUNTRIES OF LATIN AMERICAN AND THE CARIBBEAN

Argentina

Argentina is a country of migrants. Hundreds of thousands of poor Italians and Spaniards arrived in Buenos Aires in the early years of this century. At the same time that they were creating the now world-famous *tango*, the Argentinian army was busy subjugating the last remnants of Indian resistance in the northern provinces. The city of Resistencia in the Chaco commemorates the last battle against the Toba Indians in 1912.

Argentina returned to a democratic political system after the military government led by General Galtieri was discredited by defeat in the 1982 Malvinas-Falklands conflict. The elections of October 1983 were won by the veteran Radical Party politician, Raúl Alfonsín. It marked the end of sixteen years of military rule, interrupted for two-and-a half years by the presidencies of Juan Domingo Perón and, after his death, by his second wife, Isabel. The military régime of 1976-83 and the presidency of Isabel Perón were notorious for human rights violations – the so-called 'dirty war', waged against left-wing guerrilla groups and, inevitably, non-violent opponents of the government.

Argentina grew rich from the cattle and cereals that prospered on the extraordinarily fertile pampas. The owners of the huge agricultural estates (*estancias*) dominated the economic life of the nation and still exercise disproportionate influence. Since the 1930s, however, governments have encouraged industrialisation, especially the first Perón government in the late 1940s. Government-sponsored development spawned state corporations, often administered by political cronies, under whom they ran up huge deficits. President Carlos Menem, though elected in 1989 as a Perónist pledged to soften the impact of IMF-inspired structural adjustment policies, has reduced inflation almost to single figures by a drastic programme of privatisation and economic liberalisation. The cost has been spreading poverty and extensive unemployment. These problems, however, seem to be less unpopular than the desperate uncertainties of rampant inflation because in the mid-term elections of October 1991 Menem's Perónists successfully beat off opposition challenges.

appendix 1

Belize

Belize, formerly British Honduras, is one of the two English-speaking countries (the other is Guyana) on the mainland of Latin America. With its predominantly Afro-Caribbean population, Belize culturally looks eastwards to the Caribbean rather than westwards to Guatemala and the other countries of Central America. This isolation was exacerbated for many years by Guatemala's territorial claim to the whole of Belize. To this day, Guatemalan maps depict Belize as a department of Guatemala. The claim led the British government to place a permanent garrison of British troops and Harrier jump jets in the country. The civilian government of Guatemala has now renounced its claim, started bilateral talks with Belize and is restoring diplomatic relations with the United Kingdom after an interruption of more than twenty years.

Belize is gradually becoming more typically 'Central American': its minority Spanish-speaking population is growing and has been boosted by several thousand Salvadorean refugees. Sugar is the main 'official' export crop but is reportedly beaten into second place by marijuana and coca, which are said to have been worth $100 million in 1990.

Bolivia

Although Bolivia has become a by-word for political instability, it should be appreciated more for its people's supreme courage and resistance in the face of adversity. Since the Spanish Conquest Bolivia has constantly been at the mercy of foreign interests – first because of the enormously rich silver mine that by 1600 had made Potosí the richest city in the world and, later, because of its tin. Now coca and cocaine are Bolivia's major exports, estimated at $750 million in 1987 and worth more than all its other exports combined. Bolivia's main legitimate economic interest to the outside world continues to be its extensive and only partially-mapped mineral reserves. With little capital, however, Bolivia remains dependent on foreign companies and foreign aid.

Bolivia has lost much of its territory since independence in 1825 through concessions to Brazil and defeats in wars against Chile (1879-83) and Paraguay (1932-35). In the War of the Pacific against Chile, Bolivia lost its outlet to the sea and the rich nitrate deposits of Antofagasta, while in the Chaco war against Paraguay it was forced to surrender three-quarters of its Chaco territories, along with the region's rumoured oil deposits. Both defeats left a lingering bitterness. All Bolivian schoolchildren learn about their country's rights to its Pacific shore and on 23 March commemorate the 'Day of the Sea'.

There were eight coups or unconstitutional changes of government between 1978 and 1982, when Hernán Siles Suazo finally came to power after having won the largest vote but not an absolute majority in the elections of 1979. The Siles government was ineffectual, however, and by allowing inflation to reach 24,000 per cent a year by the time he left office in 1985, paved the way for the drastic anti-inflationary policies adopted by his successor, Victor Paz Estenssoro. These policies included a 95 per cent currency devaluation; a tenfold rise in fuel prices, the laying off of state-sector workers, a freeze on wages and the removal of subsidies. Inflation was reduced to double figures but real wages were halved and unemployment passed 30 per cent. Paz Estenssoro was replaced by Jaime Paz Zamora in 1989. Although Paz Zamora came third and won only 19.6 per cent of the vote in the 1989 elections, he was voted into power after intense horse-trading in Congress because no candidate secured an absolute majority. He has continued his predecessor's economic policy.

Brazil

With its huge economy Brazil is set to become a 'sub-imperialist' power in South America, dominating the region's industrial production. Brazil is already a major trading partner for all the countries with which it shares a border, as well as Chile and Ecuador. Yet Brazil is beset by internal difficulties which threaten its leadership: it is experiencing an acute urban crisis, growing polarisation between the rich and the poor, and unresolved tensions in the rural areas between small farmers and the owners of huge estates. The symptoms are unemployment; millions of homeless (an estimated 6 million children live on the streets); rising crime, including the killing by death squads of street children (a Brazilian parliamentary commission reported that some 7,000 were had been killed between 1987 and 1991); and pollution and environmental destruction.

Brazilian history is the history of its successive booms – sugar, rubber, cocoa, coffee, industrial development based on import substitution and mining. Each boom has sucked in the ingredients required by the landowners and industrialists – slaves, industrial machinery, transnational corporations and international loans. The military government (1964-85) identified the advancement of large commercial business interests with national security. By repressing the political opposition, trade unions and peasants, and by providing unprecedented subsidies and infrastructure, it saddled the country with unmanageable international debts and social problems. The contradiction between political democracy and the concentration of economic power in the hands of the few is now greater than ever. The Catholic Church in Brazil has done much to encourage popular organisation in the face of this distorted model of development and to reveal the injustices of Brazilian society.

The economic reforms of the present government of Fernando Collor will liberalise the economy and slim down or privatise bloated, loss-making state corporations, but they will do little for the millions of *favela* (shanty town) dwellers and landless peasants who have little hope of productive employment. And even now there is doubt about the government's ability to proceed with the liberalisation in the face of entrenched vested interests, including those of the military.

Chile

The dictatorship of General Pinochet came to an end in March 1990, over sixteen years after the military coup of 11 September 1973. The beginning of the end was the plebiscite of October 1988 which Pinochet lost by a margin of 54 to 43 per cent. The opposition victory opened the way for the December 1989 elections which were won by Patricio Aylwin, the veteran Christian Democrat. Aylwin stood as the candidate of a coalition that included all opposition parties except the Communist Party, which nevertheless supported him. The elections, however, were fought under a constitution devised by Pinochet which favoured the right and provided for 9 nominated senate seats (out of a total of 47). Combined with their 16 elected senators, this was enough to enable the right to block constitutional reform. Right-wing candidates in the election polled almost 43 per cent of the vote, showing that many Chileans were uncertain about their future under a government made up of people who had opposed the military régime.

The most lasting legacy of the Pinochet government is the Chilean economy, frequently cited as a model for Latin America. Today copper provides about 50 per cent of export earnings – down from more than 70 per cent 20 years ago – and the so-called 'non-traditional' exports (fruit, seafood, forestry products, cellulose and other minerals) provide the other half. These achievements were the product of cheap labour, tax write-offs, high profits, a liberal foreign investment régime and the suppression of the union movement. The economy grew at a rate of 5 per cent a year between 1984 and 1988, accelerating to 10 per cent in 1989 (the year of the presidential election) as the result of opportunist tax cuts by Pinochet. A high level of exports is still necessary to pay heavy, but not impossible, debt service charges. The result is that the democratic government is pledged to maintain the economic model. The test for the government is, as the World Bank comments, 'to fulfil its social agenda within the context of a conservative fiscal stance'. The social agenda is substantial: about 4 million Chileans live in poverty, half of whom are counted as extremely poor.

The other legacy of the Pinochet dictatorship is its record of human rights violations. In March 1991 President Aylwin presented to the nation the report of the government's Commission on Truth and Reconciliation. This gave details of 2,279 people who were executed for political reasons, died under torture or were 'disappeared' between September 1973 and March 1989.

The report, impressive and horrifying in its detail, lists only clearly-confirmed killings so its total is inevitably an underestimate. It gives no information on the far greater number of non-fatal cases of torture, arbitrary imprisonment and other excesses of the dictatorship. It is unlikely that the torturers and murderers will ever be brought to justice despite the efforts of relatives of the victims.

The temptation for politicians and church leaders alike is to withdraw from confrontation with the still-powerful military and their civilian right-wing allies, hoping that time and economic growth will heal the wounds inflicted by human rights violations.

Colombia

The Colombian writer Gabriel García Márquez, author of *One Hundred Years of Solitude,* created the genre known as 'magical realism' to deal with the complexities and contradictions of his country. On the one hand, Colombia is a success story with a growing and prosperous middle class and steady economic growth, even during the 'lost decade' of the 1980s; on the other hand, it has witnessed the longest-running guerrilla conflict in Latin America and since the late 1940s has become notorious for political and criminal violence and drug-trafficking. Poverty remains a critical problem and contributes to the spiral of violence: 25 per cent of the population suffers from a deficient diet and more than 30 per cent lacks access to safe water.

La violencia, a period of violent political conflict between Liberals and Conservatives, which acted as a prism for all sorts of other social conflicts, erupted in 1948 after the assassination of the popular Liberal politician, José Eliecer Gaitán. Around 150,000 people were killed between 1949 and 1950. The right used this period to assert itself over workers and peasants who had been stirred by Gaitán's call for change. It resulted in a system of government in which Liberal and Conservative parties agreed to alternate in power without threatening the status quo. This

appendix 1

system lasted from 1958 to 1974. Its effect was to exclude the majority of the population from any effective decision-making and ignite over thirty years of guerrilla conflict.

The two-party domination of Colombian politics has begun to break down. A new party, the *Unión Patriótica* (UP) was founded in 1985 by former FARC (Revolutionary Armed Forces of Colombia) guerrillas to challenge the Liberals and the Conservatives. The UP paid a high price for challenging the system – 70 of its leaders have been killed by extreme right-wing death squads and by the end of 1989 it had lost over 1,000 activists. Nevertheless the trend towards greater openness continues: in 1990 the M-19 guerrilla group re-entered civilian life as a political party, winning 12.5 per cent of the vote in the presidential election of May 1990 and, in December, 19 seats in the 70-member Constituent Assembly convoked to amend the Constitution. Violence, however, continues to disfigure Colombian political life. Much of it is drug-related but many people fall victim to the death squads and the security forces, acting for traditional right-wing political bosses and sometimes in collusion with the drug mafias. According to unofficial estimates, there were over 12,500 political killings and disappearances in Colombia in 1990.

Costa Rica

Costa Rica is renowned for having disbanded its armed forces after the brief civil conflict of 1948. José Figuéres, founder of the National Liberation Party, fought in the name of anti-communism but subsequently adopted all the social reforms initiated by the former president (1940-44) Rafael Calderón, the major figure of the losing side. Costa Rica has since been an oasis of peace in a region notorious for political upheaval and repression. It has a record of social and education expenditure which contributes to its tenth ranking among all developing countries in the 'Human Development Index', devised by the United Nations Development Programme.

During the period of Sandinista government in Nicaragua, Costa Rica was pressured by the Reagan administration to support its policy of military aggression through the *contras*. Under the presidency of Oscar Arias (1986-90), however, Costa Rica distanced itself from the more extreme *contras* and initiated the Arias Plan for peace in Central America, which came to fruition as the eleven-point 'Esquipulas II' agreement, winning him the Nobel Peace Prize in 1987.

The strains imposed by structural adjustment and growing concentration of wealth in Costa Rica do not augur well for the future. The differences in income between the richest and the poorest are comparable to other Latin American countries renowned for social injustice. There is a danger that increasing economic and social tensions could threaten Costa Rica's so far robust political democracy. This can be seen in the Costa Rican press which is almost uniform in its shrill and extreme conservative pronouncements.

Cuba

Cuba lies about 135 kilometres to the south of Florida. Throughout the twentieth century Cuba has been more pressured and buffeted by the United States than any other country in Latin America. After US intervention and subsequent victory over Spain in the Cuban war of independence in 1898, the US government did not allow the Cubans to attend the peace conference. The United States repeatedly intervened in Cuban affairs, or threatened to do so, until the revolution of 1959. As long as US interests (mainly those of the US sugar companies) were assured, the United States tolerated both corruption and dictatorship.

The guerrilla war, started in the Sierra Maestra by the 12 survivors of the 82 fighters who had set out from Mexico in the *Granma*, blossomed into victory in January 1959 because the revolutionary cause was taken up by students, urban workers and a significant proportion of the middle class. The antagonism of the United States became open hostility when Fidel Castro demonstrated that his government would not bend easily to US pressures. The economic embargo was imposed in October 1960; the abortive Bay of Pigs invasion, approved by President Eisenhower but allowed to continue by Kennedy, took place in April 1961; in January 1962 the United States orchestrated the expulsion of Cuba from the Organisation of American States; on 14 October 1962 US spy planes revealed the presence of Soviet rockets on Cuban soil; and after the deployment of the US fleet and tense negotiations the Soviet leader Kruschev agreed, without consulting his Cuban allies, to withdraw the missiles.

Cuba became a faithful, if somewhat wayward, ally of the Soviet Union until its collapse. The advances of the revolution – health and social standards on a par with developed countries – were funded by subsidised exchanges with the Soviet Union and other members of COMECON, which provided Cuba with oil at below world market prices and bought Cuban sugar, paying several times world market prices. The collapse of this system is a gigantic challenge for Cuba. In the modern world of free markets and open economies, in which the price of sugar is below the cost of production of even the most efficient producers, Cuba faces bankruptcy. The United States maintains its hostile stance, seemingly waiting for Castro and all he stands for to be swept away before throwing a lifeline to the beleaguered Cubans. Castro, who continues to dominate the revolutionary government, seems unwilling to compromise in the face of these obstacles.

Dominican Republic

The Dominican Republic occupies the eastern two-thirds of the island of Hispaniola, the first major landfall of Columbus's first voyage. Under the leadership of its eighty-five-year old president, Joaquín Balaguer, the Dominican Republic is celebrating the fifth centenary by building a lighthouse in the capital, Santo Domingo, for which an entire neighbourhood has been levelled.

The United States invaded the Dominican Republic in 1916 and remained in occupation until 1924. The consequence of that invasion was the thirty-one-year dictatorship of Rafael Trujillo, a former telegrapher and small-time thief, who rose to become the commander of the US-trained army in 1927. He was murdered in 1961 in a CIA-orchestrated plot. A second US invasion was launched in 1965 to prevent a group of nationalist officers from reversing a military coup which had prevented Juan Bosch, the winner of the 1963 elections, from taking power. In his place, the invasion installed Joaquín Balaguer, a close associate of Rafael Trujillo.

Today, the Dominican economy is in decline: between 1981 and 1986 income fell by 10 per cent and officially-acknowledged unemployment rose to 27 per cent. Prices of the main exports, sugar and nickel, are either declining or stagnant. The result is that the country has one of the highest infant mortality rates in Latin America: 70 deaths per 1,000 live births. The government is trying to adapt economic policies to unfavourable international trends but the outlook for the future is bleak.

Ecuador

Ecuadorean politics have been dominated by rivalry between the coastal region and the capital, Quito. The coastal region contains more than half the population and the city of Guayaquil, the commercial centre for bananas, rice and coffee. Ecuador's main resource is oil. It has been exploited only since the 1970s, and is found in the country's Amazonian territories, thus reinforcing the power of the capital.

Ecuador has escaped the political extremes of other Latin American countries. Even its period of military rule, 1972-78, was markedly milder. Military governments at least removed the last remnant of colonial rule – the system of tenancy or rent paid for in labour. Ecuador is still one of the least developed countries of Latin America, with over half the population (5.5 million) living below the poverty line. The Quechua-speaking Andean Indians, who make up the majority of the rural population, have become more politically organised in recent years and, together with Amazonian Indian groupings, are planning to commemorate the five-hundredth anniversary of Columbus's arrival in the New World with a wave of land occupations to recover what they see as rightfully theirs.

The present government is headed by a Social Democrat, Rodrigo Borja, but is increasingly unpopular because it is administering austerity policies forced on it by the difficult economic situation inherited from the previous government. The oil price rise caused by the Iraqi invasion of Kuwait provided windfall gains of $180 million which, despite pressures to reactivate the economy, were tucked away in an oil stabilisaton fund. Presidential elections are due in 1992.

El Salvador

In January 1992, twenty months of negotiations between the FMLN (Farabundo Marti National Liberation Front) guerrillas and the right-wing ARENA government culminated in a peace agreement and ceasefire, thus bringing the eleven-year civil war to an end. If fully implemented, this agreement will integrate the FMLN into civilian life as a moderate left-wing political party and break the power of the army. The agreement, reached in New York under the auspices of the UN Secretary-General, is an acceptance by the Salvadorean government that it cannot defeat the FMLN on the field of battle and that continuing the war will destroy the economy. It is also an indication of a change in US policy, with the Bush administration seeking to withdraw from a conflict in which the United States has failed to impose its will. Furthermore, it is a reflection of the end of super-power rivalry between the United States and the USSR and of the US government's insistence on detecting the influence of 'international communism' at the root of every third world conflict. Finally, the agreement indicates that the FMLN have acknowledged that revolution, as they originally conceived it, is not possible in El Salvador and that future economic prospects for Salvadoreans depend on finding a working relationship between all social forces and with the United States and neighbouring countries.

The far right, entrenched in the oligarchy and the armed forces, is by no means resigned to the agreement. There will be tense moments before it is put into effect, especially those parts dealing with the reduction in size of the armed forces and the creation of a

appendix 1

new civilian police force which will integrate former FMLN members with currently enlisted police officers. One issue that has not been settled is the question of those responsible for killing six Jesuits and two women in November 1989. A colonel and a lieutenant were found guilty, while six others who took part in the killings were acquitted by the jury on the grounds that they were obeying orders. It is widely suspected that ultimate responsibility rests with the army high command. Many other atrocities cry out for justice. The great majority of the 75,000 deaths in the civil war have been unarmed civilians, many of them killed in cold blood by the armed forces in a deliberate attempt to deprive the guerrillas of civilian support.

El Salvador will now have to begin the task of rebuilding its shattered economy, completely dependent on the United States, which over the past eleven years has channelled $4 billion in economic and military aid to this tiny country. Currently exports stand at $580 million a year, less than half the total annual import bill of $1,262 million.

Guatemala

Although the guerrilla war still smoulders on after thirty years in the more remote northern parts of the country, the URNG guerrillas have not been strong enough to force a negotiated settlement from the government in peace talks. The armed forces handed over to a civilian government in 1985 but they retain effective veto power over many areas of policy. Moreover, in the late 1970s and early 1980s the army waged its largely successful counter-insurgency war against the URNG guerrrillas without the benefit of US aid, which was spurned because it came with human rights conditions attached.

At the root of the armed conflict is the centuries-old domination of Guatemala and its Mayan Indian population by a white or *mestizo* landowning élite. Cheap rural labour is crucial to the plantation economy (producing coffee, sugar, cotton and bananas) which provides the basis of the landowners' fortunes and, in 1990, 48 per cent of export earnings.

The present cycle of Guatemala's misfortunes began with a CIA-organised military coup in 1954, mounted to oust a government committed to moderate agrarian reform. The Mayan Indians stood aside from the guerrilla conflict of the 1960s but were drawn in during the late 1970s when they saw that all attempts to win change by peaceful means were met with violence and when they came to believe that the guerrillas could actually win. The ensuing conflict was 'won' by the army in a campaign of extreme cruelty: villages were razed; entire communities massacred; and thousands of people were herded into strategic 'model villages'. Repression still continues: any person or group seen as an active defender of the poor is liable to be the target of death squads.

The new democracy of Guatemala consists largely of competitive elections between different right-of-centre factions, none of which is prepared to address the serious structural problems of the country. The World Bank admits that Guatemala 'is characterised by a very uneven distribution of land and income. The native American population – comprising more than half the population – lives in extreme poverty and at the margin of the money economy.' But the Bank does see hope for the future in non-traditional exports and tourism, 'given the country's attractive natural and cultural resources'. For these 'cultural resources' to flourish, there must be a convincing opening to participation and social justice for the Mayan Indians.

Guyana

Years of maladministration and vulnerability to international price fluctuations have made Guyana, with a gross national product (GNP) per head of $310 a year, the poorest country in the Americas. Since 1975 income (gross domestic product, or GDP) per head has fallen by 25 per cent and exports by 20 per cent. The population has declined over the past decade because of a low birth-rate and heavy emigration.

Forbes Burnham, leader of the People's National Congress (PNC), became president after the elections of 1964. He retained power until his death in 1985 largely as a result of electoral fraud. His successor is Desmond Hoyte whose election in December 1985 was widely criticised as fraudulent. Burnham nationalised the bauxite and sugar industries and maintained a virtual monopoly of the press. Continuing economic decline has forced Hoyte to reverse these economic policies and open up the economy to outside interests. Elections promised for the end of 1991 have been postponed. Opposition parties have welcomed the postponement because this will give more time to draw up an accurate register of voters.

Haiti

Haiti, occupying the western third of the island of Hispaniola, won its independence in 1804 – the first Latin American country to do so – as a result of a slave rebellion against the French colonial rulers. Haitian sugar production had made it one of France's richest colonies and was the source of much of the wealth that built Versailles. As a republic of freed slaves, Haiti isolated itself from and was isolated by the slave-owning and

appendix 1

slave-trading nations of the Western world. In 1915, in response to growing internal violence and instability and the possibility of German intervention (German residents outnumbered Americans two-to-one), the United States landed troops in Haiti, maintaining an occupying force until 1934. Subsequently, politics was dominated by the rivalry between the pale-skinned mulatto élite, which had co-operated with and done well out of the US occupation, and the emerging black opposition. François Duvalier ('Papa Doc'), the leader of the black movement, was elected president in 1957. He soon became renowned and feared for his willingness to use extreme violence against his enemies. The *Tontons Macoutes* (creole for 'bogeymen' who kidnap children) were his police. In 1964 he had himself declared 'President for Life'. After his death in 1971, Duvalier was succeeded by his son, Jean-Claude ('Baby Doc'), after approval in a referendum which gave him 2,391,916 votes in favour to one against. Jean-Claude remained in power until he was forced to flee to France in February 1986.

Politics since then has been a struggle between the remaining Duvalierists and the army on one side, and the reform movement on the other. In a climate of increasing violence the army aborted the elections of 29 November 1987 by firing on voters. New elections, held in January 1988 and marked by 80 per cent abstention, were 'won' by Leslie Manigat who was himself deposed by Prosper Avril, an army general, in September. Avril stepped down in 1990 in response to popular and international pressure. The elections on 16 December 1990 gave a landslide victory to Aristide Bertrand ('Titid'). Aristide, a former Salesian priest (expelled from the order in 1989), had won the support of the poor with his fiery preaching and had himself had narrowly escaped death at the hands of the *Tontons Macoutes*. Aristide was deposed by the army in September 1991. Haiti is now totally isolated internationally and starved of the aid on which it depends. The army and its rich backers are desperately casting about for a solution which will not mean an end to military ascendance and the political system which has given riches to the few and kept the great majority in terrible poverty.

Honduras

Until recently Honduras was the poorest country in Central America, before Nicaragua, its economy ruined by war, slipped below it. Some 40 per cent of the population over ten years of age is illiterate, 72 per cent of children under five years suffer from malnutrition, the infant mortality rate is 79 per 1,000 live births and 60 per cent of the population is inadequately housed. Unlike other Central American countries where coffee became the main export crop and underpinned the power of local ruling groups, bananas were the main export crop of Honduras. The entire operation was controlled by US companies which, in the early years of this century, made and unmade governments as they wished – hence the contemptuous term 'banana republic', coined to describe Honduras. Production increased from 6 million branches in 1910 to 30 million in 1929. By 1913, bananas accounted for 66 per cent of Honduras's exports. Today, they still make up more than a third of exports.

The influence of the banana companies caused chronic instability in Honduras until United Fruit bought out its rival Cuyamel in 1929. The crash of 1929 and the ensuing Great Depression ushered in the sixteen-year dictatorship of Tiburcio Carías who, facing lesser challenges than leaders of neighbouring countries, was less brutal. In the 1960s and 1970s the armed forces became the most important group in politics. Close contacts with the United States paved the way for Honduras, which has common borders with Guatemala, El Salvador and Nicaragua, to become the lynchpin of US military and covert operations in Central America. The Nicaraguan *contras* were based in Honduras where they were supplied by the United States. In recognition of these services total US aid to Honduras increased from $16.2 million in 1978 to $231 million in 1986; over the same period military aid increased from $3.2 million to $88.2 million. In 1981, after almost twenty years of military rule, Honduras elected a civilian government. The military, however, retained great influence while the *contra* war against Nicaragua continued. The current president, Rafael Callejas, who won the 1990 elections, was the first elected opposition candidate in fifty-seven years to assume power peacefully.

Jamaica

Michael Manley, a leading figure in the non-aligned movement in the 1970s, returned to power in Jamaica after the 1989 election which reduced Edward Seaga's right-wing Jamaica Labour Party (JLP) to 15 seats in the 60-seat assembly. Manley's People's National Party (PNP) was voted out of power in 1980 in the face of strong opposition, open and covert, from the United States. Since then he has shed most of the socialist aspirations which marked his government in the 1970s. He now has the task of restoring an economy burdened by debts incurred under the Seaga administration and satisfying the aspirations of poorer Jamaicans, who have witnessed their standard of living fall during the 1980s. The economy has diversified increasingly away from Jamaica's traditional exports, with non-traditional exports and tourism now accounting for 55 per cent of export earnings as against 40 per cent in the 1970s. Tourism now brings in more foreign exchange than alumina and bauxite.

appendix 1

Mexico

Mexico is the third-largest country in Latin America, after Brazil and Argentina, and the most populous Spanish-speaking nation. Its relationship with the United States and its 2,400-kilometre shared border exercises an enormous influence in Mexican life. This relationship will receive a further jolt when Mexico joins the United States and Canada in the North American Free Trade Area (NAFTA).

Present-day Mexico owes its form to, firstly, the Mexican revolution of 1910 – which carried out a land reform, emphasised the rights of urban labour and instituted a rigid separation of Church and state – and, secondly, to the establishment of the Institutional Revolutionary Party (PRI) which dates from 1928. Under a series of presidents elected for only one term every six years, the PRI became a formidable instrument of political patronage, making each Mexican president in effect an elected dictator. The PRI has no ideology as such, except perhaps for a vague nationalism, manifested in the liking of successive governments for state enterprises, although this has been brought to an end by the debt crisis and its remedies – structural adjustment and the liberalisation of the economy. President Salinas is now privatising the same banks that were nationalised in 1982.

The privatisation programme and cuts in remaining governmental bodies have reduced deficits and made available more resources for the relief of poverty, softening some of the effects of a decade of negative growth. The austerity measures have had a disproportionate effect on the 41 million Mexicans living on or below the poverty line.

President Salinas claims that he is the true nationalist. 'Modernisation is', he said, '... nationalistic.' This modernisation consists in the reform of the *ejido* system, inherited from the revolution, whereby peasants have the use of the land, which they can pass on to the next generation, but not the ownership. Salinas wants to turn the *ejido* lands over to private ownership to create a free market in land and encourage investment. He also wants to restore legal recognition of the Catholic Church. These proposals, together with his reforms in education and the liberalisation of the economy, will change the structure of Mexican politics: Salinas is wooing the northern middle class which has traditionally voted with the right-wing PAN party against the PRI.

Nicaragua

The Sandinistas were defeated in the elections of February 1990 by the UNO (*Unión Nacional Opositora*), an opposition coalition headed by Violeta de Chamorro, the widow of Pedro Joaquín Chamorro, a campaigning newspaper-owner who was murdered in 1978 on the orders of the dictator Anastasio Somoza. The election offered the Nicaraguans a clear choice: continuing war, scarcity and US hostility with the Sandinistas, tempered by a measure of national dignity; or a negotiated peace, the end of the US economic embargo and a renewal of US aid with Chamorro. The electoral victory of the UNO won peace but US aid was miserly, with the result that many Nicaraguans are now much worse off than they were under the Sandinistas. The new government has had to tackle the economic ills caused by the war and carry through its own programme of economic liberalisation with little external aid. New sources have not been found to replace Soviet-bloc aid, which allowed Nicaragua under the Sandinistas to import twice as much as it exported.

The Sandinistas remain the single largest force in politics, with 39 seats in the 92 seat National Assembly as against the UNO's 51 and one seat each for two small independent parties. The UNO has not changed its name because its fourteen constituent parties, ranging from the far right to the communists, could never agree on a replacement. The transitional period has been managed by an agreement between Violeta de Chamorro's team, headed by her son-in-law Francisco Lacayo, and the Sandinistas. This, to the fury of the more extreme faction of the UNO, leaves in place the major Sandinista reforms and the Sandinista army, headed by Humberto Ortega, the brother of the former Sandinista president, Daniel Ortega.

The economy is still in chaos. The year 1990 closed with a 4 per cent decline in output (a cumulative fall of 11.7 per cent between 1987 and 1990) and inflation of 7,400 per cent. Unemployment is very high and state services have been pruned drastically. Economic hardship has sharply raised political tension. Demobilised *contra* soldiers, seeking more generous treatment from the government and, in particular, good land (often in the hands of pro-Sandinista co-operatives) have reformed into military units and are known as *recontras*. They are opposed by units of Sandinistas called *recompas*.

Panama

Panama became an independent state as a result of a secessionist war against Colombia in 1903. The previous year Colombia had refused to ratify a treaty giving the United States rights to the Panama Canal route. In 1903 the new government of Panama gave the United States the right to build a canal and ceded in perpetuity the Canal Zone, the strip of land extending 8 kilometres on either

appendix 1

side of the canal. This agreement has since been revised several times, most recently in 1977 by the Carter-Torrijos treaty, which gave Panama full control over the Canal Zone. The US will surrender full operational control of the canal at midnight on 31 December 1999, when US personnel stationed in Panama – currently about 11,000 troops – must withdraw.

The United States invaded Panama on 20 December 1989 to arrest Manuel Noriega, the head of the National Guard and ruler of the country, on charges of drug-trafficking. The invasion involved 26,000 troops, causing the deaths of between 4,000 and 7,000 Panamanians. There were 23 US casualties. Noriega took refuge in the papal nunciature but gave himself up to US forces on 3 January 1990 and was extradited to Miami. Total losses were estimated at $2 billion, of which $1 billion alone was a result of looting. The operation was widely condemned in Latin America and the Organisation of American States endorsed a motion deploring the invasion by 20 votes to 1. Guillermo Endara, who was generally believed to have won the election of 1989 but was prevented from taking office by Noriega, became president after the invasion.

Panama's main income derives from off-shore banking. This declined rapidly in the two years of political instability and US economic sanctions which preceded the US invasion. In 1988 GDP contracted by 16 per cent as deposits were withdrawn from the 130 international banks established in Panama; there was a 1 per cent decline in 1989. The economy is now growing again (by 3.4 per cent in 1990, returning it to 1981 levels) but it has a long way to go before it recovers pre-1987 levels of income. By June 1990 deposits in the banking system were $15 billion, up on 1989 but still a long way short of the $40 billion placed in Panama in pre-Noriega days. Promised US aid, to make good damage caused by the invasion, has not materialised.

Paraguay

Paraguay is a land-locked country bounded by Brazil, Argentina and Bolivia. It was first settled, not by *conquistadores*, but by the Jesuits, who founded the capital city Asunción in 1537 and remained there for 239 years until their expulsion in 1776. The country is divided by the River Paraguay, from which it takes its name. Most of the population (95 per cent) lives in the third of the country lying to the east of the river. The River Paraná, on which stands the Itaipú dam, the largest in the world, forms the border with Brazil.

Paraguay continues to be a mainly agricultural country, although it has traditionally enjoyed illicit income from smuggling into the protected markets of neighbouring Argentina and Brazil. There was strong economic growth in the 1970s and early 1980s as a result of dam-building programmes. Growth has since slowed, as these programmes have tailed off and the anticipated pay-back of large electricity sales to Brazil has not yet materialised.

After ruling Paraguay for thirty-five years, the ailing dictator, General Alfredo Stroessner, was ousted by a coup in 1989. The coup leader, General Andrés Rodríguez, was sworn in immediately as president and proceeded to govern, as his predecessor had done, with the support of the Colorado Party's majority in the legislature. This *continuismo* was reaffirmed in December 1991 when the Colorados won a majority in the elections for the constituent assembly charged with writing a new constitution. The main opposition party, the Authentic Radical Liberal Party, which under its leader Domingo Laíno had provided the leadership of opposition to the dictatorship, won only 28 per cent. Free elections are scheduled for 1993.

Peru

Peruvian political life is dominated by the vicious eleven-year war between *Sendero Luminoso* ('Shining Path') guerrillas and the security forces. Another guerrilla group, the MRTA (*Movimiento Revolucionario Tupac Amaru*) started operations in 1984. A third, much smaller group, the Patriotic Liberation Front, an offshoot of the Communist Party, became active in January 1990.

Sendero Luminoso believes in 'prolonged popular struggle' and draws its inspiration from Mao Tse Tung. In its utter ruthlessness it is similar to the Khmer Rouge: *Sendero* targets all figures of government authority, development workers and anyone whose activities might benefit the status quo and therefore prove an obstacle to ultimate revolution. *Sendero* is responsible for a high proportion of the 23,000 political killings since 1980. It began its military activities in the highland department of Ayacucho and subsequently extended into other departments in the Andes. Now it also operates in Lima and other coastal cities where there are large Quechua-speaking commmunities. *Sendero* is supported by cocaine money which it collects as 'taxes' from drug traffickers in the Upper Huallaga valley. The background to these conflicts is the centuries-long exploitation of the Quechua-speaking rural population by the largely white ruling class entrenched in the major cities. Successive governments have responded with increasingly harsh military tactics: a number of the massacres attributed to *Sendero* are thought to have been carried out by counter-insurgency forces. The brutality of the government's campaign and rapidly falling living standards bring a steady flow

appendix 1

of recruits to the guerrilla movements. The thirteen most populous of Peru's twenty-four departments are now emergency zones ruled by the army.

There were full presidential and congressional elections in 1980, after a controlled period of transition from military to civilian rule initiated in 1978 with the election of a constituent assembly. Under the APRA government of Alan García, elected in 1985, the economy grew rapidly for two years, but this was achieved at the expense of a large balance of payments deficit and the controversial refusal to use no more than 10 per cent of export earnings to service the debt. Belated efforts to adjust the economy failed and inflation rose to 12,000 per cent in the twelve months up to August 1990.

A new government took office in July 1990, headed by the political outsider Alberto Fujimori, the son of Japanese immigrants. In his electoral campaign Fujimori had promised a moderate austerity programme, in contrast to the orthodox stabilisation advocated by his right-wing opponent, the novelist Mario Vargas Llosa. In the event, Fujimori's economic policy, known as 'Fujishock', was much more drastic: petrol increased in price by 3,200 per cent and all subsidies on food were removed. These and other liberalisation measures have stabilised the economy. Fujimori has a long way to go, however, before his policies begin to benefit the poor.

Suriname

Suriname was once a Dutch plantation colony with two classes: planters and slaves. After the Dutch abolished the slave trade – but not slavery itself – in 1814, more than 1,000 slaves were imported illegally each year. When slavery was abolished in 1863, the plantation slaves were replaced by imported labourers from Portugal, Java, the West Indies and later, as a result of a contract with Britain, from India.

After full independence was granted in 1975, between 100,000 and 150,000 people left the country. These were, generally speaking the most highly qualified, who took advantage of their Dutch citizenship.

Since the military coup of 1980 there has been political confusion and conflict. The Dutch government suspended aid after the military leader, Lieutenant-Colonel Desi Bouterse, shot fifteen prominent citizens in December 1982. Constitutional rule was restored in 1987, but there was another army coup on 24 December 1990, led again by Bouterse. The economy remains dependent on bauxite and alumina exports, which have suffered because of sporadic guerrilla fighting throughout the 1980s.

Trinidad and Tobago

Trinidad and Tobago became independent in 1962 and a republic within the British Commonwealth in 1976. As an oil-rich state, Trinidad and Tobago enjoyed huge prosperity in the 1970s and early 1980s, reflected in ambitious public-works programmes, the construction of iron- and steel-works and widespread corruption and misspending of public money. In 1986 the petroleum industry accounted for 25 per cent of GDP, 42 per cent of government revenue and 80 per cent of export earnings. Trinidad also has the biggest natural asphalt reserves in the world.

After 1983, with falling oil prices and the depletion of oil reserves, real income fell each year for six years, culminating in a 7 per cent decline in 1987 and a further 4 per cent in 1988. The government was forced to implement an adjustment programme, cutting government expenditure and liberalising and privatising the economy. The World Bank foresees that recovery will be gradual, since it will depend on investments in chemicals and the oil industry which will take some time to come on stream.

Dr Eric Williams, an austere and autocratic academic, dominated Trinidad and Tobago from independence until his death in 1981. Williams nevertheless presided over the excesses of the oil-boom years. His party, the People's National Movement (PNM), was defeated in local elections in 1983 and finally lost power to the National Alliance for Reconstruction (NAR) in 1986. The PNM was returned to power in December 1991 on a tide of discontent with the NAR's austerity policies. It is unlikely, however, to introduce any major changes in economic policy.

Despite its wealth Trinidad and Tobago has suffered strikes and upheavals, reflecting deeply-felt grievances at social and economic inequality. In 1970 there was a black-power uprising, supported by elements within the army and in 1990 a black Muslim group held the Cabinet and Prime Minister hostage to protest against government indifference to economic hardship.

Uruguay

Uruguay was once known as 'the Switzerland of Latin America' because of its extensive social security system built up between 1910 and 1930. Uruguay's prosperity depended on the export of beef, wool and hides. As these declined, the welfare system and standards of living generally came under great strain.

Frustration with electoral politics and the inability of the traditional parties – the Blancos and the Colorados – to halt Uruguay's decline set the scene for the emergence of the National Liberation

appendix 1

Movement, the Tupamaros, in the early 1960s. The Tupamaros mounted spectacular urban guerrilla raids and distributed food to the poor. They gained international attention by abducting and murdering the CIA agent, Dan Mitrione, and in 1971 by kidnapping and holding the British ambassador, Geoffrey Jackson. As police methods became more ruthless and the army was drawn into the conflict, the balance swung against the Tupamaros. Congress was dissolved in 1973 and the military assumed power, setting up a police state and using arbitrary arrest, widespread repression and torture to break the guerrilla movement and stifle opposition to military rule.

Civilian rule was restored in 1985 and all political prisoners were released. Controversy over whether military officers responsible for human rights violations should be amnestied continued for some time. The Congress approved an amnesty law in 1986 but opposition forces, taking advantage of a law which permits an issue to be made the subject of a referendum if more than a quarter of the electorate signs a petition, organised a campaign which gathered 630,000 signatures.

The amnesty law was submitted to referendum in April 1989. The government campaigned fiercely for the amnesty throughout the country and won by 1,008,925 votes to 770,221. The opposition did not have the resources to mount a nationwide campaign but did win in the capital, Montevideo. The presidential elections of November 1989, however, were won by the Blanco (Nationalist) candidate, Luis Lacalle. Unlike the previous Colorado Party president, Lacalle had opposed both the military government and the amnesty law. The left-wing *Frente Amplio* (Broad Front) carried Montevideo.

Both the present and the previous governments have been administering IMF-type stabilisation policies, privatising and liberalising the economy. Future growth will depend on exports and these, in turn, will depend on stability and growth in its South American trading partners. Traditional exports – such as wool, meat, fish and hides – still account for around 50 per cent of all exports, but are unlikely to find new markets.

Venezuela

Venezuela is one of only four countries in Latin America (together with Colombia, Costa Rica and Mexico) to have avoided direct military rule between 1970 and 1991. After a turbulent history, Venezuela celebrated its first free elections in 1947. The newly elected president, the novelist Rómulo Gallegos, was deposed eight months later by a military coup. The new dictator, Marcos Pérez Jiménez, was himself ousted in a popular uprising in 1958.

Since then two major parties, Acción Democrática (AD) and the Social Christians (COPEI), have competed for government, with AD winning five terms in office to COPEI's two.

Venezuela, confident of its economic power, has played a relatively independent role in Latin America. Under a COPEI government, Venezuela renewed diplomatic relations with Cuba in the early 1970s and began supplying oil, replacing Soviet oil that had been shipped at huge cost across the Atlantic. In the late 1970s the AD government of Carlos Andrés Pérez, negotiated with Mexico to set up the Latin American Economic System, a forum for co-operation and development which was not to be dominated by the United States. The Pérez government also aligned Venezuela with General Torrijos in Panama, in his attempts to renegotiate the Canal Treaty, and provided assistance to the Sandinista rebels in Nicaragua. Subsequently, Venezuela became a member of the Contadora group of countries – together with Colombia, Mexico and Panama – which sought, against the wishes of the Reagan administration, a negotiated solution to the conflicts in Central America.

Oil, and its ability to generate huge revenues, has underpinned Venezuelan democracy. Venezuela, however, after borrowing heavily in the expectation that oil would continue to provide this enormous income, was ensnared in the debt crisis when the price of oil fell in 1983. The austerity plan announced by the AD president, Carlos Andrés Pérez, after taking office in February 1989, provoked a wave of rioting and looting in major cities. Around 300 people died when the army was brought in to restore order. The attempted military coup of February 1992 was a further indication of discontent.

Argentina

Area: 2,767,000 sq km[1]
Population (1990): 32.3 million[2]
Population (2000, projected): 36.2 million[2]
Proportion under 15 years (1989): 29.9%[1]
Proportion urban (1990): 86%[2]
Population density: 11.8 persons/sq km[2]
Ethnic origins (1980): European 85%; Mestizo 10%; Amerindian between 1% and 6%[3,18]

Life expectancy – male (1989): 68 years[1]
Life expectancy – female (1989): 74 years[1]
Infant mortality per 1,000 live births (1989): 31[2]
Literacy (1985): 95%[1]
Women as proportion of labour force (1988-89): 21%[2]

GNP per head (1989): $2,160[1]
GNP per head – annual growth rate 1980-88: -1.6%[2]
Foreign debt (1989): $64,700 million[1]
Foreign debt per head (1989): $2,003
Total debt as proportion of GNP (1989): 119.7%[1]
Total debt as proportion of exports (1989): 537.0%[1]
Debt service as proportion of exports (1988): 36.1%[1]

Income distribution
- GNP per head, poorest 40% (1987): $840[2]
- share of income of wealthiest 20% (1970): 50.3%[3]
- share of income of poorest 20% (1970): 4.4%[3]

Land distribution (1969)[16]
- farms of less than 25 hectares (41.2%) occupy 0.9% of land
- farms over 1,000 hectares (6.1%) occupy 74.9% of land

Education spending[2]
- as proportion of public expenditure (1987-88): 8.9%
- as proportion of GNP (1986): 3.3%

Military spending[2]
- as proportion of GNP (1986): 1.5%
- arms imports (1987): $30 million

Main exports (1987): animals & meat 16%; food industry residues & animal feed 14%; cereals 12%; base metals & manufactures 8%; hide, skins etc 7%; oilseeds & nuts 5%[4]

Five main trading partners (1987)[4]
- imports: USA, Brazil, W. Germany, Japan, Bolivia
- exports: USA, USSR, Netherlands, Brazil, W. Germany

appendix 2

Belize

Area: 20,000 sq km[2]
Population (1989): 200,000[2]
Proportion urban (1990): 50%[2]
Population density: 10 persons/sq km
Ethnic origins (1980): more than 50% Afro-Caribbean; Amerindian (Maya) 12.5%; Carib 4%[3]

Life expectancy – male (1990): 69.5 years
Life expectancy – female (1990): 69.5 years
Infant mortality per 1,000 live births (1989): 50[2]
Literacy (1985): 91%[1]
Women as proportion of labour force (1988-89): 33%[2]

GNP per head (1988): $1,500[2]
GNP per head – annual growth rate 1980-88: 0.7%[2]
Foreign debt (1989): $137 million (Americas only)
Foreign debt per head (1989): $685
Debt service as proportion of exports (1988): 13.3%[2]

Education spending
- as proportion of public expenditure (1986): 15%[2]

Main exports (1989): sugar & molasses 37%; citrus concentrate 21%; fresh fish 12%; fresh fruit 5%[5,6]
Five main trading partners (1989)[5]
- imports: USA, European Community, Canada, Mexico, Caribbean
- exports: USA, UK, Canada, Mexico, Caribbean

Bolivia

Area: 1,099,000 sq km[1]
Population (1990): 7.3 million[2]
Population (2000, projected): 9.7 million[2]
Proportion under 15 years (1989): 43.9%[1]
Proportion urban (1990): 51%[2]
Population density: 6.7 persons/sq km[2]
Ethnic origins (1980): Amerindian 54% (3.65 million); Mestizo 32%; European 14%[3]

Life expectancy – male (1989): 52 years[1]
Life expectancy – female (1989): 56 years[1]
Infant mortality per 1,000 live births (1989): 105[2]
Literacy (1985): 74%[2]
Women as proportion of labour force (1988-89): 33%[2]

GNP per head (1989): $620[1]
GNP per head – annual growth rate 1980-88: -4.3%[2]
Foreign debt (1989): $4,349 million[1]
Foreign debt per head (1989): $597
Total debt as proportion of GNP (1989): 102.2%[1]
Total debt as proportion of exports (1989): 333.6%[1]
Debt service as proportion of exports (1989): 20.5%[1]

Income distribution (1980-88)
- proportion of rural population below poverty line: 85%[2]
- share of income of poorest 20%: 4% (av. $59 p.a.)[16]

Education spending[2]
- as proportion of public expenditure (1987-88): 20.1%
- as proportion of GNP (1986): 2.9%

Military spending[2]
- as proportion of GNP (1986): 2.4%
- arms imports (1987): 0

Main exports (1988): minerals 45.5%; natural gas 35.8%; agricultural produce 16.1%[4]
Five main trading partners (1987)[4]
- imports: Brazil, USA, Argentina, Japan, Chile
- exports: Argentina, USA, UK, Belgium, W. Germany

appendix 2

Brazil

Area: 8,512,000 sq km[1]
Population (1990): 150.4 million[2]
Population (2000, projected): 179.5 million[2]
Proportion under 15 years (1989): 38.2%[1]
Proportion urban (1990): 75%[2]
Population density: 17.8 persons/sq km[2]
Ethnic origins (1980): African/mulatto 50%;
  European 50%; Amerindian under 0.2% (150,000)[3]

Life expectancy – male (1989): 63 years[1]
Life expectancy – female (1989): 69 years[1]
Infant mortality per 1,000 live births (1989): 61[2]
Literacy (1985): 78.5%[2]
Women as proportion of labour force (1988-89): 27.9%[2]

GNP per head (1989): $2,540[1]
GNP per head – annual growth rate 1980-88: 1.2%[2]
Foreign debt (1989): $111,290 million[1]
Foreign debt per head (1989): $740
Total debt as proportion of GNP (1989): 24.1%[1]
Total debt as proportion of exports (1989): 301.6%[1]
Debt service as proportion of exports (1989): 31.3%[1]

Income distribution (1983)[1]
- share of income of wealthiest 10%: 46.2%
- share of income of wealthiest 20%: 62.6%
- share of income of poorest 20%: 2.4%

Land distribution (agricultural census 1985)
- farms of less than 10 hectares (52.5%) occupy 2.5% of land
- farms over 100 hectares (10%) occupy 89% of land
- farms over 1,000 hectares (0.9%) occupy 54% of land

Education spending[2]
- as proportion of public expenditure (1987-88): 17.7%
- as proportion of GNP (1986): 3.4%
Military spending[2]
- as proportion of GNP (1986): 0.9%
- arms imports (1987): $100 million

Main exports (1988): minerals 15%; machinery 10%; soya beans & products 9%; transport equipment 9%; coffee 7%[4]
Five main trading partners (1988)[4]
- imports: USA, W. Germany, Iraq (oil), Japan, Saudi Arabia
- exports: USA, Netherlands, Japan, W. Germany, Italy

Chile

Area: 757,000 sq km[1]
Population (1990): 13.2 million[2]
Population (2000, projected): 15.3 million[2]
Proportion under 15 years (1989): 30.7%[1]
Proportion urban (1990): 86%[2]
Population density: 17.6 persons/sq km[2]
Ethnic origins (1980): Mestizo 70%; European 25%; Mapuche Amerindian 5%-7.5% (550,000-830,000)[3]

Life expectancy – male (1989): 68 years[1]
Life expectancy – female (1989): 75 years[1]
Infant mortality per 1,000 live births (1989): 20[2]
Literacy (1985): 92%[2]
Women as proportion of labour force (1988-89): 22.2%[2]

GNP per head (1989): $1,770[1]
GNP per head – annual growth rate 1980-88: -0.1%[2]
Foreign debt (1989): $18,241 million[1]
Foreign debt per head (1989): $1,381
Total debt as proportion of GNP (1989): 78.3%[1]
Total debt as proportion of exports (1989): 187.7%[1]
Debt service as proportion of exports (1989): 27.5%[1]

Income distribution (1985)[15]
- share of income of wealthiest 20%: 56%
- share of income of poorest 20%: 3%

Education spending[2]
- as proportion of public expenditure (1987-88): 15.3%
- as proportion of GNP (1986): 5%

Military spending[2]
- as proportion of GNP (1986): 3.6%
- arms imports (1987): $30 million

Main exports (1989): copper 50%; foodstuffs 13%; agricultural & fish products 10%; other minerals 9%[4]
Five main trading partners (1989)[4]
- imports: USA, Japan, Brazil, W. Germany, Argentina
- exports: USA, Japan, W. Germany, Brazil, UK

Colombia

Area: 1,139,000 sq km[1]
Population (1990): 33 million[2]
Population (2000, projected): 39.4 million[2]
Proportion under 15 years (1989): 35.9%[1]
Proportion urban (1990): 70%[2]
Population density: 30.6 persons/sq km[2]
Ethnic origins (1980): Mestizo 50%; African/mulatto 29%; European 20%; Amerindian 1.4% (400,000)[3]

Life expectancy – male (1989): 66 years[1]
Life expectancy – female (1989): 72 years[1]
Infant mortality per 1,000 live births (1989): 39[2]
Literacy (1985): 84.7%[2]
Women as proportion of labour force (1988-89): 34.1%[2]

GNP per head (1989): $1,200[1]
GNP per head – annual growth rate 1980-88: 1.2%[2]
Foreign debt (1989): $16,887 million[1]
Foreign debt per head (1989): $511
Total debt as proportion of GNP (1989): 45.8%[1]
Total debt as proportion of exports (1989): 208.3%[1]
Debt service as proportion of exports (1989): 45.9%[1]

Income distribution (1988)[1]
- share of income of wealthiest 20%: 53%
- share of income of poorest 20%: 4%

Land distribution (1984 census, excludes Antioquia & Chocó)
- farms of less than 3 hectares (56.9%) occupy 2.8% of land
- farms over 100 hectares (3.36%) occupy 61.3% of land

Education spending[2]
- as proportion of public expenditure (1987-88): 22.4%
- as proportion of GNP (1986): 2.8%

Military spending[2]
- as proportion of GNP (1986): 1%
- arms imports (1987): $10 million

Main exports (1988): coffee 32.5%; petroleum & derivatives 20%; textiles, clothing, leather & footwear 7%; coal 6%; bananas 5%; flowers 4%[4]

Five main trading partners (1988)[4]
- imports: USA, Japan, W. Germany, Brazil, Mexico
- exports: USA, W. Germany, Japan, Netherlands, Venezuela

Costa Rica

Area: 51,000 sq km[1]
Population (1990):   3 million[2]
Population (2000, projected):   3.7 million[2]
Proportion under 15 years (1989):   36.2%[1]
Proportion urban (1990):   47%[2]
Population density: 59.5 persons/sq km[2]
Ethnic origins (1980):   European 92%; Mestizo 7.5%; Amerindian under 1% (14,000)[3]

Life expectancy – male (1989):   73 years[1]
Life expectancy – female (1989):   77 years[1]
Infant mortality per 1,000 live births (1989):   18[2]
Literacy (1985):   92%[2]
Women as proportion of labour force (1988-89):   21.2%[2]

GNP per head (1989): $1,780[1]
GNP per head – annual growth rate 1980-88:   0.2%[2]
Foreign debt (1989): $4,468 million[1]
Foreign debt per head (1989): $1,489
Total debt as proportion of GNP (1989):   91.2%[1]
Total debt as proportion of exports (1989):   236.2%[1]
Debt service as proportion of exports (1988):   19.2%[1]

Income distribution (1986)[1]
- share of income of wealthiest 10%:   38.8%
- share of income of wealthiest 20%:   54.5%
- share of income of poorest 20%:   3.3%

Land distribution (1984)[21]
- farms averaging 1.8 hectares (46.6%) occupy 2.4% of land
- farms averaging 183.5 hectares (13.3%) occupy 75.8% of land

Education spending[2]
- as proportion of public expenditure (1987-88):   20.8%
- as proportion of GNP (1986):   4.5%

Military spending[2]
- as proportion of GNP (1986):   0%
- arms imports (1987):   0

Main exports (1988):   coffee 26%; bananas 20.5%; cattle & meat 4.5%[4]

Five main trading partners (1984)[4]
- imports: USA, Japan, Guatemala, W. Germany, El Salvador
- exports: USA, W. Germany, Guatemala, El Salvador.

Cuba

Area: 11,000 sq km[1]
Population (1990): 10.6 million[2]
Population (2000, projected): 11.5 million[2]
Proportion urban (1990): 75%[2]
Population density: 30.6 persons/sq km[2]
Ethnic origins (according to 1981 census): white 66%; mixed race 22%; black 12%[7]

Life expectancy – male (1990): 75.4 years[2]
Life expectancy – female (1989): 75.4 years[2]
Infant mortality per 1,000 live births (1989): 11[2]
Literacy (1985): 96%[2]
Women as proportion of labour force (1988-89): 31.7%[2]

GNP per head (1989): $2,000[2]
Foreign debt, to West only (1988): $6,260 million[7]

Education spending[2]
- as proportion of public expenditure (1987-88): 14.1%
- as proportion of GNP (1986): 6.2%

Military spending[2]
- as proportion of GNP (1986): 5.4%
- arms imports (1987): $1,800 million

Main exports (1983): sugar & sugar products 75%; re-exported Soviet oil 9%; seafood 4%; nickel 3%[10]
Five main trading partners (1989)[4]
- imports: USSR, E. Germany, China, Czechoslavakia, Spain
- exports: USSR, E. Germany, China, Bulgaria, Czechoslovakia

Dominican Republic

Area: 49,000 sq km[1]
Population (1990): 7.2 million[2]
Population (2000, projected): 8.6 million[2]
Proportion under 15 years (1989): 23.2%[1]
Proportion urban (1990): 60%[2]
Population density: 148.2 persons/sq km[2]
Ethnic origins (1980): African 84%; mixed race or white 16%[3]

Life expectancy – male (1989): 65 years[1]
Life expectancy – female (1989): 69 years[1]
Infant mortality per 1,000 live births (1989): 63[2]
Literacy (1985): 80%[2]
Women as proportion of labour force (1988-89): 14.5%[2]

GNP per head (1989): $790[1]
GNP per head – annual growth rate 1980-88: -1.6%[2]
Foreign debt (1989): $4,066 million[1]
Foreign debt per head (1989): $565
Total debt as proportion of GNP (1989): 63.3%[1]
Total debt as proportion of exports (1989): 165.5%[1]
Debt service as proportion of exports (1989): 13%[1]

Income distribution (1980-88)[2]
- proportion of total population below poverty line: 44%
- proportion of rural population below poverty line: 43%

Education spending[2]
- as proportion of public expenditure (1987-88): 10%
- as proportion of GNP (1986): 1.6%

Military spending[2]
- as proportion of GNP (1986): 1.4%
- arms imports (1987): $5 million

Main exports (1988): sugar & molasses 23%; gold & silver 10%; coffee 9%; cocoa 5%. Earnings from tourism were $657 million, three times the earnings from sugar ($217 million)[5]

Five main trading partners (1985)[4]
- imports: USA, Venezuela, Mexico, Japan, W. Germany
- exports: USA, Puerto Rico, Belgium & Luxembourg, Netherlands, Canada

Ecuador

Area: 284,000 sq km[1]
Population (1990): 10.6 million[2]
Population (2000, projected): 13.3 million[2]
Proportion under 15 years (1989): 40.1%[1]
Proportion urban (1990): 56%[2]
Population density: 38.9 persons/sq km[2]
Ethnic origins (1980): Amerindian 40%; mixed race 40%; white 15%; black 5%[12]

Life expectancy – male (1989): 64 years[1]
Life expectancy – female (1989): 68 years[1]
Infant mortality per 1,000 live births (1989): 61[2]
Literacy (1985): 83%[2]
Women as proportion of labour force (1988-89): 20.4%[2]

GNP per head (1989): $1,020[1]
GNP per head – annual growth rate 1980-88: -1.1%[2]
Foreign debt (1989): $11,311 million[1]
Foreign debt per head (1989): $1,067
Total debt as proportion of GNP (1989): 117%[1]
Total debt as proportion of exports (1989): 392.3%[1]
Debt service as proportion of exports (1988): 36.2%[1]

Income distribution (1980-88)[2]
- proportion of total population below poverty line: 51%
- proportion of rural population below poverty line: 65%

Education spending[2]
- as proportion of public expenditure (1987-88): 21.3%
- as proportion of GNP (1986): 4.2%

Military spending[2]
- as proportion of GNP (1986): 1.6%
- arms imports (1987): $90 million

Main exports (1988): petroleum 40%; seafood 19%; bananas 14%; cocoa & products 8%; coffee 7%; petroleum derivatives 5%; seafood products 4%[4]

Five main trading partners (1988)[4]
- imports: USA, Japan, Brazil, W. Germany, Spain
- exports: USA, W. Germany, Chile, Japan, Taiwan

El Salvador

Area: 21,000 sq km[1]
Population (1990): 5.3 million[2]
Population (2000, projected): 6.7 million[2]
Proportion under 15 years (1989): 44.7%[1]
Proportion urban (1990): 44%[2]
Population density: 2,535 persons/sq km[2]
Ethnic origins (1980): Mestizo 89%;
  Amerindian 5% (190,000); European 1%[3]

Life expectancy – male (1989): 59 years[1]
Life expectancy – female (1989): 67 years[1]
Infant mortality per 1,000 live births (1989): 61[2]
Literacy (1985): 69%[2]
Women as proportion of labour force (1988-89): 25.1%[2]

GNP per head (1989): $1,070[1]
GNP per head – annual growth rate 1980-88: -1.8%[2]
Foreign debt (1989): $1,851 million[1]
Foreign debt per head (1989): $349
Total debt as proportion of GNP (1989): 32.1%[1]
Total debt as proportion of exports (1989): 177.3%[1]
Debt service as proportion of exports (1989): 16.6%[1]

Income distribution (late 1970s)[20]
- share of income of wealthiest 20%: 66%
- share of income of poorest 20%: 2%

Land distribution (1971, modified by 1985 agrarian reform)[20]
- farms lass than 3 hectares (71%) occupy 10.4% of farmland
- farms over 100 hectares (0.7%) occupy 38.7% of farmland

Education spending[2]
- as proportion of public expenditure (1987-88): 12.5%
- as proportion of GNP (1986): 1.9%

Military spending[2]
- as proportion of GNP (1986): 3.7%
- arms imports (1987): $50 million

Main exports (1988): coffee 58%; textiles & textile manufactures 9%.[4] Remittances from Salvadoreans living abroad bring in over $500 million per year.
Five main trading partners (1988)[4]
- imports: USA, Guatemala, Mexico, Japan, Costa Rica
- exports: USA, W. Germany, Guatemala, Costa Rica, Japan

appendix 2

Guatemala

Area: 109,000 sq km[1]
Population (1990): 9.2 million[2]
Population (2000, projected): 12.2 million[2]
Proportion under 15 years (1989): 45.7%[1]
Proportion urban (1990): 40%[2]
Population density: 8.48 persons/sq km[2]
Ethnic origins (1980): Amerindian (Maya) 54%; Mestizo 42%; European 4%[3]

Life expectancy – male (1989): 60 years[1]
Life expectancy – female (1989): 65 years[1]
Infant mortality per 1,000 live births (1989): 56[2]
Literacy (1985): 51.9%[2]
Women as proportion of labour force (1988-89): 16.2%[2]

GNP per head (1989): $910[1]
GNP per head – annual growth rate 1980-88: -3.1%[2]
Foreign debt (1989): $2,601 million[1]
Foreign debt per head (1989): $283
Total debt as proportion of GNP (1989): 32.6%[1]
Total debt as proportion of exports (1989): 171.1%[1]
Debt service as proportion of exports (1988): 19%[1]

Income distribution (1979-81)[1]
- share of income of wealthiest 10%: 40.8%
- share of income of wealthiest 20%: 55%
- share of income of poorest 20%: 5.5%

Land distribution (1979)[8]
- farms less than 1.4 hectares (54%) occupy 4% of farmland
- farms over 45 hectares (2.6%) occupy 65% of farmland

Education spending[2]
- as proportion of public expenditure (1987-88): 12.4%
- as proportion of GNP (1986): 1.4%

Military spending[2]
- as proportion of GNP (1986): 1.3%
- arms imports (1987): $5 million

Main exports (1989): coffee 33%; sugar 8%; bananas 8%; cotton 2.4%; cardamom 2.4%[4]
Five main trading partners (1988)[4]
- imports: USA, Mexico, W. Germany, Japan, El Salvador
- exports: USA, El Salvador, W. Germany, Costa Rica, Italy

Guyana

Area: 22,000 sq km[2]
Population (1990): 800,000[2]
Population (2000, projected): 900,000[2]
Proportion urban (1990): 35%[2]
Population density: 36.4 persons/sq km[2]
Ethnic origins (1980): Asian 50%; Afro-Caribbean 30%;
  Amerindian 5%; others – Mestizo, European, Chinese[18]

Life expectancy – male (1989): 64 years[1]
Life expectancy – female (1989): 64 years[1]
Infant mortality per 1,000 live births (1989): 54[2]
Literacy (1985): 95%[2]
Women as proportion of labour force (1988-89): 21%[2]

GNP per head (1989): $310[9]
GNP per head – annual growth rate 1980-88: -5.5%[2]
Foreign debt (1988): $1,764 million[5]
Foreign debt per head (1988): $2,500[5]
Total debt as proportion of GNP (1988): 302%[2]
Total debt as proportion of exports (1988): 18.2%[2]

Education spending
- as proportion of GNP (1986): 9.6%[2]

Main exports (1989): sugar 37%; bauxite 33%; rice 6%[5]
Main trading partners (1988)[6]
- exports: European Community, Latin America, USA, Japan

appendix 2

Haiti

Area: 28,000 sq km[1]
Population (1990): 6.5 million[2]
Population (2000, projected): 8 million[2]
Proportion under 15 years (1989): 40.1%[1]
Proportion urban (1990): 28%[2]
Population density: 236 persons/sq km[2]
Ethnic origins (1980): African/mulatto 99%

Life expectancy – male (1989): 54 years[1]
Life expectancy – female (1989): 57 years[1]
Infant mortality per 1,000 live births (1989): 94[2]
Literacy (1985): 48%[2]
Women as proportion of labour force (1988-89): 33.6%[2]

GNP per head (1989): $360[1]
GNP per head – annual growth rate 1980-88: -2.1%[2]
Foreign debt (1989): $802 million[1]
Foreign debt per head (1989): $123
Total debt as proportion of GNP (1988): 34.2%[1]
Total debt as proportion of exports (1989): 203%[1]
Debt service as proportion of exports (1988): 8.8%[1]

Income distribution (1980-88)[2]
- proportion of total population below poverty line: 76%
- proportion of rural population below poverty line: 80%

Education spending[2]
- as proportion of public expenditure (1987-88): 20.6%
- as proportion of GNP (1986): 0.4%

Military spending[2]
- as proportion of GNP (1986): 1.5%
- arms imports (1987): $30 million

Main exports (1988-89): light manufactures 67.5%; coffee 21.6%[4]
Five main trading partners (1988-89)[4]
- imports: USA, Japan, France, Canada, W. Germany
- exports: USA, Italy, France, Belgium, W. Germany

Honduras

Area: 112,000 sq km[1]
Population (1990): 5.1 million[2]
Population (2000, projected): 6.8 million[2]
Proportion under 15 years (1989): 45%[1]
Proportion urban (1990): 44%[2]
Population density: 46 persons/sq km[2]
Ethnic origins (1980): Mestizo 92%; Amerindian 5% (202,000); African/mulatto 2%; white 1%[3]

Life expectancy – male (1989): 63 years[1]
Life expectancy – female (1989): 67 years[1]
Infant mortality per 1,000 live births (1989): 79[9]
Literacy (1985): 68%[2]
Women as proportion of labour force (1988-89): 18.3%[2]

GNP per head (1989): $900[1]
GNP per head – annual growth rate 1980-88: -1.7%[2]
Foreign debt (1989): $3,350 million[1]
Foreign debt per head (1989): $657
Total debt as proportion of GNP (1989): 72.5%[1]
Total debt as proportion of exports (1989): 303%[1]
Debt service as proportion of exports (1989): 13.1%[1]

Income distribution (1980-88)
- proportion of total population below poverty line: 37%[2]
- proportion of rural population below poverty line: 55%[2]
- share of income of wealthiest 20% (late 1970s): 60%[20]
- share of income of poorest 20% (late 1970s): 4%[20]

Land distribution (agrarian census 1974)[8]
- farms of less than 2 hectares (37%) occupy 3% of land
- farms greater than 100 hectares (2%) occupy 44% of land

Education spending[2]
- as proportion of public expenditure (1987-88): 19.5%
- as proportion of GNP (1986): 5%

Military spending[2]
- as proportion of GNP (1986): 5.9%[2]
- arms imports (1987): $60 million[2]

Main exports (1989): bananas 36.5%; coffee 20%; lead & zinc 9%; shellfish 8%[4]
Five main trading partners (1989)[4]
- imports: USA, Japan, Venezuela, Mexico, Netherlands
- exports: USA, W. Germany, Japan, Italy, Belgium

appendix 2

Jamaica

Area: 11,000 sq km[1]
Population (1990): 2.5 million[2]
Population (2000, projected): 2.7 million[2]
Proportion under 15 years (1989): 33.8%[1]
Proportion urban (1990): 52%[2]
Population density: 232.8 persons/sq km[2]
Ethnic origins (1980): more than 90% Afro-Caribbean

Life expectancy – male (1989): 71 years[1]
Life expectancy – female (1989): 75 years[1]
Infant mortality per 1,000 live births (1989): 16[2]
Literacy (1985): 98%[2]
Women workers as proportion of labour force (1988-89): 31%[2]

GNP per head (1989): $1,260[1]
GNP per head – annual growth rate 1980-88: -2.1%[2]
Foreign debt (1989): $4,322 million[1]
Foreign debt per head (1989): $1,728
Total debt as proportion of GNP (1988): 133.8%[1]
Total debt as proportion of exports (1989): 188%[1]
Debt service as proportion of exports (1988): 26.4%[1]

Income distribution
- proportion of rural population below poverty line (1980-88): 80%[2]
- share of income of wealthiest 20% (1988): 49.2%[1]
- share of income of poorest 20% (1988): 5.4%[1]

Education spending[2]
- as proportion of public expenditure (1987-88): 11%
- as proportion of GNP (1986): 5.6%

Military spending[2]
- as proportion of GNP (1986): 1.5%
- arms imports (1987): $5 million

Main exports (1989): alumina 45%; bauxite 13%; sugar 7%[5]
Five main trading partners (1986)[4]
- imports: USA, UK, Canada, Japan, Ecuador
- exports: USA, UK, Canada, Netherlands, USSR

Mexico

Area: 1,958,000 sq km[1]
Population (1990): 88.6 million[2]
Population (2000, projected): 107.2 million[2]
Proportion under 15 years (1989): 38.1%[1]
Proportion urban (1990): 73%[2]
Population density: 46.1 persons/sq km[2]
Ethnic origins (1980): Mestizo 75%; European 15%; Amerindian 10% (3.5 million)[3]

Life expectancy – male (1989): 66 years[1]
Life expectancy – female (1989): 73 years[1]
Infant mortality per 1,000 live births (1989): 41[2]
Literacy (1985): 84.7%[2]
Women as proportion of labour force (1988-89): 23.1%[2]

GNP per head (1989): $2,010[1]
GNP per head – annual growth rate 1980-88: -1.4%[2]
Foreign debt (1989): $95,642 million[1]
Foreign debt per head (1989): $1,079
Total debt as proportion of GNP (1988): 41%[2]
Total debt as proportion of exports (1989): 264%[1]
Debt service as proportion of exports (1988): 25.5%[2]

Income distribution (1977)[3]
- share of income of wealthiest 20%: 57.7%
- share of income of poorest 20%: 2.9%

Education spending[2]
- as proportion of public expenditure (1987-88): 16.6%
- as proportion of GNP (1986): 4.3%

Military spending[2]
- as proportion of GNP (1986): 0.6%
- arms imports (1987): $240 million

Main exports (1987): crude petroleum 38%; motor engines 6%; coffee 2.4%; shrimps & prawns 2.1%[4]
Five main trading partners (1988)[4]
- imports: USA, W. Germany, Japan, Canada, France
- exports: USA, Japan, Spain, France, W. Germany

appendix 2

Nicaragua

Area: 12,000 sq km[2]
Population (1990): 3.9 million[2]
Population (2000, projected): 5.3 million[2]
Proportion urban (1990): 60%[2]
Population density: 32.6 persons/sq km[2]
Ethnic origins (1980): Mestizo 76%; African/mulatto 11%; European 10%; Amerindian 3% (105,000)[3,10]

Life expectancy – male (1989): 65 years[2]
Life expectancy – female (1989): 65 years[2]
Infant mortality per 1,000 live births (1989): 59[2]
Literacy (1985): 78%[2]
Women as proportion of labour force (1988-89): 21.5%[2]

GNP per head (1988): $830[2]
GNP per head – annual growth rate 1980-88: -4.7%[2]
Foreign debt (1990): $10,400 million[9]
Foreign debt per head (1989): $2,564
Total debt as proportion of GNP (1988): 309%[1]
Total debt as proportion of exports (1989): 2,653%[1]
Debt service as proportion of exports (1989): 8.6%[1]

Income distribution (1980-88)[2]
- proportion of total population below poverty line: 20%
- proportion of rural population below poverty line: 19%

Land distribution (1983)[20]
- 10.5 % of farms are 7 hectares or less
- 26.5 % of farms have 70 hectares or more (excluding state farms)

Education spending[2]
- as proportion of public expenditure (1987-88): 12%
- as proportion of GNP (1986): 6.4%

Military spending[2]
- as proportion of GNP (1986): 16%
- arms imports (1987): $500 million

Main exports (1987): coffee 44.7%; cotton 15.5%; meat 4%[10]
Five main trading partners (1984)[4]
- imports: USA, USSR, Mexico, Cuba, Spain
- exports: Japan, W. Germany, USA, France, Spain

Panama

Area: 77,000 sq km[1]
Population (1990): 2.4 million[2]
Population (2000, projected): 2.9 million[2]
Proportion under 15 years (1989): 35.4%[1]
Proportion urban (1990): 53%[2]
Population density: 31.8 persons/sq km[2]
Ethnic origins (1980): Mestizo 70%; Afro-Caribbean 14%; white 9%; Amerindian 7%[19]

Life expectancy – male (1989): 65 years[1]
Life expectancy – female (1989): 69 years[1]
Infant mortality per 1,000 live births (1989): 23[2]
Literacy (1985): 86.4%[2]
Proportion of women in the labour force (1988-89): 27%[2]

GNP per head (1989): $1,760[1]
GNP per head – annual growth rate (1980-88): 0.1%[2]
Foreign debt (1989): $7,418 million[1]
Foreign debt per head (1989): $3,090
Total debt as proportion of GNP (1989): 142.5%[1]
Total debt as proportion of exports (1989): 257.8%[1]
Debt service as proportion of exports (1988): 0.1%[1]

Income distribution (1980-88):
- proportion of total population below poverty line: 25%[2]
- proportion of rural population below poverty line: 30%[2]
- share of income of wealthiest 20% (1980): 60.3%[22]
- share of income of poorest 20% (1980): 2.7%[22]

Education spending[2]
- as proportion of public expenditure (1987-88): 26.7%
- as proportion of GNP (1986): 5.4%

Military spending[2]
- as proportion of GNP (1986): 2%
- arms imports (1987): $5 million

Main exports (1988): bananas 28%; shrimps 21%; coffee 4%; sugar 3%[4]
Five main trading partners (1989)[4]
- imports: USA, Free Zone of Colón, Ecuador, Japan, Costa Rica
- exports: USA, W. Germany, Costa Rica, Italy, Puerto Rico

Paraguay

Area: 407,000 sq km[1]
Population (1990): 4.3 million[2]
Population (2000, projected): 5.5 million[2]
Proportion under 15 years (1989): 41.1%[1]
Proportion urban (1990): 50%[2]
Population density: 10.8 persons/sq km[2]
Ethnic origins (1980): Mestizo 76%; European 20%; Amerindian 3%; African/mulatto 1%[3]

Life expectancy – male (1989): 65 years[1]
Life expectancy – female (1989): 69 years[1]
Infant mortality per 1,000 live births (1989): 41[2]
Literacy (1985): 88.3%[2]
Women as proportion of labour force (1988-89): 38.1%[2]

GNP per head (1989): $1,030[1]
GNP per head – annual growth rate 1980-88: -2.1%[2]
Foreign debt (1989): $2,490 million[1]
Foreign debt per head (1989): $579
Total debt as proportion of GNP (1989): 61.1%[1]
Total debt as proportion of exports (1989): 181.3%[1]
Debt service as proportion of exports (1989): 11.9%[1]

Income distribution (1980-88)[2]
- proportion of total population below poverty line: 35%
- proportion of rural population below poverty line: 50%

Education spending[2]
- as proportion of public expenditure (1987-88): 14%
- as proportion of GNP (1986): 2.9%

Military spending[2]
- as proportion of GNP (1986): 1%
- arms imports (1987): 0

Main exports (1989): soya beans 35%; cotton 32%; timber 3%[4]
Five main trading partners (1986)[4]
- imports: Brazil, Argentina, USA, Algeria, W. Germany
- exports: Brazil, Argentina, Netherlands, Switzerland, Chile

Peru

Area: 1,285,000 sq km[1]
Population (1990): 21.6 million[2]
Population (2000, projected): 26.3 million[2]
Proportion under 15 years (1989): 38.4%[1]
Proportion urban (1990): 70%[2]
Population density: 17.4 persons/sq km[2]
Ethnic origins (1980): Amerindian 49%; Mestizo 33%; white 12%; African/mulatto 6%[3]

Life expectancy – male (1989): 60 years[1]
Life expectancy – female (1989): 64 years[1]
Infant mortality per 1,000 live births (1989): 84[2]
Literacy (1985): 82%[2]
Women as proportion of labour force (1988-89): 33.1%[2]

GNP per head (1989): $1,010[1]
GNP per head – annual growth rate 1980-88: -1.2%[2]
Foreign debt (1989): $19,875 million[1]
Foreign debt per head (1989): $920
Total debt as proportion of GNP (1989): 173.5%[1]
Total debt as proportion of exports (1989): 432.2%[1]
Debt service as proportion of exports (1989): 6.8%[1]

Income distribution[1]
- share of income of wealthiest 10%: 35.8%
- share of income of wealthiest 20%: 51.9%
- share of income of poorest 20%: 4.4%

Education spending[2]
- as proportion of public expenditure (1987-88): 22.9%
- as proportion of GNP (1986): 2.2%

Military spending[2]
- as proportion of GNP (1986): 6.5%
- arms imports (1987): $430 million

Main exports (1987): copper 20%; petroleum & derivatives 10.5%; lead 10%; zinc 9%; fishmeal 9%; coffee 5.5%[4]
Five main trading partners (1980)[4]
- imports: USA, Japan, W. Germany, Argentina, Brazil
- exports: USA, Japan, USSR, W. Germany, Belgium & Luxembourg

Suriname

Area: 163,000 sq km[1]
Population (1990): 400,000[2]
Population (2000, projected): 500,000[2]
Proportion urban (1990): 47%[2]
Population density: 2.5 persons/sq km[2]
Ethnic origins (1990): East Indian 35%; Creole 32%;
  Indonesian 10%; Bosneger (Bush Negro) 10%; Chinese 3%;
  Amerindian 3%[18]

Life expectancy – male (1990): 72.4 years[2]
Life expectancy – female (1990): 72.4 years[2]
Infant mortality per 1,000 live births (1989): 32[2]
Literacy (1985): 92.7%[2]
Women as proportion of labour force (1988-89): 29%[2]

GNP per head (1989): $3,010[1]
GNP per head – annual growth rate 1980-88: -6.8%[2]
Foreign debt (1989 – estimated): $80 million
Foreign debt per head (1989 – estimated): $200[11]

Education spending
- as proportion of public expenditure (1987-88): 22.8%[2]

Main exports: bauxite, alumina, aluminium[11]

Trinidad and Tobago

Area: 5,000 sq km[1]
Population (1990): 1.3 million[2]
Population (2000, projected): 1.5 million[2]
Proportion under 15 years (1989): 33.6%[1]
Proportion urban (1990): 69%[2]
Population density: 250 persons/sq km[2]
Ethnic origins (1980): Afro-Caribbean 50+%; Asian 45+%; European between 1% and 2%[3]

Life expectancy – male (1989): 69 years[1]
Life expectancy – female (1989): 74 years[1]
Infant mortality per 1,000 live births (1989): 15[2]
Literacy (1985): 95%[2]
Women as proportion of labour force (1988-89): 27.3%[2]

GNP per head (1989): $3,230[1]
GNP per head – annual growth rate 1980-88: -7.3%[2]
Foreign debt (1989): $2,012 million[1]
Foreign debt per head (1989): $1,548
Total debt as proportion of GNP (1989): 53.9%[1]
Total debt as proportion of exports (1989): 107%[1]
Debt service as proportion of exports (1989): 12.3%[1]

Income distribution (1980-88)
- proportion of rural population below poverty line: 39%[2]

Education spending[2]
- as proportion of public expenditure (1987-88): 15.3%
- as proportion of GNP (1986): 4%

Military spending[2]
- as proportion of GNP (1986): 1%
- arms imports (1987): 0

Main exports (1988): petroleum products 60%; chemicals 21%; basic manufactures 9%[4]
Five main trading partners (1988)[4]
- imports: USA, UK, Canada, W. Germany, Japan
- exports: USA, Barbados, UK, Jamaica, Japan,

Uruguay

Area: 177,000 sq km[1]
Population (1990): 3.1 million[2]
Population (2000, projected): 3.3 million[2]
Proportion under 15 years (1989): 25.9%[1]
Proportion urban (1990): 86%[2]
Population density: 18 persons/sq km[2]
Ethnic origins (1980): European 90%; Mestizo 7.5%; African/mulatto 2.5%[3]

Life expectancy – male (1989): 69 years[1]
Life expectancy – female (1989): 76 years[1]
Infant mortality per 1,000 live births (1989): 23[2]
Literacy (1985): 95.3%[2]
Women as proportion of labour force (1988-89): 30.9%[2]

GNP per head (1989): $2,620[1]
GNP per head – annual growth rate 1980-88: -1.4%[2]
Foreign debt (1989): $3,751 million[1]
Foreign debt per head (1989): $1,210
Total debt as proportion of GNP (1989): 46.5%[1]
Total debt as proportion of exports (1989): 170.5%[1]
Debt service as proportion of exports (1989): 29.4%[1]

Education spending[2]
- as proportion of public expenditure (1987-88): 15.1%
- as proportion of GNP (1986): 6.6%

Military spending[2]
- as proportion of GNP (1986): 1.6%
- arms imports (1987): 0

Main exports (1988): wool 25%; meat 11%; hides 7%[4]
Five main trading partners (1989)[4]
- imports: Brazil, Argentina, USA, W. Germany, Mexico
- exports: Brazil, USA, W. Germany, Argentina, USSR

Venezuela

Area: 912,000 sq km[1]
Population (1990): 19.7 million[2]
Population (2000, projected): 24.7 million[2]
Proportion under 15 years (1989): 38.5%[1]
Proportion urban (1990): 91%[2]
Population density: 22.4 persons/sq km[2]
Ethnic origins (1990): Mestizo 65%; European 21%; Amerindian 7%; African/mulatto 7%[3]

Life expectancy – male (1989): 67 years[1]
Life expectancy – female (1989): 73 years[1]
Infant mortality per 1,000 live births (1989): 35[2]
Literacy (1985): 85.7%[2]
Women as proportion of labour force (1988-89): 21.5%[2]

GNP per head (1989): $2,450[1]
GNP per head – annual growth rate 1980-88: -2.4%[2]
Foreign debt (1989): $33,144 million[1]
Foreign debt per head (1989): $1,682
Total debt as proportion of GNP (1988): 79.9%[1]
Total debt as proportion of exports (1989): 211.5%[1]
Debt service as proportion of exports (1988): 25%[1]

Income distribution (1987)
- share of income of wealthiest 10%: 34.2%[1]
- share of income of wealthiest 20%: 4.7%[2]
- share of income of poorest 20%: 50.6%[2]

Education spending[2]
- as proportion of public expenditure (1987-88): 16.6%
- as proportion of GNP (1986): 4.3%

Military spending[2]
- as proportion of GNP (1986): 1.6%
- arms imports (1987): 0

Main exports (1989): petroleum & derivatives 75%[5]
Five main trading partners (1988)[4]
- imports: USA, W. Germany, Italy, Japan, Brazil[4]

United Kingdom

Area: 245,000 sq km[1]
Population (1990): 57.2 million[2]
Population (2000, projected): 58.4 million[2]
Proportion under 15 years (1989): 19%[1]
Proportion urban (1990): 89%[2]
Population density: 235.7 persons/sq km[2]

Life expectancy – male (1989): 73 years[1]
Life expectancy – female (1989): 79 years[1]
Infant mortality per 1,000 live births (1989): 9[1]
Literacy (1985): 99%[2]
Women as proportion of labour force (1988-89): 38.7%[2]

GNP per head (1989): $14,610[1]
GNP per head – annual growth rate 1980-88: 3.8%[2]

Income distribution (1979)[1]
- share of income of wealthiest 10%: 23.3%
- share of income of wealthiest 20%: 39.5%
- share of income of poorest 20%: 5.8%

Education spending
- as proportion of GNP (1986): 5.3%[14]

Military spending
- as proportion of GNP (1986): 5%[14]
- arms exports (1988): $2,900 million[2]

Main exports (1989): machinery & transport equipment 40%; other manufactures 40%[1]

United States of America

Area: 9,373,000 sq km[1]
Population (1990): 249.2 million[2]
Population (2000, projected): 266.1 million[2]
Proportion under 15 years (1989): 21.6%[1]
Proportion urban (1990): 75%[2]
Population density: 28.4 persons/sq km[2]

Life expectancy – male (1989): 72 years[1]
Life expectancy – female (1989): 79 years[1]
Infant mortality per 1,000 live births (1989): 10[1]
Literacy (1985): 99%[2]
Women as proportion of labour force (1988-89): 41.5%[2]

GNP per head (1989): $20,910[1]
GNP per head – annual growth rate 1980-88: 2.7%[2]

Income distribution (1985)[1]
- share of income of wealthiest 10%: 25%
- share of income of wealthiest 20%: 41.9%
- share of income of poorest 20%: 4.7%

Education spending
- as proportion of GNP (1986): 5.3%[14]

Military spending
- as proportion of GNP (1986): 6.7%[14]
- arms exports (1988): $14,300 million[2]

Main exports (1989): machinery & transport equipment 43%; other manufactures 34%[1]

appendix 2

Sources

1. *World Development Report, 1991*, World Bank, Oxford University Press.
2. *Human Development Report, 1991*, United Nations Development Programme (UNDP), Oxford University Press.
3. *The Cambridge Encyclopaedia of Latin America and the Caribbean*, Cambridge University Press, 1985.
4. *South America, Central America and the Caribbean, 1991*, Europa Publications, London, 1990.
5. *The Americas Review 1990/91*, World of Information, Saffron Walden, 1990.
6. *Third World Guide 1991/92*, Instituto del Mundo, Montevideo, Uruguay.
7. *Cuba: the Test of Time*, Jean Stubbs, Latin America Bureau, London, 1989.
8. *Guatemala: False Hope, False Freedom*, James Painter, CIIR/ Latin America Bureau, London 1987.
9. *Trends in Developing Economies, 1991*, The World Bank, Washington D.C.
10. *Dictionary of Contemporary Politics of Central America and the Caribbean*, P.Gunson, G.Chamberlain & A.Thompson, Routledge, London, 1991.
11. *Dictionary of Contemporary Politics of South America*, P.Gunson, G.Chamberlain & A.Thompson, Routledge, London, 1989.
12. *Ecuador: Fragile Democracy*, D.Corkill & D.Cubitt, Latin America Bureau, London, 1988.
13. *Peru: Paths to Poverty*, Latin America Bureau., London, 1985.
14. *World Military and Social Expenditures, 1989*, Ruth Leger Sivard, World Priorities, Washington D.C., 1989.
15. 'Chile after Pinochet: Aylwin's Christian Democrat Economic Policies for the 1990s', David E. Hojman in *Bulletin of Latin American Research*, Vol.9, No.1, 1990.
16. 'The River Plate Countries', J. Colin Crossley, in *Latin America: Geographical Perspectives*, Harold Blakemore & Clifford Smith (eds.), Methuen, 1983.
17. World Bank estimates, quoted in James Dunkerley, *Rebellion in the Veins*, Verso, London, 1984.
18. *Political and Economic Encyclopaedia of Latin America and the Caribbean*, Peter Calvert (ed.), Longman, London, 1991.
19. *Panama: Made in the USA*, John Weeks and Phil Gunson, Latin America Bureau, London, 1991.
20. *Forging Peace: the Challenge of Central America*, Richard Fagen, PACCA / Basil Blackwell, New York, 1987.
21. *Censo Agropecuario*, San José, Costa Rica.
22. *Notas sobre la evolución del desarrollo social del istmo centroamericano hasta 1980*, UN Economic Commission for Latin America, Mexico City, 1982.